Campaign Inc.

Campaign Inc.

How Leadership and Organization Propelled
Barack Obama to the White House

Henry F. De Sio, Jr.
2008 OBAMA FOR AMERICA COO

University of Iowa Press | Iowa City

University of Iowa Press, Iowa City 52242
Copyright © 2014 by Henry F. De Sio, Jr.
www.uiowapress.org
Printed in the United States of America
Design by Sara T. Sauers

The University of Iowa Press is a member of Green Press Initiative
and is committed to preserving natural resources.

Printed on acid-free paper
ISBN: 978-1-60938-269-8 (pbk)
ISBN: 978-1-60938-287-2 (ebk)
LCCN: 2014004815

For Sine, Dante, and Zane
The first steps of our journey together as a family.

Contents

Preface

EVERYTHING I KNOW about the physics of winning and success I learned from the campaign trail. There is always a winner and a loser. The campaign world, just like the business world, is highly competitive. And because political campaigns are launched from scratch every election cycle, they provide the ultimate entrepreneurial showcase.

We tend to think about the political campaign as this big blob—a marketing machine that spits out the ads we see on TV, the canvassers we get at our doors, the endless stream of phone calls, and the emails that barrage our inboxes. But if you pull back the curtain, what you will discover is a complex, dynamic environment filled with motivated and fiercely passionate people executing a vast array of tasks. It is a highly charged environment with a million things going on at once.

This plays out in full view for the world to examine in real time. There is always a camera on the candidate, and the organization's financial books are open to the public in the form of regular election filings that are required by law. Here you can find every dollar, every donor, and every dime spent. All of this combines to create a sensitive dynamic inside the campaign—and it's all too human.

It is in this hothouse environment under the scorching glare of the media spotlight that leadership is on full display for everyone to see. It's like a leadership reality show. Imagine coming to work every day to a place where everything your boss says, every decision you make, and every action your organization takes is constantly scrutinized. You are always one misstep away from sparking a media firestorm. You are the buzz of the Internet on Friday, the newspaper headlines on Saturday, the talk of the morning political shows on Sunday, and the water cooler chatter on Monday. And you are the conversation at America's dinner table every night.

When you understand the campaign in this context, it becomes quite awesome. What you have, then, is a laboratory that is rich with examples of why winners win and why losers lose. It is the perfect observatory for understanding the characteristics that separate the successful from the aspiring. Some people learn the timeless principles of leadership in the boardroom. Others get them in the workplace. And still more from the classroom or on the battlefield. Mine have been born from the campaign trail, where the edge goes to those who have a clear command of the principles that drive personal and organizational success. I have seen how the precepts I write about in this book offer a noticeable edge for entrepreneurs, innovators, and executives across sectors.

Why I Wrote This Book

I realize the release of this book six years after the historic election of 2008 may seem somewhat oddly timed. Admittedly, it would probably have fit better with the crop of other published accounts that rolled off the presses during the ensuing eighteen months.

In my defense, when I was first approached to write a book about my experience helping to build and manage our campaign, I chose instead to accept the invitation to serve in the Obama administration. My choice was between two passions; always a good thing, but never easy to deliberate over. While my enthusiasm for the idea of writing this book never diminished, interest around me had certainly waned by the time I was finally ready to take up the matter two and a half years later. Even the same publishing representatives that had initially contacted me were understandably cool to the idea they had pitched me a few years earlier.

I went ahead and wrote the manuscript anyway. My motivation was twofold. First, I didn't want to forget the incredible experience I'd had; nor did I want to lose the rich lessons I'd gleaned from our campaign journey. Second, this was an election for the ages, one that will be talked about a century from now. I wanted to offer my two boys a firsthand account of what it was really like to work in this historic and groundbreaking effort. I missed out on many of their earliest days in this world, first to help birth a president and then to support him during his formative years in the White House. I thought this was the best gift I could give my two sons in return.

As I set out to write *Campaign Inc.*, I had one core objective. I wanted to answer the question I faced regularly in the months following the election: how did you do it?

This book is my answer for why Barack Obama won the election of 2008. A specific theme I felt compelled to convey was the importance of leadership and organization in the success formula. It's what propelled Barack Obama to the White House. Despite his talents and charisma on the campaign trail, those qualities alone wouldn't have earned him the presidency. Therefore, woven into the story line of this book is a central focus on the building of the operation that took down the Clinton machine and then went on to defeat the powerful Republican apparatus in the fall. Good candidates don't win elections—great campaigns do. That makes this less the story of citizen Obama's rise as a candidate, and more a tale that introduces us to Barack Obama, CEO.

For these reasons, *Campaign Inc.* is a story that I am uniquely qualified to write. I have been writing, speaking, teaching, and coaching others how to build winning campaigns and highly effective organizations for more than a decade. My background, mixed with my vantage as the campaign's day-to-day manager from its start until the very end, afforded me a view like none other. But, to be clear, these writings are not the simple, starry-eyed musings of someone who just can't let it go. Nor is this an account written by someone still drunk on the elixir of that victory. *Campaign Inc.* is a forward-looking commentary that offers important lessons for achievement-oriented readers while still maintaining relevance to the current political discourse.

Campaign Inc. is the inside story about the making of Obama for America; it is a case study for building and leading high-performance organizations. The political playing field is intense. For the Obama campaign, the competition couldn't have been greater nor the odds longer. We couldn't afford to run our operation based on the traditional ways of doing things. Senator Obama himself was direct about his vision from the outset when he said to "run it like a business." This book documents the ascent, in just twenty-one months, of an entrepreneurial start-up that grew to become the largest campaign in American political history—ultimately approaching the size of a Fortune 1000 company. It is an account that is instructive for business executives and students alike because it offers a glimpse into the culture, systems, and inner-workings of an organization that dared to be different.

This book is also quite relevant to the current political discourse. I have outlined a blueprint for building and running a winning national campaign operation. This makes the content contained herein quite appropriately timed to coincide with the 2016 presidential election. While every campaign must be shaped differently, this story presents a model that will long be the standard for measuring similar organizations in the future. Political watchers will never view presidential campaigns the same, and they will have a new lens for understanding and evaluating the state of the national race.

For those wanting insight into Barack Obama's approach to leadership, read on. Very clear examples illustrate how the president positions himself for political success. *Campaign Inc.* reveals a man driven by principles, not events. It also highlights his longheaded perspective and discipline. Barack Obama doesn't chase public opinion; rather, he moves steadily forward.

Finally, this is a book about commanding change. From the early days of chaos, to the rapid-fire demands of a grueling nomination fight stretching five months and fifty-seven contests, to the final days of unprecedented scale that positioned us to compete against our muscular general election adversary, *Campaign Inc.* describes how our staff navigated constant organizational transition and uncertainty. We were working in an environment of "change on steroids." This story documents how we met that challenge by tearing down the walls of our initial departmental silos that had been carefully built in our formative months to transition into an organization that worked in fluid, collaborative teams that transcended preexisting boundaries to achieve unexpected success.

Let me add a few caveats at the outset. First, I refer to the president quite informally throughout this book. I even call him by his first name. Today, he is "Mr. President" to me (though my kids still call him "Mr. Barack") but back then, he was just "Barack." That's what we all called him. We referred to his rival simply as "Hillary," even though during the more than two years I worked in the administration with her she was, of course, "Secretary Clinton." And the emerging medium we labeled "new media"? That is now commonly known as digital communications. You will also notice in the story that I introduce my colleagues Steve Hildebrand and David Axelrod as "Hilde" and "Ax" respectively, in the same way they were addressed by the rest of us in the organization at the time. The point is that I am writing in my 2008 campaign voice. Things change and the world moves on, but this is a story about life as it was, so I speak in that voice.

Second, I have recounted events as I remembered them. My intention was to tell the best story I could and share the lessons I learned about winning and success, relying primarily on the journal I kept at the time. In fact, you will notice that every chapter begins with an entry that was pulled from those pages. I didn't read David Plouffe's best seller, *The Audacity to Win*, until years after it was released—after I completed my own manuscript. I lived it, quite frankly. I also knew we had two very different views of the campaign given our respective roles, and I didn't want his account to affect mine. The story I tell is primarily based on my experience and my personal impressions. This is not to say I wasn't influenced by the news reporting of the time and, where possible, I make every effort to credit specific references inside the text. Mostly, however, when I wanted to remember a speech or an event, I visited the running blog of our relentless in-house historian, Sam Graham-Felsen.

The third thing you will notice is that this book contains no photographs. I never took any, sadly. I hope someday somebody will publish a photo book that depicts what life was like inside Chicago headquarters. In the meantime, I will do my best to narrate this account in a way that will make you feel like you were right there with us.

Okay, I think we're ready. Let's go!

Campaign Inc.

Introduction

Checkout

ON MARCH 1, 2011, I DETERMINED it was time for me to begin making plans to leave the White House. This triggered a series of meetings in the West Wing later that day in an effort to ensure there would be enough time to accommodate a transition of my responsibilities. While I'd logged over two years of service to the president as his deputy assistant for management and administration, the day also marked my four-year anniversary with Barack and Michelle Obama, dating back to the beginnings of his presidential campaign. Serving as the 2008 chief operating officer at Obama for America and then as a senior aide in the Obama White House was the professional experience of a lifetime. And my family was blessed with many precious memories. Now, it was time for me to spend more time with my wife and two young children.

On my last day at the White House four months later, I meandered through the vast complex as I began the lengthy checkout process, which involved getting signatures from different department representatives in exchange for government assets and documents. It was all very surreal. You could always tell when it was someone's last day. Like others before me, I wandered the halls holding the checklist at arm's length in front of me, as if it was a map that offered clues to the next stop on a treasure hunt.

It occurred to me as I searched for signatures to complete my off-boarding that I had actually spent more time in the administration than the twenty-two months I'd devoted to the president's historic election campaign. The nation had long since moved on from the 2008 election, just as I was moving on with my life. The political climate and national mood was noticeably different from when Barack Obama had been sworn in over two years earlier. Despite a dizzying two-plus years that featured the appointments of two women to the Supreme Court, the end of Osama bin Laden's reign of terror, and major legislative achievements—saving the American auto industry from extinction, pulling the economy from the brink of a depression, reforming financial industry regulations, and expanding access to affordable health care among them—there was widespread speculation that the president's back was against the wall. While his accomplishments were indisputable, it is also fair to say that some of his policies were controversial.

Adding to the turbulence, unemployment remained locked at just over 9 percent and the economy could only be generously characterized as anemic. Voters were weary of war and wary of the nation's growing debt. Most importantly, the administration was still regrouping after the results of the midterm elections that ushered in a Republican majority in the House of Representatives and paved the way for contentious battles over national priorities. Uncertainty surrounded the president's future as his approval ratings dipped to 45 percent, down from 85 percent in the days just before his inauguration. A dominant narrative steadily surfacing in the media probed the possibility that his would be a one-term presidency. What a difference just a couple of years had made.

At the beginning of 2011, the national press corps had already been in speculative overdrive about the prospects for the 2012 presidential elections. Familiar names from our race in 2008 were surfacing early. The media seemed obsessed with the intentions of Sarah Palin. Other names—Mitt Romney, Mike Huckabee, and Tim Pawlenty, for example—were being bandied about as potential Republican presidential contenders.

On the Democratic side, Secretary of State Hillary Clinton continued to knock back questions about whether she was planning a run against President Obama in the Democratic primaries. At the same time, top aides David Axelrod and Jim Messina were preparing to leave for Chicago to lead the reelection campaign. In their wake, 2008 Campaign Manager David Plouffe came in to take up a position as a senior advisor in the West Wing.

This was the backdrop against which I prepared my own exit.

My Story

I got the call that changed my life on the day after Christmas 2006. My wife and I were shopping at a Barnes & Noble bookstore in San Luis Obispo, California, enjoying our outing with the extended family we were visiting at the time. The call was unexpected. I had no contacts at the Obama campaign, so when my cell phone rang and the voice on the other end inquired as to my interest in coming to Chicago to work for Senator Obama, I couldn't have been more surprised. It was like a scene from the television series *The West Wing*.

I flipped my phone shut at the end of the conversation in wonderment. I was stunned and excited—yet still very cautious about the serendipitous moment. While the offer to put my résumé in the right hands was appealing, I really didn't see this going very far. There might be a consulting contract somewhere in this for me, I thought, but anything more seemed like a long shot. My wife and I were both sufficiently dubious that we thought it best not to share what had just transpired with our relatives.

Though we were in California at the time of the call, my wife and I lived in Alexandria, Virginia. We had a pretty tranquil life that neither of us was interested in upsetting. Sine, pronounced See-na, worked in public relations at a prominent area university. I was managing a national advocacy campaign. The balance I was able to strike between my personal and professional lives was something I relished. Yet the idea of working in a presidential campaign still interested me. During the fall of 2006, just two months earlier, Sine and I were sitting on the banks of the Potomac River scribbling out a list of goals for our future. I'd expressed to Sine then that I thought I had one more presidential election in me.

Having worked on the previous 2004 race as a consultant for the AFL-CIO, I was excited for the upcoming political season. But as winter approached, working in a presidential campaign seemed an increasingly unlikely possibility for me. I had links to Al Gore, a candidate I liked at the time, but I'd been given clear indications from people close to him that he would not run again long before the news was public. John

Edwards's team was sending some interest my way, but nothing there seemed likely to develop into a meaningful role. None of the other candidates appealed to me.

The lone exception was Senator Barack Obama, of Illinois, but I didn't know him or anyone in his Senate office. Nor was I familiar with the people in his campaign to try to make a connection there. And because I was unknown on the national political scene, a call from their camp seemed entirely improbable.

Opening Pitch

Very soon after the New Year, I was contacted by the campaign and told to get in touch with Steve Hildebrand for a phone interview. Steve was highly regarded in political circles and one of the few names associated with the Obama campaign that I actually recognized. After several attempts at reaching him per the instructions I'd received, I finally tracked him down in Sioux Falls, South Dakota. I'd been told in advance of the call that I was under consideration for the job of national field director, though Steve never indicated that at all during our talk.

Nonetheless, when asked about my vision for the campaign, I made my case to Steve that I thought new developments in technology would dramatically change the nature of voter contact in a campaign. We could now put electronic tools in the hands of our supporters that would let them customize and download literature from our website and create talking points for use when phoning and door-knocking their neighbors. I mentioned to him that I'd even begun testing a product that could make it possible with just a cell phone, a computer, and an Internet connection to transform any kitchen table into a high-tech, auto-dialing "virtual" phone-bank terminal. We had the potential, I enthusiastically proclaimed, to convert homes into campaign offices. This would revolutionize the nature of the relationship between volunteers and the candidate's organization.

At the time, I thought my interview went well, and soon after I received word that when asked, Steve told the campaign manager that I had some "very interesting ideas." Then several weeks passed without my hearing anything. When the candidate officially announced his intention to seek the presidency on February 10, 2007, my phone had long been silent. I held out little hope that I would ever hear from the campaign again.

But in the days immediately following Barack Obama's announcement, my conversation with the campaign reemerged. This time they were talking about a senior role in the campaign's management. I was thrilled. Though I was relatively new to national politics, I had been running campaigns of various stripes for more than twenty years on two continents. There was no function of a campaign that I didn't know and nothing I hadn't already seen. I had also built and run organizations my whole career—although not to the size and scope that the Obama campaign would ultimately become—so I was confident in my ability to lead a large organization. I felt certain that my whole career had prepared me for this moment.

I was finally made an offer in late February. The problem was that the pay fell shy of what I thought my wife and I could afford to make the move. I felt very uncomfortable going back with a counteroffer, but I felt I had to try because I knew I would regret walking away from this opportunity. The bargaining was a bit contentious, frankly, even though I hadn't yet met or even spoken to the person with whom I was supposedly negotiating. The campaign manager was a guy named David Plouffe. At first I mispronounced his name and called him "Ploof," but I was quickly corrected by Hildebrand. Turns out that it sounds like *puff*, as in Plouffe the Magic Dragon. Anyway, I was told that when David finally agreed and signed the paperwork authorizing an offer of employment, he hastily scribbled out his signature and announced, "He'd better fuckin' be worth it!"

March 1

Just a couple of days later on March 1, 2007, my wife and I emerged from her doctor's office in Washington, D.C., where it was confirmed that Sine was pregnant. We had agreed in advance that we would put off any final decisions about enlisting with the campaign until we knew that our baby was healthy. There was sound reasoning behind our caution since her first pregnancy a year before had ended sadly in a miscarriage. Our happy news that morning triggered a series of actions that we'd agreed to in advance if all was well. I immediately began the process of shutting down my consulting practice, gave the required thirty-day notice on our housing lease, and jumped on a plane to Chicago to sign my employment paperwork with Obama for America—all in the same day.

It was late in the afternoon when I stepped out of a cab and approached the tall building on Michigan Avenue. I remember looking up at that high-rise for the first time and thinking, "I got this!" I felt nervous about meeting a whole new group of people but unwaveringly confident in the difference I would make in this organization. I found my way through the building up to a small reception area of the campaign's offices, where I was warmly greeted by one of the many volunteers swarming the small space. She didn't flinch when I introduced myself and, in fact, leapt to her feet and loudly announced, "Mr. De Sio, of course!" I was impressed. I immediately felt like a VIP.

I was ushered behind the counter into a larger office space that was bustling with people. Still, the blaze of activity all around us could not distract the small team at a table along the side of the room that was firmly focused on processing my required staff paperwork and issuing me new computing equipment. Above the noise I heard one of my new colleagues in a nearby side office sounding out my name as if reading it for the first time. "Henry De Sio, Henry De Sio," he mused. "Can someone tell me what I am supposed to do with this résumé?" the gentleman shouted loudly. He seemed confused. So was I, since it wasn't clear to me who had my résumé. I learned later that the voice belonged to Temo Figueroa, the person who ultimately had been hired as the national field director.

I was quickly given an orientation to my new BlackBerry and laptop computer by a cheerful attendant who introduced herself as Alison Stanton (soon to become one of my key aides). Next she escorted me through the maze of people and past the makeshift desks to my office. As we walked, Alison explained that the small temporary space we were navigating couldn't support the entire cadre of staff and volunteers. Many were farmed out to area hotels and law firms, where they packed into conference rooms and accessed the Internet from their laptops. In my case, I was shown to a ratty desk in a stuffy, crowded side room. And that's where I worked for the first month until our permanent headquarters were readied a few floors up.

Answering the Call

A month after I had signed on to the campaign, I returned home to Alexandria to help my wife pack up the house, relieved that the physical distance between us would soon be closed. We put most of our belongings into a storage facility in Maryland. Only the things we absolutely needed and that could fit into our two cars came along with us to Chicago. Some last minute cleaning of the house preceded our cramming the two dogs, Caesar and Mia, into the back of the Ford Escape. Sine would drive the SUV, and I would drive the Saturn. Our hope was that we would make it as far as Pittsburgh by nightfall. Bad weather was expected on both ends of our journey, so we were eager to get on the road. But there were still family and friends to say our good-byes to on our way out of town. Time felt like it was working against us as we left the house and slowly navigated the small streets of Old Town Alexandria for the last time.

When I accepted this position, I promised my wife that I would do this for just one year. Our baby was due in October, the primaries would begin in early January, and well more than half the races would be completed by the end of February. Those last few months would be challenging for us with a new baby, but I assumed at that point we would know our fate. If we lost, well, that was that. If we won, I could step out of the campaign knowing there would be plenty of support from the national party and the stampede of established campaign pros who would likely come in and take over. That was the logic behind throwing our belongings in storage rather than shipping everything to Chicago. We would be without our possessions for only a year.

While we thought we had considered and carefully planned out all of the aspects of this move when we first talked about my taking the job, during the long drive alone in the car I suddenly developed some serious doubts about our future. I ended up spending the better part of the two-day drive from Alexandria to Chicago second-guessing our decision to uproot. This newfound uncertainty magnified the voices of skeptics still fresh in my mind, who had actively questioned how we could leave our lives and jobs behind to risk so much for a candidate that everyone agreed would never win.

Also contributing to my noticeably cold feet, Sine wasn't feeling well when we left. Her current flu-like symptoms were alarmingly similar to those she had when she miscarried. She was about twelve weeks pregnant, and we were both very concerned about the baby. In addition to that, I didn't like her driving the long distance alone in her car, especially given the high winds we battled throughout much of the journey. As someone who gets paid to anticipate the worst, I began to tease out a troubling set of what-ifs in my head. I suddenly worried about what we would do if something went wrong with this pregnancy or if the campaign went off the tracks and we found ourselves out of the race early. We didn't know anybody in Chicago, and we wouldn't have a support network there. Neither of us would have jobs or income if things went awry. I had long known that I was in a very tenuous line of work, but I began to really come down on myself for putting us in such a vulnerable position.

My brain was also replaying recent conversations that further underscored my vulnerable situation working in a risky campaign start-up. Almost as soon as I signed on, some of my new co-workers confided to me personal fears over job security. It was a hard time for many around me. Some battled to balance family relocation with their new work demands. Others felt over their heads in new, unfamiliar roles and struggled with the speed at which new problems came at them. There were even those who worried that the campaign's inability to get control of the chaos we faced in those earliest days was an indicator of mismanagement that might lead to some kind of shake-up which would directly affect them somehow. And, of course, nobody could know if something might happen to force our candidate out of the race unexpectedly.

None of this had been happy news for my wife to hear when I reported these conversations on our regular late night phone calls during that first month. This whole process was already unnerving enough for her. I felt secure with my performance, but then again, I really didn't know anybody in the campaign who might cover my back if things around me came unhinged. I did my best to write off the jitters of some of my co-workers to being in an unformed environment that was flooded with new people still trying to get their footing. At the same time, I struggled to imagine what impact any dramatic changes inside the organization might mean for me. Pondering these impressions as I drove, glancing occasionally at my wife in the rearview mirror, I suppose the reality of what I had committed us to was finally sinking in.

The journey to Chicago was unbearably long.

Lakeview

Sine and I finally pulled into Chicago on Sunday afternoon. The house that we had rented in Lakeview, near Wrigley Field, wasn't ready in spite of what we had been promised. We were forced to take a hotel room. I was particularly annoyed because we were planning to buy furniture for our new home later that day at a local IKEA. This was the only time I had in my schedule to do so. This wrinkle in our housing situation meant we would have to go a whole week without any furnishings. I had missed enough time with the move and didn't see how to get free until the following weekend. And Sine, now running a fever, clearly wasn't well enough to take on this responsibility alone.

What followed was perhaps, personally, the most difficult week in the entire campaign. On Monday morning, I left for the office at 7:00 A.M. Sine was still asleep in the small but comfortable hotel room. I hoped that a good day's rest would help her feel better. Instead, she only got worse. Though the house was now ready, she couldn't get out of bed to go over there. I arranged to keep the pricey room for another night, and later that evening I took both cars over one at a time and emptied the boxes at the new place while she slept at the hotel. I was already exhausted after my long day. Some time close to 9:00 P.M., I brought a Chicago-style pizza back to the hotel room. Sine didn't eat any.

On Tuesday, I left her again early in the morning. At some point during the day, Sine at least felt well enough to make her way to the new house. Unfortunately, when I came home that night to our large three-bedroom residence, I found her lying quietly in the dark on an inflatable mattress in one small corner of the living room. Our two dogs were curled up very near to her, next to the glowing nine-inch television that carried one fuzzy channel.

Meanwhile, at work, where I confidently commanded my new environment, none of my co-workers understood the full extent of my dilemma. I was stepping into my leadership at the office as spectacularly as I was abandoning it at home. I was reluctant to openly share my personal problems with my colleagues for fear of what that might communicate about my competence. We were all still new to each other and I thought it important to earn the trust and confidence of the people who were still evaluating me as their leader. On the other hand, I felt horrible about leaving Sine alone all day, and she wasn't getting any better. We were also worried for the baby.

On Wednesday morning, I finally decided to miss work so I could take Sine to an area hospital emergency room. We didn't have a local doctor yet, so the ER had to pass as our general health care provider for the moment. The nurses and doctor carefully checked Sine and then they turned their attention to the baby. To our relief, the heartbeat was fine. Everything was okay.

For the rest of the week, I continued my routine of leaving Sine early in the morning and returning home sometime after 9:00 P.M. She was still very ill. I left her lying in the same corner of that big, empty house on the inflatable bed every morning and returned to the same scene, with the dogs at her side and the glow from the tiny TV screen piercing the darkness in front of her, every night. We had to squeeze in one more visit to the emergency room since Sine's unrelenting fever had gotten even worse. She never once complained.

That Friday night, after a very long week, we got our first piece of furniture for the new house: a big screen television from Costco. During the remainder of the weekend we filled out the rest of our home. Sine started feeling better, and things began to look up as we settled in. Candidly, I have never felt more derelict or selfish as a husband than I did that week. I know I was reacting to the pressures at work and the anxieties expressed by others around me. In hindsight, I wish I had considered my options and priorities differently.

I was so relieved to get that week behind me. I was terrified the whole time for the baby and for Sine's health. I pushed through at work, knowing that my concern would be paralyzing if I let myself dwell on our personal situation. Instead, I stayed focused on the problems right in front of me and hoped for the best at home. Now, with the whole weekend to get our home and lives in order, I felt quite confident that we would both feel much better and things would normalize.

For my wife and me, these were the first steps of a journey that forever changed us. One moment we were living quiet, unassuming lives in Alexandria, Virginia, and the next we found ourselves navigating the bustling city of Chicago in pursuit of a dream we hoped would change history. It was unnerving and exhilarating at the same time.

We were not alone in our bewilderment. Everyone who answered the call to work in the Obama campaign had a similarly compelling tale of sacrifice and risk. Each of my new co-workers brought with them a fascinating mix of grit and motivation portrayed in their own personal stories. The pressures on every one of us and our loved ones would only grow as we journeyed further and further down the campaign trail together. Though difficult to measure, the dynamics of the workplace were undoubtedly affected by the factors that weighed on each individual outside of it.

Here is where the story truly begins. Against this backdrop of uncertainty and sacrifice, I tell the story of the campaign team that set out to propel a little-known senator from Illinois to the most powerful office in the land.

1

No Drama Obama

APRIL 5, 2007: *The note from Campaign Manager David Plouffe flashed from my BlackBerry this morning. Subject line: Stop the Spending.*

Chaos

I dreaded my new campaign BlackBerry, yet habitually fumbled for it immediately upon waking each day. The device delivered the regular dose of SOS's that as the "organization guy" I could not avoid. I was the fireman. When people needed my help it was often an emergency, and at this early stage of the campaign, it seemed like every morning there was an appeal that was sure to consume the first couple hours of my day.

Some of the requests were to facilitate cooperation between certain staff or departments. At other times I was needed to sooth tensions that had grown from the confusion over roles and responsibilities. Then there were the frustrated leaders in Iowa who couldn't navigate Chicago for needed services because they didn't have reliable points of contact at a time when our staff and volunteers were constantly shuffling into new positions. On top of all this, there were the myriad problems associated with the physical move from the campaign's temporary quarters into our new national headquarters.

Mostly, though, I was on alert for messages from David Plouffe, our campaign manager, who stayed up late into the night working through the many unique challenges of a complex campaign start-up. On the morning of April 5, he was rightly worried about the spending appetite of this growing and ambitious organization.

At the time I'd received David's email appeal, I was still battling to get people and systems in place. Only about a hundred of us were on payroll at this point, though the number of volunteers buzzing around was an indicator of the many more wanting to be hired. And while most of our staff were located at headquarters, the four early primary states of Iowa,

New Hampshire, Nevada, and South Carolina were also building up. The eleventh floor of the downtown Chicago high-rise, only days ago empty and silent, was now quickly being overtaken by complete chaos as people moved in from temporary office locations around the city.

We were still mostly strangers to each other. Phones and computers were being installed by Sam Falkoff, known by many of us as "Sam the Red Sox fan" since we all had yet to learn last names. He tried his best to fulfill his duties while taking care not to intrude on the staffers who feverishly worked to get their newly assigned seating areas put together.

As soon as folks had their workstations up and running, they were off, scurrying past each other and moving quickly between desks to get answers to pressing questions. There was motion to be sure; progress, on the other hand, was still difficult to discern. This is always a challenging time in a campaign. Like any good business, you would ideally like to have key systems and personnel in place before you launch. But our campaign was still very much unformed and struggling to catch up to the high volume of inquiries and demands that had been generated from our candidate's announcement that he would run for president just weeks earlier.

The crush of enthusiasm from outside increased the pressure on us inside. Our reception desk was overrun with phone calls. The small correspondence team was collecting a mountain of print mail to go with an incredible volume of incoming email. Our staff in the political department and others of us in the campaign attempted to manage the many requests coming our way from influential leaders and organizational representatives who wanted time with the candidate or a signal of support for their core objectives. And our fundraisers had the daunting challenge of competitively raising money behind a little-known Barack Obama brand in a clear mismatch against Clinton, who was quite literally the "Campbell's Soup" of politics, with the high name recognition and deep relationships that came with her two decades of national service.

Building the Airplane in Midflight
The weight bearing down on all of the other departments increased their reliance on those that I oversaw. Looking back on my work, even

from the earliest days, I thought of myself as one part chief executive officer, one part chief people officer, and one part chief firefighter. If I properly tended to the first two, I had fewer fires to fight. At the outset, however, I mostly battled both brush fires and blazes.

The teams I managed struggled to get a handle on the flurry of demands coming our way. With only about a dozen staff around me at the beginning of April, managing the surge with so few people was a Herculean undertaking for all of us. The chief financial officer (CFO), Marianne Markowitz, had a small staff at the beginning and was still setting up the financial infrastructure. Marianne was going to be outstanding in her new role, but she had very little support back then. She diligently worked to establish budgets while pulling together spending and accounting processes. Not distant from her memory were her very first days of the campaign when she hastily opened bank accounts to accommodate the deluge of checks that were suddenly flooding in.

We also had a very capable chief technology officer (CTO) in Kevin Malover, our big catch from Orbitz. However, by the first week of April, he had only hired a handful of people. His team was racing to get servers up and the technology infrastructure built out, while also laboring to service newly issued personal computing equipment. Our Iowa HQ was often on the phone clamoring for urgently needed help with ordering phones, computers, and BlackBerry devices for their staff as well as equipment for the offices that were quickly beginning to dot that state.

Our personnel department had only three people at this point. It was ridiculously shorthanded at a time when every headquarters department and each of the four early state offices were desperate to hire. Director Jenn Clark and company had to do everything manually on spreadsheets, while managers with skeleton crews pressured her to expedite their priority hiring requests. Approaching paydays were particularly stressful as last-minute, unreported roster changes were handed to her by distracted department heads just as her team was preparing to process the payroll. This always caused a scramble to finalize the payee list against pressing deadlines to hit the "send" button so that money could be transmitted into employee bank accounts on the promised day.

The other departments that I oversaw within campaign management—including national field operations, legal, correspondence, the call center, headquarters management, and travel—were still mostly stacked with volunteers and also overwhelmed. With insufficient staff, limited technology, and undefined systems for hiring, spending, and contracting, we were building the airplane in midflight.

Impatience Erupts

The mounting challenges facing the staff in my departments were of little concern to others around us, who had their own fires to fight. Impatience quickly became epidemic in this pressure-filled environment, where systems were underdeveloped and communication was lacking. A get-it-done-at-any-cost attitude emerged, evident in the alarming instances of rogue spending and hiring that began to surface.

For example, occasional unknown hires that should have been pre-approved and processed through personnel were only uncovered after our IT staff received random requests for computing and communications equipment. A trickle of unauthorized campaign purchases were discovered by the CFO only after she'd received questionable invoices or unexplained shipments. She also stumbled across some contracts that had been signed by individuals who didn't have the authority to do so. Lastly, we had intermittent reports that staff was occupying some field offices before the leases had been finalized. This particular piece of news caused me extra heartburn. Similarly, the organizers in the states who had properly followed the prescribed office-opening procedures became aggravated at the protracted negotiations and lease reviews by us in Chicago that kept them working out of local coffee shops.

These kinds of incidents were limited and mostly born from the confusion of the time. But they were indicative of the tensions resulting from competing demands within the campaign between those at HQ who had to be deliberative and the managers in our states who had time-sensitive matters that required speedy resolution. We were all working toward a common cause, but the unique pressures on every one of us had the potential to create unfortunate missteps that only increased frustration and further flared tempers.

The campaign's management, my units in particular, had to quickly finalize proper systems and processes so that we could close these gaps in our operation. Our early work in this regard was critical to producing the structural capacities, work flow efficiencies, and collaborative advantages required to compete at the highest level against the daunting Clinton machine. How gracefully the organization moved through this awkward phase would have a direct impact on its future development and ultimate performance.

But the enormity of that challenge cannot be fully comprehended without my first offering a tutorial on the peculiar forces at work within the environment of the campaign start-up that, for us, was primarily driven by its explosive early growth.

Arrival

The migration to the campaign is a testament to the lure and reward of entrepreneurship. It is the uniquely American phenomenon of leaving everything behind to pursue the unimaginable. For many of us, the pilgrimage culminated at Obama for America (OFA) headquarters in Chicago, making it a gathering place for idealists, innovators, and risk takers. While it may be true that the campaign was a magnet for the young who had more to believe in and less to risk, we had folks walk through our doors who left behind high-paying employment at law firms, Wall Street companies, private businesses, and consulting practices. Personally witnessing the number of people streaming in without the promise of a job but who were instead motivated by a higher purpose was inspiring.

As is typical in campaigns, getting hired in the earliest days was mostly based on whom you knew. Friends, confidants, and trusted associates circled the candidate first. Next in were the reputable campaign and policy experts who were slotted into the top spots. They often recruited proven colleagues from their pasts to fill key positions under them. Finally, the self-selected arrived, eager to volunteer for anything with the hope that they would get noticed and quickly picked up. There was no time in this fast-moving environment for the conventional practice of interviewing candidates who'd responded to thoughtfully written job postings. When hiring in a pinch, managers tapped the high achievers they'd worked with previously or one of the impressive volunteers directly in front of them. It was a crude screening process, often referred to internally as "try and buy."

Everybody who got in the door had somebody open that door. This fostered strong loyalties around the directors, creating a tribal feature that is not uncommon in the campaign setting. Like any large or growing enterprise, a departmental identity is a natural development. In the campaign start-up, this characteristic is more sharply sculpted by the race against the others for expanded responsibilities and the competition for limited resources. The imperative for us in higher campaign management was to ensure that budding rivalries didn't take hold. If periodic outbreaks of infighting were to develop into serial disputes, entrenched camps could emerge threatening any possibility for enduring internal harmony. The ensuing drama would become crippling over time.

Managing in Silos

We were organized into predictable units for a political campaign. The communications team handled our public messaging and traditional media outreach, as well as monitoring campaign-related news in real time. New media was a flagship unit that wouldn't have existed independently in previous cycles. Giving it a unique and autonomous place in our structure signaled the innovative spirit of our campaign, while also recognizing digital communications as a maturing medium. This team had responsibility for our email communications, our innovative website, and our online organizing activities. The scheduling and advance department—we casually called it "Schedvance"—was essentially divided into two pieces. One part of that unit managed the candidate's appearances and, frankly, his time, while another section was focused on precisely organizing the activities around him in the communities he visited. As the campaign progressed, managing the surrogates—the VIP supporters who spoke on the candidate and campaign's behalf—became another major responsibility. Along with campaign operations I led, those were the larger shops.

Beyond that, we had smaller departments in headquarters that numbered about four or five staff in each. They included research, political, and national field, the latter with the mission of identifying and mobilizing local volunteers in the non-early-states and organizing our initial canvassing activities there. Lastly, we had a paid media department that was comprised of a very small team that coordinated our message activities and managed a universe of contracted firms for polling, producing TV and radio ads, and other related services.

We struggled from the outset with a type of tunnel vision and departmental isolation that quickly hardened into a series of individual silos inside headquarters. This was reinforced by our traditional organizational structure featuring clear lines of authority flowing through department heads to teams assembled around defined functional responsibilities. This system suited the management style of David Plouffe, who typically liked to work individually with the respective shop leaders to move projects forward.

His approach frustrated a few of the more collaborative-minded among us, who would have preferred that ideas be presented in our morning senior management meeting so that details and differences could have been hashed out together. These folks seemed to crave dialogue and, frankly, a more strategic role. That just wasn't David's way. But absent such a platform, communications between the departments and within the campaign generally were disjointed in the beginning, which made it feel at times like our right hand didn't know what our left hand was doing. New initiatives that had been launched by a given department just appeared suddenly on the headquarters floor, usually in the form of very last-minute requests for assistance that were then difficult for others to fulfill. These might take the form of door-to-door canvassing projects or fundraising house party blitzes, for example, requiring multidepartment involvement to be carried off effectively. At a time when we were still learning how to work and communicate together, the resulting pandemonium could lead to occasional and sometimes contentious skirmishes between staff.

Over time, our top management adapted to David's leadership style. We became better at talking offline together, and we shared information more immediately. This formed the basis for what would, in the long run, become unique, nimble, and proactive partnerships that ultimately served the organization well. Problems were solved informally and meetings occurred only as needed with just the necessary stakeholders attending. Work eventually got done more efficiently in this brand of management ecosystem.

Working without Boundaries

It was an electric time in the campaign: spirited, innovative, and hopeful. A highly driven, uninhibited group of people had been unleashed into this competitive environment. The mix of pace, purpose, and passion they brought with them was intoxicating, but in a workplace without boundaries it was a combination that had the potential to become toxic. We didn't have intrinsic parameters or organizational history to direct us.

Unlike the traditional business start-up where the assimilation of the work force can be modulated and the corporate culture systematically shaped, campaigns are hastily constructed and grow from these seeds of early turmoil and disarray. This causes a Wild West atmosphere in the beginning. What we were attempting was the organizational equivalent of creating a village from scratch, where a stream of people arrived all at once to a place that had no rules, no norms, and no structure. Chaos was the immediate consequence.

Everyone had their own personal tactics for getting what they wanted, and in an immature setting, even good people lost control of their "inner jerks." This resulted in failed first impressions and missteps that mortally wounded some very decent people early on. When reputations were on the line, blame could fly. Without systems or standards in place to help employees resolve their personal grievances, relationships risked being spoiled.

The casual atmosphere of the new campaign work environment could also be confusing. Headquarters, mostly fashioned by the young and the young-at-heart, sometimes felt more like a college dorm or living room than a national headquarters that would one day grow into a mammoth enterprise. At irregular intervals during the day, the frenetic tapping sound of a ping-pong ball cut through the noise of the floor, as those needing an outlet for the weighty demands of their work frequented the large green table that sat in the middle of our fundraising department.

Toward the end of every day, dozens of staff routinely congregated near Field Director Temo Figueroa's office for an informal golf-off. The cheers could even be heard on the other side of the building, as one by one people took their shot at making the fifteen-foot putt on the green carpet rolled out across the front of his door. Staff in the different departments also occasionally organized brief weekly happy hours on Friday afternoons, after which many went back to work until late at night. Long days stretched deep into evenings, contributing to frayed nerves and the blurring of lines between the personal and professional within our workplace.

Do It Differently

Behind the scripted candidate movements and disciplined messaging that voters see and hear on TV, the unpredictable human response to this complicated work environment can affect staff and ultimately each organization differently. My charge, and that of the rest of us in management, was to corral discord. From chaos, order must rise or the operation will fail.

I trace our early edge over the other campaigns to the success we had in getting control of these systemic idiosyncrasies. This gave our candidate all of the advantages that came with a highly effective work force and operation. We further benefited from the decision to set up headquarters in Chicago instead of Washington, D.C. Being next door to the key early battleground state of Iowa gave us a strategic boost, but it also spared us from the Washington ways and personality types that could have stunted our organizational development.

Even this early in the campaign, word was already circulating that sharpened knives were being wielded freely inside of rival Hillary Clinton's Washington-based operation, which was stacked with well established politicos. Much later, when internal disputes were publicized in the media, we learned the extent to which her campaign never properly matured following its organizational infancy. It occurred to me then that their leaders failed to move beyond the early mayhem; rather, they brought it along with them as the enterprise grew.

I directly credit our candidate for setting the right tone early. Barack Obama was adamant from the start that he wanted to run his campaign differently. Honestly, every candidate says this, which made the pronouncement sound a bit cliché. But what set Barack apart from others before him was that he went further than to simply say we would do it differently—he gave us a road map for how that should happen. He communicated a set of organizational principles that reflected his values, offering specific guidance for our campaign that calibrated it differently and positioned us more competitively. Herein was the first secret to our organizational success: *No drama. Respect everyone. Build it from the bottom up.*

These words rippled through the campaign until it became our mantra. With them, Senator Obama took command of his fledgling organization. This is not insignificant, as public office seekers often struggle to balance their dual roles as candidate and CEO of the campaign organization. Some cede the management entirely to a campaign manager or to consultants, even detaching completely from it. Others are overly involved in the daily affairs and routine decisions, becoming a distraction to staff and often neglecting their own duties at the same time. Though he may have battled in the early days to fully command his role as a national candidate, from the outset Senator Obama communicated a clear vision for his organization and he demonstrated a firm grasp of its management.

Barack Obama delegated authority over the campaign to a person he trusted, David Plouffe. However, the culture—the ethos of the organization—that, he wholly influenced. We all knew what the boss expected. Infighting or unhealthy competition would not be tolerated. Respect was a cornerstone for how we should relate to one another. The senator's desire for a bottom-up organization offered us all a stake in the work and a call to leadership. His words were all we had to start with, but at the end of the day, they provided us with a clear code of conduct.

This wasn't simply a prescription for a pleasant work environment. It changed the personality and character of our work force. Beyond telling us how to do it differently, Senator Obama also described the type of individual that he wanted in his organization. While other campaigns sought proven career organizers with long political résumés and deep Washington experience, we were looking for hungry, unselfish individuals with positive attitudes (no drama) and varied backgrounds (respect everyone) that had the capacity to own the work (build it from the bottom up). For those of us in management, this gave us license to hire people who offered more than a specific skill set or expertise. We hired leaders. It was an important distinction that offered our organization a subtle yet powerful edge as the competition progressed later.

The Power of Community

The most important application of this framework was that Senator Obama presented a path for us to transition from working as a group of individuals to coming together as a community. Ego calls good people forward into politics. This is true for candidates, and it is true for those who are drawn to their campaigns. While people first pass through the doors of headquarters alone, once inside, the aspirations of the individual must be subjugated to and aligned with those of the larger community. Organizational success relies on capable individuals coalescing around a unique set of shared values. The Obama axiom of no drama, respect, and bottom-up organization facilitated an important transformation that lifted our prospects in the race because the passion that motivated each of us was quickly harnessed into the power of a unified and cohesive community.

In full disclosure, there wasn't universal comfort with the candidate's prescribed principles. One of my fellow senior colleagues lamented that "no drama" silenced voices and openly expressed displeasure that this candidate didn't want to hear all views. Many months later, a former Clinton staffer who'd recently joined our organization was less indignant but equally resigned when she expressed her exasperation over an issue that bothered her. "I want to be more forceful, but you guys have this 'no drama Obama' thing going on that I don't want to challenge too aggressively," she told me.

In the end, however, we succeeded in giving people more than a voice. We gave them a stake in the work. Looking back, one of our great triumphs was that in a bottom-up organization, our staff and volunteers were fully empowered and they truly made a difference. We became a no-nonsense campaign that didn't spend a lot of time squabbling over direction. We all knew where we had to go, and we came to understand what was needed to get there.

Leading from the Inside

As a manager, I found Senator Obama's guidance helpful as I approached my own work. My job was to lead from within the organization, and his words were useful in focusing my energy and attention. The need to immediately calm this hypercharged environment required swift action. At a time when some might have worried about where they sat, what meetings they were invited to, and what decisions they were being included in or excluded from, *no drama* meant that I had to concern myself less with my own status and more with the broader good. Arriving in the early days of flaring tempers and unrestrained frustration, *respect* dictated that I confront conflict with patience and objectivity. *Bottom-up organizing* meant that my own sights had to be trained downward and across the campaign, with a central concentration on helping those at the lower rungs of the organization get the tools they needed to succeed. It was the candidate's vision that we would empower the grassroots, but this had to occur inside our own organization, as well as in the field.

I had two primary objectives during those early days. First, my teams needed to perform with speed and precision. There were systems to develop and processes to communicate outwardly. I also wanted us to execute our responsibilities reliably while resisting the urge to expand our duties beyond that which was expected of us. We needed to earn the trust of our peers.

My second goal was to quickly get people into their lanes, critical when attempting to bring order to chaos. On the shop floor, much of my time was spent wrangling wayward staff and clarifying roles wherever there was confusion. I defined responsibilities and made sure all parties involved understood them. This kept everyone accountable for results and saved me from having to spend valuable time mediating time-consuming personal disputes that had the potential to become a distraction from core activities.

During the early stages of the campaign, I was also concerned about survival—my own and that of my staff. Asserting leadership among strangers is a risky proposition. One must proceed with caution. It is difficult for those who enter campaigns in positions of leadership to retain their stature all the way to the end. I'd once heard of an experiment that demonstrated how an assertive monkey was never allowed to climb toward a bunch of bananas at the top of a ladder without being punished and pushed down by fellow caged primates. The same dynamics are at work in organizational leadership. In a fluid and volatile environment, managing one's authority so that it is effective and lasting requires proper tuning. Even as a senior-level manager, I was careful to assert my authority in ways that would be viewed by others as evenhanded and proportional.

I was especially protective of the people I managed in those earliest days and was very direct with my instruction that even as scuffles erupted around us, staff who worked with me were prohibited from actively participating in them. I didn't want us to be regarded as confrontational, particularly since other departments were counting on us to help them. Teamwork and collaboration were our primary goals. We needed to contribute to maintaining harmony.

More importantly, I wanted to ensure that my folks didn't spoil relationships at the beginning that would jeopardize their ability to assert their leadership later, when it was truly needed. Where there was employee conflict, I was quick to step in. In an unformed environment, this was a time to educate staff on how to constructively assimilate, collaborate, and effectively resolve differences. Our workplace would eventually mature and render such intervention unnecessary, but acquainting employees with acceptable protocols wasn't a small part of my job in those first days.

Sadly, not everyone in the campaign emerged from this period unscathed. Some managers habitually overstepped their authority, and in doing so, undermined their own credibility. Others avoided the fray too willingly and unwittingly gave away their power to others who were all too eager to fill the leadership gap. There were also a fair number of junior staffers who, because of their strident conduct toward some of their peers, struggled to overcome damaged reputations. In this environment, your credibility is all you have. Yet, even as some fell, others rose. Talent was always finding its way to the top.

As the thaw of spring began to take noticeable effect in Chicago, we saw real signs of cooperation and collaboration emerging between our staff and departments. Systems were quickly laid down, and by the end of April, operational processes had been developed, communicated, and were being effectively implemented. There was evidence that we were getting control of our rapidly growing operation. Most importantly, we had successfully completed the transition from self to community.

Big!

"It's so big," the voice boomed from the other side of the building. The tall, thin gentleman sporting a black White Sox ball cap repeated those words over and over as he gazed wonderingly at his surroundings. Drawing nearer, he seemed uncomfortable with the mammoth dimensions of our new headquarters. I patiently waited for him to approach and noted that the smattering of staff he'd strolled past appeared to be drowning in office space.

It was hard for any of us at that moment to imagine that we could ever really fill all of the empty desks. Phones had yet to be installed. Computer monitors and keyboards dotted the landscape of what looked like a large desk farm. The walls were awash in sunlight, which only emphasized their barrenness as they waited to be dressed with campaign signage that hadn't yet arrived. As a stopgap, Mrs. Obama soon convened the children of staff for a pizza and poster-drawing party that produced the kids' artwork that long decorated our workspace.

When the candidate finally made it across the floor to me, I reached for his outstretched hand and welcomed the senator on his first visit to our new headquarters. We exchanged the usual pleasantries, and then he stiffened his grip and sharpened his gaze. "Now listen, keep it tight, Henry," the senator remarked with his typically warm smile. "You know I like it run tight." This was consistent with his previous instruction that he wanted the campaign to be run like a business. He then dropped his hand and slapped me on the shoulder, ambling slowly past me and shifting his sights upward. "This is sure big," he announced again, his voice trailing off as he marched on.

That moment stuck with me for the rest of the campaign. Barack seemed quite relaxed that day as he freely wandered through HQ unescorted. In the not-too-distant future, he would be assigned a secret service detail, which would limit his movements even in his own headquarters. It was a development that I'm sure forever changed him.

Of course, I didn't escape untouched either. As the campaign mushroomed over the coming weeks and months, I too would become constrained by it. During the course of the next nineteen months, I'd not have the luxury of casual weekends or uninterrupted time with my wife. Instead, I became beholden to the demands of the hundreds—and later, thousands—of staff and volunteers who eventually populated our organization.

The flashing red light on my BlackBerry served as a constant reminder.

2

Stick to the Plan

JULY 7, 2007: *The irony of working for a media-dependent, communications-driven organization is the noticeable isolation I feel from the general news events of the day. I work in a bubble. A small screen on the building's elevator rotating the day's top headlines serves as my primary news source. Whatever it delivers during the eleven-story ride is my fix.*

Chicago, Iowa

"The states are unhappy." That was the first thing Steve Hildebrand told me when I joined the campaign. Steve was very specific with his concerns about a lack of responsiveness at headquarters to our staff in the early states. He was particularly worried about Iowa and asked for my help in straightening out the problem. His request was important because our leadership team was dedicated to a simple strategy for securing the Democratic nomination: win Iowa.

Despite the fact that we'd trailed well behind in the polls from the outset, we believed that if we prevailed in Iowa, the force of that win would propel us through the early contests and on to victory. David Plouffe was supremely confident from the earliest days that Barack Obama was ideally suited to such a strategy. David often referred to the senator as the perfect momentum candidate. Though the polling numbers coming out of the Hawkeye State were daunting, Plouffe felt certain that as voters got to know Senator Obama they would quickly warm to him.

To help us overcome our long odds, Steve Hildebrand was brought on at HQ as our top field and political staffer. He also had the distinction of being the "Early States" director, meaning that he oversaw the strategy and build-out of the first states that would host primary contests in January 2008. They were Iowa (January 3), New Hampshire (January 8), Nevada (January 19), and South Carolina (January 26). Paul Tewes was hired as the Iowa state director. Steve and Paul had been business partners before the campaign and ran a highly regarded political consulting firm together. Both were aggressive organizers with long histories in Iowa politics.

Steve was adamant that our Chicago headquarters staff had to stay focused on serving the needs of those four important bases. He made it clear that we worked for the states and not the other way around. As someone who'd never really been much of a creature of national headquarters, I was an easy mark for his sermons. I'd had a long career running mostly state-based organizations and community campaigns, so Steve's philosophy was one I wholly agreed with and applauded.

With an initial fundraising target for 2007 set at $50 million, the first budget we constructed reflected our commitment to this early state strategy. It was a spending plan that was supposed to take us through the end of the calendar year, but it wasn't a national budget. It didn't even fund the twenty-two states and the U.S. territory that were scheduled to have contests on February 5, a big day on the 2008 election calendar known as Super Tuesday. Instead, our money was to be spent only on those first four January races. At David's direction, we dedicated the money we hoped to raise to building and operating the early states and Illinois.

This triggered weeks of haggling with a dozen national HQ department leaders and the four early state heads. In that lineup, however, often to the consternation of the other state directors, Iowa was always considered to be first among equals. Not surprisingly, this was where the bulk of our early-state resources were targeted.

Even the national headquarters and our Illinois field operations just down the street from us were viewed largely as appendages of our neighbor to the west. Jon Carson, then the Illinois state director, was building a program that had a mission not of identifying local support for our own statewide election on February 5, but of getting volunteers from Illinois across the state line every weekend. And at headquarters, we were so deliberately trained on Iowa that I may as well have listed "Chicago, Iowa" as my work address.

We were all in for Iowa.

The Ops Desk

Steve's heartburn over the lack of support for the states was, therefore, something of an organizational crisis. Fortunately, I already had a pretty clear idea of what was wrong: it was a reflection of the havoc at our national headquarters. We were distracted by our own growth and staffing buildup. In the frenzy that accompanied our organization's launch, staff and volunteers in Chicago quickly shuffled through roles. Some individuals were moved into new positions to fill glaring operational gaps, others were reassigned to meet a suddenly pressing need, and there were still more that dropped everything to accept a coveted paid job in another area of the campaign.

For our state colleagues, this meant that the helpful person on the other end of the phone one day might suddenly be absent the next. That would spawn a fresh round of calls coming from the field to find a new contact that might once again offer needed support. They struggled to navigate the maze at HQ for help with hiring staff, processing office leases, procuring contracts, securing Internet and phones, and ordering general office equipment. This search was made infinitely more difficult by the fact that we were not structured for ease of access to outside users, whose range of questions usually crossed departmental lines. For example, the stranger offering them assistance with office leases couldn't provide technology support or help with personnel matters.

While state managers were stalled in their efforts to get up and running, their newly on-boarded staff got grumpier in the coffee shops where they were temporarily parked. From there they accessed the Internet on their personal laptops until they could be issued campaign computers and get clearance to move into new field offices. There was frustration on our side, as well. Our HQ staff was peppered with calls from an array of unfamiliar individuals with different temperaments seeking answers to the very same questions. This only contributed to the cycle of confusion.

I recognized this as a common problem in organizational start-ups and knew precisely what we had to do to solve it. The states needed a sole point of contact at headquarters that could help them access the myriad services they relied upon to facilitate their growth and ongoing effectiveness. I immediately sketched out a plan whereby a single individual would be assigned to assist them with all of their organizational needs. I named this the Early States Operations Desk. One call to the Ops Desk would offer state leaders access to a suite of services that included specialized legal, financial, technology, and personnel support. Gone were the days of phone surfing or sprayed emails to our headquarters for help.

One of the reasons this plan fit so well within our structure is that it capitalized on our organizational architecture, with our day-to-day campaign management functions all falling under my purview. Though we had a technology department with a CTO, a personnel office managed by a director, and a financial operation headed by a CFO, those departments along with legal, travel, HQ management, and a handful of others all flowed to me. While each functioned autonomously, they didn't exist independently of the others, as can often be the case in campaign organizations. This meant that I had the inherent ability to bring all of those services together in one package for the states.

I quickly enlisted the help of a sensational young organizer, Dan Jones, to manage the Ops Desk. Dan was still a volunteer when the two of us designed the Ops Desk system. During that time, Dan created a large binder for the state directors and operations managers that served as a toolkit for all of their organizational needs. Inside were detailed instructions for state leaders on opening offices, securing Internet and telecommunications services, hiring staff, ordering individual computers and office equipment, and obtaining travel and expenditure approvals. Accompanying the guidance for each of these activities were the necessary forms to initiate the respective processes.

Of course, these systems were still being formed even as Dan was compiling the written documentation into a binder. And because processes were constantly modified at this time, producing paper updates for the early state representatives was a burden. As a solution, Dan also found a web-based platform that offered a private digital space for communicating with his leaders. Here he could house an electronic toolkit, upload the most current versions of the request forms, message leaders in real time, and host project management calendars tailored uniquely to the specific needs of the respective states.

During this time, I fiercely lobbied Plouffe to create a new position in my staffing plan so I could hire Dan to be our national field operations director. I knew we needed this role and he was just the person for the job. The title was big, but I wanted one that reflected the importance of his responsibilities and not the size of the department. Dan would need some authority behind him to execute this role effectively.

After formally joining our staff, Dan was fully available as the designated contact to each of the four early states twenty-four hours a day, seven days a week. There was now seamless two-way communication occurring between each of the states and my shops via the Ops Desk. Dan even had a special phone sitting next to the general campaign phone on his desk that served as a designated line for the four state operations managers. He consistently delivered for them, and his service ethos became the hallmark of our operation. In the later days of the campaign, the Ops Desk grew in staff and responsibility. But throughout 2007, it was a one-man enterprise impressively executed by Dan, who had an easy demeanor, sharp knowledge of the field, and a commitment to quick responsiveness that made him a natural in the role.

Super Tuesdays

One of the first things we did as part of the Ops Desk response was set up a weekly one-hour conference call between HQ and the leadership in each of the early states. The second day of the workweek came to be known as "Super Tuesday" because that's when our CTO, CFO, personnel director, and chief staff counsel from legal were pulled away from their many demands and busy schedules to sit in on four consecutive hours of phone meetings. Dan meticulously accepted agenda items in advance, and our senior managers and supporting staff all crowded into Kevin Malover's office for the exhaustive summits.

These were often thorny exchanges during which we resolved budget issues, untangled clauses holding up lease agreements, and endured painfully long discussions about specific phone and office equipment needs. We drilled down to the most basic details to ensure movement on all fronts so that the week ahead could be devoted to getting things done. Super Tuesday turned out to be an invaluable offering for our state leaders. Typically the forgotten constituency of most campaigns, these folks had a direct line to our most senior headquarters staff and got the highest level of attention from them in our organization.

Some of our first operational advantages over the Clinton campaign were made possible by the Ops Desk system. Later, I learned that while Senator Clinton's organization ultimately drifted toward a similar model for communicating these types of needs between the states and headquarters, they lagged behind us by a full six months. This meant that we had the advantage of twenty-six weeks of direct work with the states before her team even began to engage at the same level. That's one hundred hours of dedicated phone meetings in which, every week, we scoped out requirements and were held accountable for delivering on our commitments.

I've been told that even after the Clinton campaign consolidated their services and stepped up their field support program, scheduled phone calls were poorly attended by the states, and high-level headquarters staffers were never made available the way ours had routinely been. The end result was that Clinton's organizers languished on the ground for long bouts. I am certain this contributed to the stories I heard about the strained relations between their state and headquarters staffs.

Conversely, the support and attention we gave to the states meant that our operations on the ground were quickly up and running. While we weren't wholly spared some of the normal tensions between headquarters and field offices, our system facilitated remarkably strong coordination and collaboration. This offered us an incredible early, if unnoticed, edge, and it made us faster and more nimble on the ground.

The Tale of Two Memos

We made all the right moves in those first days to position ourselves to be competitive organizationally. Things were beginning to settle down, and we were proactively shaping our programs and systems. But while the best plans can be made and followed, there always looms the potential for an unexpected event to distract and overwhelm the environment. I've heard it said that an airplane crash is the result of not one, but a series of mistakes. Organizational crises materialize the same way, and like any emergency, they come on very fast.

The typical crisis follows a predictable pattern. First, there is the initial miscue, usually born from human error or emotion. Next is the mistake that is often linked to some sort of attempted cover-up, which was why I always instructed staff that they were to report problems "when they first happened and not when they second happened." Finally, add into the mix a bad reaction from somewhere else or introduce the inevitable finger-pointing, and you have the common characteristics of an organization that has or will soon topple into a crisis. Such developments typically play out behind the scenes and away from public view. Sometimes they make news.

The D-Punjab Memo

It was late in the week; a typical morning for me in mid-June. I didn't get any kind of advanced warning from Plouffe or Hildebrand. It wasn't a topic in our senior staff meeting. I first heard about the problem from Marianne, our chief financial officer, when she came over to ask me what I knew about "the memo in the press." Staff was coming to her with something they referred to as the "Punjab memo." I probed her on this topic a bit, but quickly diverted my attention back to my own issues at hand. I was a little embarrassed that I didn't know anything about it, but I didn't. Maybe something had come across my email that I hadn't yet seen, I thought to myself.

Soon I was getting the same questions. During the course of my conversations and after some light investigation online, I discovered that the source for the alarm was a memo that had been leaked to the press titled: "Hillary Clinton (D-Punjab)'s Personal Financial and Political Ties to India." The title pretty much speaks to the cause for the furor that soon followed. The document was filled with facts and numbers suggesting Hillary's support for outsourcing American jobs.

To me, the leak appeared to be intentional on our part. The purpose for discreetly delivering a document like this to the media would have been to prompt an investigation into these issues without it being directly attributed to us. This is a common campaign practice, but not one I had thought we would engage in much, frankly.

I continued to pay little attention to the brewing tempest. It seemed a very unfortunate public relations problem that was well outside of my lane. If there had been an internal breakdown somewhere, Plouffe didn't approach me, so I didn't insert myself. My rule was that if it didn't involve me, I didn't involve me either. This kept my attention where it needed to be during that frenetic time.

As the controversy progressed, it became clear that our research department was being fingered for producing the piece, along with our communications team for leaking it. This was a problem. The Indian American community was outraged and publicly demanded the names of those on our staff who were responsible. This led to a spate of articles calling out two of our employees specifically by name and accusing them of similarly questionable tactics while working on previous elections. A narrative began to form in the media that while his speeches were filled with lofty rhetoric calling for a new kind of politics, Senator Obama was surrounded by old-school "hacks" and long-established dirty tricksters. Although the evidence produced of these individuals' so-called previous transgressions seemed pretty flimsy, the prospect of our friends actually being personally singled out in the press was unnerving. Once the media goes down that path, it's never quite clear where the prospecting will end. When staff and high-profile stakeholders feel vulnerable or exposed, the organization gets jittery.

As the external pressures built over the ensuing days, doubts about Senator Obama's leadership emerged in the media. These were developing on three fronts in particular. First, our candidate's personal reputation was in peril. This story directly slammed against the image our campaign was presenting: that Barack Obama was someone who would change the nature of our public discourse. Second, his credibility with Indian Americans and other minority communities had been suddenly thrown into question. Therefore, his treatment of these events would be of particular interest to key parties in our budding coalition. Finally, the senator's capability as an executive was on full display. How he guided his fledgling organization through this firestorm—how he managed his own leadership—would leave an impression on voters.

The story hung around in the news over the weekend before Senator Obama finally addressed the matter himself on Monday, June 18. The *Des Moines Register* reported that our boss described the event as a "screw-up on the part of our research team." He added that it wasn't anything that had been seen by him or his senior staff. He also characterized the matter as "stupid and caustic."

This created a new direction for the controversy. The media, which always sniffs out tension in a story, immediately pounced on the candidate-versus-the-campaign angle. They began to focus on past instances when our candidate had been at odds with his own staff. For example, in February he distanced himself from a verbal swipe taken at the Clintons by our communications director, Robert Gibbs, after the defection of one their loyal Hollywood backers. Reporting also highlighted that, in May, our scheduling staff was blamed for not booking the senator into a New Hampshire fire fighter's event.

Chatter on the headquarters floor quickly kicked into overdrive. As we got deeper into Monday and on into Tuesday, murmurings of indignation that the candidate could so easily "throw his staff under the bus" could be heard everywhere. Whether some were easily influenced by these news reports and blogs or people really had suffered hurt feelings, the outside stories had clearly become an inside distraction.

"This Is My Organization—I Take Responsibility"

The drumbeat soon faded as Senator Obama's reported remarks to the *Register* were buttressed with a separate statement of apology issued to the Indian American community. "I consider the entire campaign—and in particular myself—responsible for the mistake," he said. The seriousness of the statement was illuminated by his explicit instruction that David Plouffe and chief strategist David Axelrod were being tasked with reviewing all materials prior to their public release to avoid future mistakes. Having now assumed personal accountability, the controversy in the media slowly dissipated. At headquarters, the storm among staff passed as quickly as it had surfaced.

As a campaign moment, this incident went mostly unnoticed by voters, and devoting this much ink to it arguably exaggerates its significance. On the other hand, it was a defining moment in our short organizational history. While this may have seemed like a simple public relations crisis requiring little more than a textbook management response, these events ultimately presented something far more foreboding. This played on one of the subtle tensions woven into the fabric of all campaigns that probes whether the candidate views himself as being of or apart from the organization—whether, in this case, he worked for the campaign or the campaign worked for him. At stake was Senator Obama's credibility as a manager and as the CEO of his organization. It was a delicate balance. He had to navigate the outside pressures while holding the respect of his own employees.

The press had aggressively probed this relationship, and frankly, staff waited on the answer. We wanted to know as much as anyone else how our chief would respond—whether there would be firings, forced resignations, or even a good public shaming as was all speculated in the media. These were very early days, but staffers were already tired from the long hours and slightly less influenced by the stars in our eyes. As events unfolded, the campaign's employees were still searching for clues as to how the boss regarded the work force. His reaction mattered.

Barack stepped up as the CEO of his organization and addressed these concerns head on. He didn't cast blame; rather, he accepted ownership of the failure that led to the fallout. In doing so, he took the spotlight off our staff and calmed the fraying nerves inside our organization. In this moment, Senator Obama also answered the question about his relationship to the rest of us by demonstrating that he could lead from the front as the candidate and from above as the chief executive officer. Most importantly, he was one of us and not apart from us. His response was revealing, not just to his staff, but also to political watchers who wanted to understand his capacity as a leader.

Our campaign manager was equally deserving of praise for his role in navigating the crisis after the initial error had occurred. David Plouffe never made the event an issue within the campaign. Instead, he played it very low key. He didn't dwell on it in private conversations or in senior staff meetings. Any big reactions from him would surely have triggered a blame game within the organization and that would have been toxic. We were feeling enough heat from the outside; we didn't need the temperature to rise inside. David's nonreaction kept the controversy contained to whatever was playing out in the headlines. Also, by keeping the drama down, Plouffe gave the candidate the space he needed in those initial days of the crisis to get the facts before addressing the matter publicly. This allowed the campaign to continue moving forward with options.

The adept handling of this matter by the candidate and our management ultimately allowed the D-Punjab memo foible to pass as a mostly unremarkable event. That kept the rest of the campaign staff focused on Iowa and the other early states. Operational unity had been our greatest single defining characteristic to date. Had the crisis been mismanaged—and there were many opportunities for that, particularly with the press fanning the flames—it could have distracted us from the vital work at hand and ultimately led to enduring acrimony. That was a recipe for failure.

Clinton's Memogate

The Clinton campaign had a sensitive document of its own spill out into the public domain just three weeks before ours had. On May 23, 2007, a memorandum from Clinton Deputy Campaign Manager Mike Henry exploded onto the Internet. In the leaked memo, titled "An alternative nomination strategy," the experienced politico pitched a forceful case that his campaign should pull up stakes in Iowa so that resources could be directed to states where Senator Clinton "might have a better chance of winning."

If our campaign was all in for Iowa, this memo conversely described something more reflective of a "Leave Iowa" strategy. The following is an excerpt from the memo obtained and run by the *New York Times*, in which Mike Henry stated:

> The caucus process in Iowa, once grounded in grassroots and volunteer organizing, has out priced [*sic*] itself (estimated campaign costs = minimum $15 million between field and TV). We will not have a financial advantage or an organizational advantage over any of our opponents. Further, the results are likely to be inconclusive on caucus night (first, second, and third place decided by a point or two) and they will provide little or no bounce for anyone. Worst case scenario: this effort may bankrupt the campaign and provide little if any political advantage.

This was a bombshell coming out of that campaign! Many of us knew Mike, which only added to the intrigue surrounding the controversy. But the motives for the leak—it initially looked to me like somebody was being thrown under the campaign bus—mixed with the astonishing revelation that there was still an internal debate raging inside that camp about strategy, made the whole thing curious. These were issues that should have long been settled. Also, the concerns Mike expressed that committing to the nation's first contest might potentially bankrupt their organization only added to the fascination over exactly what was going on over there.

According to David Yepsen of the *Des Moines Register*, Senator Clinton described the ordeal as a "kerfuffle" within her campaign. This was a striking admission, but not a surprising one given the comments of some of her other senior aides who, according to *Politico.com* and speaking on the condition of anonymity, said it was unlikely that their boss would follow Mike's prescribed guidance. Still, with the activity-laden Memorial Day weekend looming, the timing couldn't have been worse. The trip would be uncomfortable for Hillary, I expected, not unlike offending your mother-in-law before an approaching holiday visit.

From my perspective, getting this memo via the media was like intercepting a rival football team's playbook before the big playoff game. It was an attention-grabber in Chicago and somewhat inexplicable to us. Here was evidence that the internal unity and discipline that would emerge from our own controversy weeks later was clearly lacking inside of Camp Clinton. The fact that the campaign's senior management was not in agreement on a way forward must have had a powerfully negative effect inside of that organization—the kind that rips a staff apart. Without consensus around a plan, victory would hang in the balance. Despite this revelation, however, the press continued to report for many months about the professional, polished, and overpowering Clinton machine.

Boom!

As the summer passed, our campaign moved into the final stages of preparation for full engagement. After having focused for six months on building a competitive organization from scratch, I worked diligently with the staff in my departments to tighten our systems in front of the rapidly approaching primary contests. To this end, I wanted to run a few diagnostic checks and enlisted the help of a volunteer, Josh Gray, whom I later hired as assistant COO. Together, he and I cooked up a plan we called Operation Campaign Mystery Shopper. The idea was to have Josh poke around and look for soft spots in our operating structure.

Drawing on his organizational expertise, Josh developed a performance checklist that would help us evaluate the speed and responsiveness of our operation to common requests. His list included: (1) inquiring with some of our local field offices about volunteer opportunities; (2) emailing questions to the campaign's information center to learn about our candidate's policy positions; (3) calling the 800 number to gauge customer responsiveness; (4) navigating the website to assess ease of use and access to important information; and (5) making an online donation. Additionally, Josh called our headquarters from an outside phone posing as a small town reporter asking to speak to our campaign spokesperson. He also dialed in as a vendor trying to sell a product to test where his inquiry would be directed.

Happily, we found that every area of our campaign earned strong marks from our mystery shopper. Well, all but one. Josh was easily passed from our switchboard directly to the press secretary, but we quickly fixed it so that there would be a proper screening process going forward.

Armed with hard data that we could use to measure and analyze our progress to date, Josh applied the same tests to the other campaigns to get a side-by-side picture of how we stacked up against the competition. The findings were stunning. While our organization was highly responsive, the others were terribly uneven. This included the campaigns of our chief rivals, Hillary Clinton and John Edwards. Phones went unanswered. Voice messages left were often not returned. Email auto replies had typos in them. Expressions of volunteer interest were ignored or follow-up was sluggish. Vendor inquiries sometimes went to high-level campaign officials who would have then been vulnerable to long, distracting sales pitches or tie-ups.

In every instance, our campaign gave a better and faster response to his queries than our competitors. Furthermore, Josh found that he had the chance to add his name to our email list with every touch on our website. Such was not the case with the other campaigns. This was evidence that we more aggressively worked at building our database of contacts. Overall, the experiment demonstrated for us the soundness of our operation, while exposing the other campaigns as loose and disorganized.

Put the Right People on the Bus

During the last weeks of summer, I began making critical personnel adjustments that would maximize overall staff performance. Not every hire from the frenzied early days was a right fit, and not everyone who came in during the start-up period was positioned ideally for the next phase: the competition. Also, the needs of the campaign were quickly changing as the primary contests approached. My intention was to have the right leaders in key roles by Labor Day in the departments I managed. These were the folks I wanted driving our operation into early March, which was when I expected the nomination would be settled.

I felt strongly that the campaign as a whole needed to make similar moves. This might even include tinkering with our higher-level HQ management lineup to open a path up for some of our proven second tier leaders. If we didn't shuffle the deck, we risked becoming flat-footed and lethargic at a time when we had to lift our game. Despite the organizational weaknesses Josh had recently exposed, the Clinton machine was still the most formidable in recent campaign memory. While we were good, we needed to quickly get to the next level in order to be competitive in the primaries.

These would not be easy issues to tackle. We didn't have newly created positions in headquarters to work with, making these kinds of adjustments difficult. And the steel ceiling that had formed at the top of the organization back in the earliest days made upward mobility a challenge. The lack of movement at the highest levels created a stagnant flow chart, common in campaign start-ups. Remember, most of our staff had been hired at the same time, during the early surge. Given that the expectant life cycle of a campaign is short, almost everyone was prepared to enlist for the duration—however long that might be. Therefore, with no shifts occurring at the top, the organizational structure was bottlenecked. There were no openings to advance toward, leaving nowhere for the second leadership tier to rise. This could leave us vulnerable to developing personal rivalries and infighting.

At the same time, we were very much aware that after the four January races the battleground map was going to suddenly expand. On February 5 alone there would be twenty-three races. This meant that we would have to begin making plans to cover more area with only marginally more staff. We needed to move people out of headquarters. Most would see the possibility as an opportunity to be where they could make the greatest contribution to our effort. Some would view their move into the states, whether temporarily or permanently, as a demotion. That made this a complicated chore.

Adding to the challenge, in our business dramatic personnel moves are pursued at the risk of rankling key supporters and provoking negative news stories. Campaign staff often have direct ties to influential people, including political figures, media personalities, and big donors. This complicates the optics associated with making noticeable shifts within the organization. These sensitivities can cause inertia at the executive level. The prospect of media scrutiny—the fear of the spotlight that is invited when shuffling high-profile staff—can result in a pileup of personnel problems that may require a broader and more dramatic response later. The outcome is usually some sort of staff shake-up, an all-too-common event in campaigns. Such activity almost always provokes unwanted stories in the most vulnerable of times.

Beginning in September, David, Steve, and I proactively waded through a number of key personnel decisions across the organization in advance of the approaching primaries. Some in higher levels of management had taken the organization as far as they could before the toll on their families and other personal demands forced them to move on from the campaign. Others were asked to transition into new roles outside of headquarters, in states where their advanced expertise would have the greatest impact. This gave us added firepower in the field since these were typically experienced staffers who could offer critical knowledge, focus on discreet projects of high strategic importance, or serve as surrogates who could confidently speak to key audiences on behalf of the campaign and candidate. In other cases, some of our midlevel staff were penciled into roles as directors and lead managers in the new states soon coming online.

As people moved out, others moved up to take their places within HQ. At the end of this process, we very effectively reorganized some of our key staff in headquarters and across the country to meet the new needs of the campaign heading into the next phase.

The Gathering Storm

Uncertainty accompanies change, and with each personnel move a sense of insecurity began to seep into our work force. Rising anxiety levels were further intensified by the realization that we were just over a dozen weeks from Iowa. We'd staked everything as a campaign on that state, and our staff was keenly aware that a loss there might also mean sudden and abrupt unemployment.

The reality of the risk that each of us had individually assumed was now staring directly at us. Our staff had endured great hardship, long hours, and in many cases, family angst. In my own case, Sine was due to give birth in just weeks. We faced the prospect of being suddenly displaced in a strange city with a newborn and no savings, given that we'd tapped deep into our nest egg to make all this possible. What we once excitedly pursued as a dream we realized could potentially become a nightmare.

We were not alone. Several hundred other staff members and stake-holders faced similar fears in one way or another. Volunteers had given countless hours to the campaign because this was a candidate and a cause they believed in. Many of our large donors, respected in their professions and communities, had put their reputations on the line when asking friends and colleagues to open their wallets. Senator Obama himself, like many on our staff, had been away from his family often for many days on end.

Now well into our eighth month, we had all grown weary from the pace and the long hours. At headquarters, beginning Labor Day weekend, I sent out a memo encouraging all of our staff to work seven-day weeks, though many of us had already been doing so for a couple months. I had asked my own staff to start that routine right after the July 4 holiday. Around this same time, we informed employees that their extended family—parents and other loved ones—should know not to expect any of us home for Thanksgiving or the December holidays. This news caused some irritation. It also meant that we would have several extra place settings around our table for Christmas dinner at my home to accommodate some of the campaign orphans on my staff who had no family in Chicago.

We began assigning more and more headquarters staff to work in states to meet the growing needs on the ground. Most going out were excited; they knew they would be where they could best help us win. But these folks also had to make decisions about what to do with the homes they were leaving behind. Many were locked into long-term leases that couldn't be broken. That forced us to scramble to find supporters who could put them up in the unfamiliar towns where they were newly assigned. There they would sleep on couches for countless weeks while paying rent on their empty apartments back in Chicago.

With these moves to the field, those of us that remained in headquarters could look forward to a reduction in staff by as much as 30 percent, coupled with anticipated workload increases due to the growing demands for our services as the primary elections approached. That we in headquarters ultimately succeeded in meeting the needs of our state colleagues was a tribute to our amazing volunteers who stepped up to close the gaping holes that opened after regular staff had been sent out.

Breaking Point

The tensions that had been building could also be partly traced to a CNN poll released in September, which indicated that Senator Clinton had increased her national lead by a margin of 46 to 23 percent. This news shot through the campaign like a rocket. The obvious unrest that accompanied these results was further exacerbated by the mainstream media's obsession with national polling numbers. Even as we saw signs of momentum developing in Iowa, panic set in because all that was being reported in the news was the nationwide data that showed us losing. It caused turbulence inside that threatened to break down the unity we'd long maintained around the Win Iowa strategy.

Key stakeholders associated with the campaign were losing faith and began to openly challenge the wisdom of our course. There was a growing chorus calling for Senator Obama to spend less time in Iowa so that he could visit more states. The same voices also pleaded to have more resources siphoned away to fund national ads that could counter the worrying trends in public opinion. Winning Iowa wasn't enough, some argued, when we were losing everywhere else.

Morale was also buckling inside headquarters, and displeasure with the campaign's leadership was being openly expressed. The murmurs of a dissatisfied few were quickly becoming louder. For example, I had to defend against complaints from other staff that David Plouffe and I needed to curb our spending appetites, a charge I found to be patently ridiculous.

The outbursts came from everywhere and were aimed at anything. On one occasion, a high-level staffer—coming from a meeting with a notable local politico—took aim at the campaign's mantra, proclaiming, "No drama, why not?" Seemingly still wound up from the recent conversation, the angry aide continued, "Conflict keeps the circle wide and voices present. Head off drama at a cost!"

There were even silly rumors swirling that Plouffe might leave or David Axelrod might lose his job.

Stay the Course

It was our turn. Like the Clinton campaign before us, doubts about our strategy were being openly aired and threatened the internal unity that had been so critical to our success. This was a watershed moment inside Obama for America. Clearly, drama was percolating. I worried about whether we could manage the voices in the candidate's ear. There were bound to be influential money people, strategists, senior staff, and confidantes who would attempt to shake his faith in his own plan.

We had one thing going for us, however. While there were rumblings within and around our organization, at the top there was still a consensus that the road we'd mapped out long ago was still the right way forward. The pressing issue, as we headed into October, was calming jitters about the strategy.

That became the next order of business. Our best opportunity to confront the mounting concerns expressed by some of our major funders would be at an upcoming national finance meeting in early October. The burden was on us to demonstrate that their collective investment in the campaign had been properly directed. This was a case that could be best made in Paul Tewes's backyard in Iowa, where our donors could see firsthand the fruit born of their financial seed. Amidst our impressive operation there and gathered in a state where polling numbers were slowly breaking our way, we could more persuasively restate the case for winning Iowa.

I remember a lot of attention paid to the preparation in advance of that meeting. And while I can't say the controversy ended with the completion of that summit, it did open up an important dialogue with our key stakeholders as things got increasingly tumultuous. In fact, the campaign seemed to reach a breaking point in the middle of October, when another CNN national poll dropped. Where Senator Clinton had posted an alarming 46 percent to 23 percent lead in September, the new survey showed the gap had grown to 51 percent to 21 percent. In just a month, we'd watched her twenty-three-point advantage over us build to thirty points.

These results fueled the drumbeat calling for a shake-up, just as reporters tried to sniff out the jump-ship stories that they typically like to write around this time in an election. When the heat is on, members of the media enjoy pointing out who is running from the kitchen and leaving the chef behind. Then, a story surfaced in late October that a big donor was breaking from our ranks and heading for the Clinton campaign. On its own, this was a quickly passing headline. If more examples piled up though, we would have a real problem.

Coincidentally, not long after that news dropped, our chief technology officer approached me to say that he was leaving the campaign to accept a private sector job. I'd grown close to Kevin Malover, and I knew that his decision was strictly personal. It was something he needed to do for his young family and was in no way reflective of any dissatisfaction with the campaign or doubts about our chances. Still, working in a media environment, I knew that the sudden departure of a senior staffer with a celebrated past at Orbitz would have been noticeable at a bad time.

Fortunately, Kevin had thoughtfully arranged to leave in early January, right after the New Hampshire primary. I asked that he keep his decision just between us. A search for a high-profile CTO, even if conducted passively, would raise red flags around us. It was the right decision, but it ended up being a secret that I'd have preferred not to have kept from our technology teams and others on our staff. Nonetheless, in the midst of the upheaval and with the Iowa caucuses nearing, we needed to keep the temperature down and the staff focused.

Moving out of October, things began to relax. The case we'd consistently presented—that we were right where we needed to be in our broader effort—was finally beginning to get traction. There were a few reasons for this easing. First, we were clearly closing the gap in Iowa. That alone was no small accomplishment and served as vindication of our strategy. Second, we could explain our poor national showing as a function of Senator Obama's low name recognition outside of Iowa and the other early states. But we remained confident that behind the credibility of an Iowa win, our national numbers would improve. Finally, we didn't shy away from the hard work of engaging our supporters and persuading them that this was no time to make major course corrections. This argument was strengthened by the resolve of our candidate, who remained steadfastly committed to the Win Iowa strategy. Through it all, we'd held up pretty well considering the enormous organizational stress.

Emergency

This wasn't just a turbulent time at the office. I had a lot going on at home as well. On Monday, October 22, Sine went in for a scheduled visit to her obstetrician. Upon examination, she was immediately rushed to the hospital for an induced delivery. I hurried home to arrange care for the dogs and then quickly returned to the hospital. It was time for our son to come out, even if he was apparently quite reluctant himself. Thirty hours later, after a dramatic effort by the doctors and nurses, Dante Francis was born.

I stayed with Sine at the hospital during her recovery that week, but rarely put the BlackBerry down. When I returned to work, we had help at home. Anticipating the demands on me heading into the primaries, Sine had carefully planned for a series of visits by family members that stretched all the way out to February 5. Even as I resumed my grueling schedule at the office, however, I also began an unexpected four-month-long stretch when I paced the hallway outside our bedroom well into the night in an ongoing effort to soothe our inconsolable baby.

Hijacked

A month later, on the afternoon of November 30, I was at the pediatrician's office with Sine and baby Dante when I got word from Dan Jones of a hostage situation at Senator Clinton's Rochester, New Hampshire, headquarters. Steps were being taken locally to calm things at our own nearby office in that town, but our field offices across the country were in a state of heightened concern. It wasn't clear what was happening in New Hampshire, and our staff was looking to me for guidance on whether they should close their offices or take other precautions.

In response, I quickly convened a conference call with our state directors and operations managers, apprising them of what we knew and providing instructions they could offer their local staff, short of closing their own offices. I didn't want to create a panic by calling for closures or suspending activity, but we did have to be vigilant in this moment while we were learning more about the exact nature of the threat. And we would definitely need to be cautious about the possibility of a copycat attempt somewhere else. I didn't want us to be fearful, but I wanted us to be careful.

I was aware that anything we sent out from HQ could find its way into the press. I didn't want to politicize our response, so I remained in close contact with state leaders and continually advised them on how they should communicate through their organizations. My team also quickly updated a detailed safety memo that state leaders could customize for their local office managers, with guidance on keeping exits safely unimpeded, addressing suspicious behavior, and immediately arranging meetings with local fire and police representatives to establish that connection. We also offered advice on how to manage offices and volunteers through uncertainty without impeding activities.

Finally, my team revisited with senior staff and state directors our internal rapid response system in place for reporting personal threats, medical emergencies, office break-ins, and lost computers and Black-Berry devices with sensitive data. We reminded them of our phone hotline and emergency email address, which went to Dan Jones. Depending on the nature and location of the emergency, Dan immediately assembled the necessary team to tackle the problems. If Dan was the first call, he made sure I was always the second. I spent many a night throughout the campaign responding to reports from that rapid response system. Fortunately, or unfortunately, I was already awake with Dante.

Sacked!

The end of the year brought more big news from the Clinton camp. With just weeks separating us from the Iowa caucuses, two of their campaign workers from that state were dismissed for circulating offensive emails about our candidate. Then, in an unrelated incident, one of their top advisors in New Hampshire was also forced to leave over his own defaming comments that were again directed at Senator Obama. Hillary Clinton's decision to let those folks go must have triggered enormous reverberations inside her organization. The timing couldn't have been worse with Iowa fast approaching. Things just seemed to be falling apart over there.

In fact, as the year closed out, this had become a tale of two very different campaigns. Both were diligently constructed from scratch. Both grew up in a similar environment with the same goals. Both were preparing for an epic battle in Iowa. But, at least from where I sat, the competing organizations seemed to be on opposite trajectories. The Clinton campaign, once widely viewed as mighty and invincible, was now beginning to show some serious cracks. We, on the other hand, were steadily rising in our confidence and competence.

Evaluating the strength of our operation against the other campaigns, however, was like looking across a poker table. The only clarity we had at the time was what we saw in the hand we held. We didn't have the same visibility into the cards of our rivals, so we couldn't be certain about whether they were winning, bluffing, or folding.

My hunch was that the Clinton campaign was playing a bluff. I had very little information on which to base this, except for what I could piece together from Operation Campaign Mystery Shopper and snippets out of the news. I envisioned theirs was an unruly campaign, still unsettled on a plan and ravaged by endless turf skirmishes between rival factions that flowed from multiple power centers at the top of their organization. But, while operational challenges and worries about money seemed present over there, I remained fearful. What hadn't changed was my profound respect for the opposition candidate and her team. I knew we were in for the fight of our lives.

Our success during 2007 was largely a function of discipline. By focusing firmly on Iowa and the early states, we clarified for our staff exactly who our key partners were. We tailored systems like the Ops Desk to specifically meet their needs. And as required, we made the hard choices necessary to position our organization to compete at its highest potential. We battled through the D-Punjab memo crisis, and later, when some of our stakeholders became uncertain about the path we'd plotted, our management remained steadfast. In that moment, we benefited from having a candidate who stuck by the strategy and stood with his leadership team. He never wavered. Instead, he boldly led us through that period of doubt by remaining fierce, focused, and resolute. We stayed the course.

If the golden rule of effective leadership is to have a plan, then rule number two is to stick to the plan.

3

Rise to Big Moments

DECEMBER 5, 2007: *Jeremy Bird, the South Carolina field director, needs a cow for the Oprah event. CTO Kevin Malover was waiting for me at my desk when I returned from a meeting to assure me that Toniann was working on it. This was the first I'd heard of the issue. I was rushing back out and couldn't talk, but I told Kevin that if Jeremy needed any more farm animals, maybe the folks in Advance (our event organizers) should help him.*

Under Pressure

"That's how you perform under pressure," Senator Obama lightheartedly joked with the news team covering his education-themed event at a South Carolina school gymnasium. Reporters weren't satisfied. They were clamoring to interview him about what had just transpired. The buzz wasn't over a speech he'd given or any pressing news issue of the day. It was *the shot* that they were scrambling to queue up for their respective media outlets.

Just moments before, the gangly candidate, with rolled-up sleeves and a tie hanging loosely off his neck, playfully teased the smattering of people that had gathered around him as he received the basketball on a dare. Without a proper warm-up he casually hunched over, methodically dribbled the ball, and from deep in three-point range, straightened up and launched it into the air. After a brief moment of disbelief, cheers erupted as the ball perfectly hit its target and fell easily through the net.

This was a man who rose to big moments.

Define Thyself Lest You Be Defined

In August 2007, Barack was still relatively unknown among the general public. And, despite the media fuss over the ensuing few hours, that particular occasion in South Carolina went mostly unnoticed. Nonetheless, the images being broadcast were helpful to our candidate. They introduced him warmly to voters as an everyday guy people could generally relate to. At the same time, we were always on alert for attacks from the opposition intended to seriously undercut him.

In a business of contrasts, the first job of the campaign is to define the candidate—yours and theirs. This is the basis for the endless messaging battles that unfold on television, in print, when knocking on doors, and during public appearances and debates. Because Barack was new to the national scene, the freshman U.S. senator was highly susceptible to being negatively framed before voters could really get to know him. Even as the Iowa caucuses were fast approaching, many Americans couldn't pronounce Barack Obama's name, let alone guess who he was or what he did.

This was not a small problem since the senator was competing in a large field of eight candidates, featuring known and respected Democrats. Hillary Clinton had been a household name for the better part of two decades. In addition to her remarkable achievement of winning election to the United States Senate in 2000, while still the sitting First Lady, she'd also topped Gallup surveys eleven times as the "most admired woman in America." John Edwards was also a familiar face, particularly in Iowa, where he placed second in the 2004 caucuses on his way to becoming the party's VP nominee. Other notable contenders included such political stalwarts as Senator Joe Biden, Governor Bill Richardson, and Senator Chris Dodd. It would certainly be a daunting challenge to help our candidate break through this imposing lineup. At the same time, we had to guard against any potential missteps on our part or damaging attacks from outside that could contribute to an ill-fated, defining moment.

The "Hope and Change" One

The campaign trail is littered with political corpses and broken dreams. During our run, it was still haunted by Howard Dean's campaign-ending scream following his Iowa loss in 2004 and the specter of a windsurfing John Kerry, who was portrayed by opponents as the serial flip-flopper prone to shifting his positions with the changing winds. The skeletons from derailed Democratic campaigns of national elections past— Gary Hart and Michael Dukakis also among them—offered a stark reminder of what became of those who were mortally wounded in political combat.

Senator Obama had actually been a difficult mark for his rivals. On one hand, he was baggage-free, which made him hard to attack. His relatively thin political résumé and limited national exposure ironically worked to his advantage. Our candidate was also buoyed by a courageous but popular stand he'd taken against the Iraq war back in 2002, while still in the Illinois Statehouse. This diffused the opposition, and absent a sustained collective offensive against him, Barack was able to skillfully dodge the random mortar directed his way.

On the other hand, Senator Clinton was a ripe target for the organized wrath of her peers. There were a few reasons for this. First, Hillary was universally considered the front-runner in the race. Second, she had a long history of service in the public eye that opened her record to a full-on assault by the others. Finally, and most importantly, Mrs. Clinton had been continually dogged by the tortured response she'd long offered explaining her vote in the Senate supporting the use of military force against Iraq in 2002. Hillary wasn't the only candidate in the Democratic field who'd cast that vote. Senators Biden, Edwards, and Dodd had also voted yes. But her stubborn defense of it uniquely distinguished her from her peers as the "unrepentant one."

We were further helped in the definition wars by having a candidate with a refreshing political outlook. He was a great communicator in the tradition of Ronald Reagan, Bill Clinton, JFK, and FDR before him, sharing with each a mastery of the communications mediums of their times. But, while it was clear that Barack had the capacity to compete at this level, the question circulating throughout the political world was whether he had the caliber of organization behind him that could propel him to victory.

B-Team

In the summer of 2007, while Senator Obama had earned the recognition he deserved, our organization wasn't getting the same due respect on the campaign trail. Working in my bubble in Chicago, I felt certain that our early mistake-free execution would have wowed political insiders. I was shocked to learn otherwise during a June visit to Washington, D.C., where I discovered that the conventional wisdom seemed to be lining up very differently.

Many of my political friends—even some who were outside of politics—attributed our early accomplishments to having an unusually gifted candidate. The theme running through most of my conversations was that our organization would not be able to compete against the Clinton machine when it really mattered in six months. One of my former associates was particularly candid, adamant in his view that Senator Obama had assembled a "B-Team" that was hopelessly mismatched against Clinton's daunting and deeply experienced organization. Ours was a no-name campaign, my friend specifically insisted, adding that Clinton's forces would quickly overpower ours when the game was on.

During that visit, the people I met continually reminded me of her imposing staff lineup. She had enlisted Terry McAuliffe, the former Democratic National Committee chairman, universally regarded as the party's preeminent fundraiser. Also on her team was Harold Ickes, a legendary operative with deep establishment ties and the sway to lock down critical endorsements. Two of President Bill Clinton's former aides and strategy gurus, Paul Begala and James Carville, as well as vaunted field organizer Michael Whouley were also said to be advising her organization, which was filled position-by-position with the best names in the business. Finally, as everyone universally pointed out to me, if all else failed, Hillary was married to the greatest mind in modern American politics.

Myth: A Good Candidate Wins Elections

These early whispers grew to a near-deafening roar throughout the fall as Washington insiders and the media elite eschewed our candidate's chances, describing Hillary Clinton's staff as a political dream team and her pursuit of the nomination as "inevitable." To be sure, we were battling a campaign Goliath. Her organization was a force in every sense, and Hillary herself was excellent on the stump.

For our part, I was convinced that our early success coming out of the gate was as much the result of the capability of our operation and staff as it was the extraordinary talent of our candidate. I think Senator

Obama would have agreed. He was refreshingly frank with us in the earliest days, admitting that he was still prone to mistakes and clumsily struggling to find his footing on the campaign trail. He occasionally gathered us for all-staff pep talks outside of David Plouffe's office, where he announced quite humbly that he was relying on us to carry him while he was still learning his job.

When you have a candidate like Barack Obama, however, it is easy to overlook the importance of the organization in winning elections. It is also difficult to fully appreciate the contributions made by the rest of the team when all of the news and views are, of course, focused on the candidate. Nonetheless, even for all of his talents, Senator Obama couldn't ultimately succeed if he were fronting a mediocre operation. Great communicators have the potential for historic presidencies, but it's the campaign—not the candidate—that wins elections. Our staff, therefore, had to be demons about the details, and our mastery of them elevated us above the competition.

I was so focused on the performance of our organization that I often lost track of the candidate's activities during the day. That made those last thirty minutes before I went to bed at night precious because I could finally sit down to watch cable news to see how Barack had done. Every morning, I joined our senior staff meeting in a small conference room where we ran through the movements and message of the candidate. It was surreal to watch TV late at night to discover that the things we'd plotted and discussed together some fifteen hours earlier had been executed in a distant city or town exactly as we'd envisioned.

I marveled at the political gymnastics Barack could perform in front of the cameras. I appreciated even more the dizzying array of tasks so precisely carried out by others in the organization that were invisible to viewers. Behind every speech was a deliberate process for vetting the content, the location, and the people who stood next to the candidate. There were endless negotiations with vendors over every detail of the event, right down to the balloons for the stage and the helium that filled them.

With every activity there was an elaborate communications operation that prepared releases for the media, tracked news stories, and kept our stakeholders constantly apprised using electronic mediums. Local field organizers were relentless in helping our advance teams locate sites, administer the ticketing, and manage an array of logistical issues. At every stop, there were additional demands for individual meetings and small klatches coming from local political figures, donors, or constituency leaders. Any mistakes or miscalculations in this regard could result in added work later soothing feelings and mending relationships.

Hundreds of staff and volunteers were critical to the management and smooth execution of these activities. Each venue and vendor contract had to be vetted and signed off on at our headquarters. Because we were strict stewards of every dollar, expenditures had to be preapproved by our CFO and myself to ensure compliance with departmental budgets, campaign standards, and federal laws. Candidate appearances and hot news items often triggered a new wave of giving by supporters that had to be personally inspected by our compliance staff to ensure there were no lobbyist donations (an internal policy) or individual contributions that exceeded the legal limits. Phone calls and email messages continuously flooded in. Technology had to be reliable, and our professional technicians worked hard at securing the infrastructure to withstand the pounding generated from the remarkable surges of traffic to our website.

These were the many complex components of the operation—currents in an elaborate system that flowed to and from the campaign manager, who was positioned at the hub of an expansive and growing organization. The smallest slipup in any area could have an effect on the whole, and any series of mistakes opened up the possibility for troubling problems later. Having hurriedly built this complex organization completely from scratch, with the many moving parts and staff, I find it remarkable that it was run so competently at all levels.

The Campaign Orchestra

Mine was the street-level perspective of the duties and tasks associated with candidate support and campaign administration. There is nothing romantic in it, which is why organization is often an overlooked factor of success. Even zooming out to the satellite view, most regard the campaign enterprise as little more than one great marketing machine that spits out the political ads we see on TV, the talking points we hear, and the volunteers we speak with on our phones and at our doors.

To appreciate the true nature of a campaign, I like to compare it to an orchestra performing a masterful arrangement. Both are similarly structured hierarchically into autonomous, yet interdependent groupings. Not unlike the famous masterpiece *Boléro*, in which the featured melody moves systematically and deliberately through each of the sections—from percussion to flute to woodwind to brass—the campaign similarly unfolds. In the final moments, just before its spectacular and abrupt conclusion, all of the parts combine to lift the organization to its full crescendo.

An effective Campaign (capital *C*) is really a series of campaigns (small *c*) played out over the course of the election cycle. The campaign manager, then, is like a conductor guiding the performance. Under his direction, all of us who headed departments were the leaders of our own sections. Our charge was to execute routine duties flawlessly—the accompaniment—and prepare to rise to our big moment: the solo. As soon as the campaign manager looked to any one of us, our teams had to be ready to step up.

Precise execution in moments big and small by all of the component parts is what separates winning campaigns from losing campaigns. Looking back, I think perhaps our organization was outmatched on paper. However, I strongly contend that the skillful execution of all our roles by every one of our departments contributed to our impressive performance in 2007. Leadership and organization were the two driving factors that positioned our candidate ideally as we approached the 2008 primary contests.

Rolling Thunder

In the first months of 2007, Senator Clinton was universally considered to be the front-runner in the race for the Democratic nomination. The question was who would emerge as the viable alternative, important since the media tends to frame its election coverage by featuring a favorite and a challenger. John Edwards was the likely number two seed.

The former senator from North Carolina had been John Kerry's VP nominee in 2004 and had remained a fixture in Iowa in the two years since that election. However, there was bad news for Senator Edwards coming from a January 2007 *Washington Post*/ABC News poll. The survey revealed that he was trailing by a very large margin to Senator Clinton, 41 percent to 11 percent.

Even more foreboding for the Edwards camp, Barack Obama found his way to a second-place showing at 17 percent. We were further helped by a Quinnipiac University poll a month later, which found that 40 percent of those surveyed hadn't yet formulated an opinion about our candidate. This bolstered our case that it was, in fact, Senator Obama who was the greater threat to Hillary Clinton. He'd have more room to rise in the polls as the Democratic electorate became better acquainted with him, while the public's impressions of the former VP nominee were already hardened based on his high-profile run in 2004. In other words, Senator Edwards's sagging numbers were already fully baked, while it was easy to point to the yeast in ours.

The Money Primary

Still, our reasoning would have to be backed up with evidence. To that end, Washington insiders and the media elite would use two tests to determine the viability of the competing campaigns during that first year: fundraising and endorsements. Specifically, every dollar and each political VIP that the respective campaigns nabbed early would be quickly brandished as new evidence of dominance over the others. This made the "invisible primaries," as they are known, of huge consequence. It also put added pressure on the organization that we were still scrambling to get up and running.

This set up the first showdown meant to measure the capacity of each campaign in attracting investors. Our fundraising team, headed by Julianna Smoot, faced long odds as it stepped up to compete against a well-established Clinton brand that featured some of the most formidable Democratic money chasers in recent memory. The senator herself had knitted together an expansive donor network during her two decades in national politics that included eight years as First Lady in the

White House and two successful bids for the United States Senate. Not surprisingly, conventional wisdom had the smart money on Clinton.

The first heat ended on March 31. That was the cutoff date for recording donations and expenditures for the quarter—data that would be packaged into a public financial disclosure filing that each campaign was legally required to submit two weeks later with the Federal Election Commission (FEC). Within twenty-four hours, on April 1, Clinton's team enthusiastically announced that their report would show a Democratic all-time record of $26 million. Edwards quickly followed with a claim of $14 million, which would also surpass the $9 million high watermark set by Al Gore during his 2000 run.

The media waited on word from us. Silence. Suspense grew as two more days passed. Then, on April 3, we finally unveiled our own results: the Obama campaign matched Clinton nearly dollar-for-dollar with a fundraising haul that was just shy of $26 million. In fact, our effort stood out even more notably when considering $10 million of Hillary's money had been transferred from her Senate campaign coffers. Also, because many of her larger contributors had blown past the individual giving limits for the primaries, $7 million would be wholly unavailable to her campaign until the general election. Conversely, just about all of our funds were immediately available to us.

But our campaign had another loaded piece of data that became the real eye-popper. We could lay claim to one hundred thousand contributors—twice the number she would be able to show. By a 2:1 margin, more people had bought a stake in our campaign.

Three months later, we proved that our first quarter success was no aberration when we posted fundraising numbers totaling $32.5 million for the second quarter, of which $31 million could be put to immediate use. This dwarfed Senator Clinton's $27 million, especially when taking into account that only $21 million of that could be tapped for the Democratic nomination period. Her campaign again accepted more than $6 million in "general election" money, donations we continued to purposely discourage. This revelation opened up doubts about the breadth of her support, as well as questions about the discipline and precision of that team's revenue-generating operation.

The strength of our fundraising performance during the first six months reverberated throughout the political world. This had to have shaken the Clinton campaign to its core. But it was testimony to the amazing work of Julianna's staff and our National Finance Committee. Together, they delivered a big boost to our campaign by bringing in big money early.

Our early successes were mostly lost on everyday voters, however. In fact, a June 2007 poll out from CNN showed Hillary with a commanding 43 percent to 25 percent lead over us. David Plouffe cleverly released a public statement in response to calm predictable jitters resulting from the news by urging a longheaded view of the contest. He wrote:

> One of our opponents is also the quasi-incumbent in the race, who in our belief will and should lead just about every national poll from now until the Iowa caucuses. Expect nothing different and attach no significance to it.

The Name Game

The race for endorsements would offer the next test for the campaigns. The Clinton strategy was hugely invested in this particular trial. Winning over major endorsers would validate their emerging claim of "inevitability." The goal of Steve Hildebrand's political outreach team in response was to keep the score close, just as our fundraisers had done. More importantly, every key name that we could pull over to our column before Labor Day would prove to be infinitely more valuable than those that came afterward because a strong early showing of support communicated viability. The problem, once again, was that we were hopelessly outmatched. Our side didn't have the long ties that Senator Clinton and her senior campaign staff had. This put a lot of pressure on our endorsement gathering efforts led by Political Director Matt Nugen.

The name chase was on. Senator Clinton gained an early edge in March when she picked up the endorsement of Tom Vilsack, Iowa's popular former governor who himself had flirted with the idea of his own presidential run very early in the race. Only two months out of office, Vilsak was a big prize for her campaign. His volunteer base would certainly be a boon to her field efforts in that state's nearly eighteen hundred precincts.

Mrs. Clinton was also making impressive headway with organized labor. In late August, she pulled endorsements from the International Association of Machinists and the Transportation Communications Union (TCU). Two weeks later she welcomed the support of the National Association of Letter Carriers. Senator Edwards matched Clinton's pickups by winning over the support of the United Brotherhood of Carpenters and Joiners of America. Then, on Labor Day, he added both the United Steelworkers and the United Mine Workers. Three days after that, the Transport Workers Union came aboard. But in October, Clinton scored two big trophies, first with the endorsement of the 1.4-million-member American Federation of Teachers and then with the equally sizeable American Federation of State, County, and Municipal Employees (AFSCME). Its thirty thousand members in Iowa alone would add significantly more juice to her ground game in that state.

Finally, Mrs. Clinton proved formidable in Hollywood's star wars. Her unveiling Steven Spielberg's endorsement in June was widely portrayed in the media as a black eye for our campaign since the renowned movie director had co-hosted a fundraiser for us just months before with his DreamWorks partners, David Geffen and Jeffrey Katzenberg. The pickup, it was speculated, would also offer a helpful edge to Senator Clinton in the lucrative Tinseltown money chase.

Progress on each of these endorsement fronts by our rivals was countered by strong performances of our own, despite the fact that we were fighting for our political life. A month before the Spielberg news, we'd rolled out our own showstopper by announcing the endorsement of Oprah Winfrey. Her fundraiser at her home in Santa Barbara later in the fall would fill our treasury with a few million dollars. Additionally, although we were getting skunked on the union-by-union endorsement scorecard, there was chaos within the rank-and-file as many members broke from their elected leadership to openly side with our candidate.

But the greatest achievement logged by our political team was its ability to hold the line in the battle for the roughly eight hundred Democratic Party superdelegates. This was an important bloc in the nomination quest for a few reasons. First, unlike pledged delegates who were selected in state primaries and caucuses based on their commitment to a given candidate at the convention, superdelegates were free to back whomever they pleased. Second, they made up 20 percent of the total pool that would decide the nomination. For context, there would be 4,050 delegates to the national convention, making 2,026, or 50 percent +1, the magic number of delegates needed to win the nomination. Finally, because they were comprised of influential party leaders, governors, and members of Congress, early individual endorsements would have a lot of sway in the nominating process. A strong showing of superdelegates for any particular candidate could very well decide this race.

As feared, Mrs. Clinton looked dominant in this category from the outset. At the end of 2007, it was being widely reported that she could count on the endorsement of 169 superdelegates, followed by only 63 for us and 34 for Edwards. But deeper analysis also revealed there was good reason for optimism on our part. First, Senator Clinton had only succeeded in piecing together the support of 20 percent of all the superdelegates. That number was unexpectedly low this deep into the election season. Second, it was also being reported as late as mid-December that only a dozen Democratic senators had publicly committed to any of the candidates in our field.

Some later used these facts to support a misguided postelection analysis that because the party's elite hadn't fallen neatly in line behind her, the establishment candidate wasn't Hillary Clinton, but rather it was Barack Obama. This was an unfortunate conclusion and completely dismissed the important role of our organization. Matt Nugen, our political director, had a better analysis. Our strong fundraising presence early on froze the political establishment into a state of uncertainty. And while we didn't outperform our key rival in the endorsement race, neither did their team achieve checkmate. For us, stalemate was victory. This created an opening for us as the game shifted to the next head-to-head challenge.

Preparing the Ground Game

Our early fundraising success not only earned us insider credibility, but it also generated revenues higher than we had budgeted. Because good managers follow the money, Plouffe and I had to beat back continual efforts by our department heads to get a share of the new spoils. In a show of discipline, David fended off these attempts and instead held everyone to our initial budgets. He made some accommodations for the early states, but generally resisted the pressure to pour additional dollars into already funded operations. The driving principle behind his money management approach was simple: live within the budget, and apply revenue overages to vital new initiatives.

David didn't get bogged down in battles over the funding of existing programs. Instead, having stuck to his guns, he was freed to begin aggressively filling in the budget line for the February 5 operation that would support those states holding contests on Super Tuesday. Heading into the fall, that part of the operation had gone unfunded. Now it quickly became our new focus. David repositioned Jon Carson, who'd been the Illinois state director, to oversee the project. Jon promptly began to populate his vast new turf covering the twenty-two states and a U.S. territory with experienced directors and eager staff, many from headquarters.

The public exuberance that greeted Carson and his team in the February 5 states created extraordinary possibilities for us. Campaign office openings, area canvassing activities, and volunteer trainings—typically uninteresting to busy everyday Americans—attracted large, energetic crowds. Jon, who never let a good opportunity go to waste, began submitting requests to open offices in some communities even before we'd really begun filling out staffs just because he knew we'd get a PR pop. The enthusiastic buzz that would accompany his office grand openings generated unusual press interest and a generous amount of ink in area newspapers. This contributed to a growing awareness of the grassroots stirring that was being incubated beneath Barack's candidacy.

As 2007 came to an end, we had full operations in the early primary states of Iowa, New Hampshire, Nevada, and South Carolina. Our fundraising success and prudent spending also made it possible for us to systematically build organizations in the twenty-two February 5 states long before our rivals. But none of that would have mattered if we lost Iowa, which was where we next flexed our organizational muscle.

Quietly and away from the eyes of the nation, our organizers prepared neighborhood house parties in precincts across the state for the same night, on December 13, just weeks before the actual caucus night. This would be a practice run for January 3—a way to test our turnout operation there. It also offered a natural opening to acquaint our local supporters with the unusual process of "voting with your feet." In advance, our new media team crushed through the production of educational videos that were to be made available on disc to the local party hosts and online for downloading and viewing. As Carson explained to me at the time, organizing such an elaborate rehearsal was an aspiration in every presidential election year, but it was an idea that had never been fully realized before.

The exercise was impressively carried out by Paul Tewes's remarkable statewide organization. Thousands of supporters turned out to homes throughout Iowa. At the designated time, house party hosts dialed into a conference line to allow their guests a chance to listen to Senator Obama deliver a message of thanks and encouragement. At the conclusion, Caucus Director Mitch Stewart had a performance readout that could help him determine where to direct resources and attention in the last days.

Linking Organization to Success

At the end of December, we'd surged past both Clinton and Edwards to a razor-thin lead in the polls in Iowa. This race was headed to a photo finish. Thanks to the work of our staff, donors, and volunteers in 2007, a race once thought unwinnable was now wide open.

Our success during that first year was in some ways separate, but never apart from our candidate. It was unnoticed by casual observers but not insignificant. A former community organizer, Senator Obama understood the connection between organization and achievement. Our operation was an energy factory that transformed the passion of individuals into power generated from a community working together toward a common cause. The senator's leadership within the campaign and his daily performance on the stump set the standard that each of us was expected to meet. Like him, we precisely executed the routine details of our jobs, and when it mattered, we consistently responded with impressive performances.

Oprahpalooza

On December 9, 2007, our organizers in South Carolina were putting the final touches on their marquee event featuring Oprah Winfrey and Senator Obama. Oprah-mania had reached fever pitch in the state and the excitement in front of the duo's appearance together was high. Adding to the pressure, we made a last-minute move to relocate from an eighteen-thousand-seat arena to the University of South Carolina's Williams-Brice Stadium as a way to accommodate the thirty thousand attendees we were now expecting. This would be our largest crowd yet.

While there was skepticism in the media about the potential for an "Oprah effect" in politics, our team on the ground fully appreciated the opportunities that came with the arrival of this popular celebrity. At the time, Winfrey's television viewership numbered upwards of eight million, 75 percent being female. Welcoming this iconic woman of day-time television was hugely helpful to us in our race against the most influential woman in American politics. Our organizers also discovered that 70 percent of those who signed up to attend the rally never had contact with the campaign before.

This sparked the imagination of our talented South Carolina field director, Jeremy Bird, who saw the possibility for our stadium audience to be transformed from interested political spectators into campaign stakeholders. His approach to this event was, therefore, very different from that which was typical of more conventional campaigns. Rather than prepare this as a regular media event with a large crowd stuffed into a venue that could deliver spectacular pictures and video footage, Jeremy set out to turn his rally into a mass phone bank.

His vision was for everyone at once to break out their personal cell phones and call at least four people to tell them where they were and use that as an opening to talk about our candidate. Everyone who entered the complex would be handed a phone script and four numbers to call. In the last hours before the event, our teams at national headquarters were crushing through a series of tasks to support this audacious aspiration.

One request in particular was important to Jeremy. He wanted a COW. Actually, he wanted two. A COW is short for Cell on Wheels. In order for the mass phone bank to be possible, we needed these additional mobile towers because existing signal transmission capacity would otherwise crash under the weight of all the simultaneous call attempts. Kevin Malover, our chief technology officer, rushed across the shop floor to inform me that his team was doing everything they could to meet this last-minute need, though it seemed that the odds for getting more than one seemed long. Still, in the end, our Chicago staff succeeded in fulfilling the demand and Jeremy went forward with his plans.

When Barack and Michelle stepped onto the stage with Oprah, they were greeted by what was described as deafening cheers. But it was the buzz that could be heard long after the rally had ended that was particularly noteworthy. Attendance reports ranged from twenty-nine thousand to thirty-six thousand, and news that a Guinness Book representative was on hand to verify the world record phone bank attempt spread wildly through the blogosphere.

Turning the event into a massive voter contact operation was important, both for the systematic expansion of our support base and for the media coverage that resulted. It helped shift momentum in that state decisively in our favor as we closed a ten-point gap from the month before. The world may have been talking about Oprah and Barack, but the day belonged to Jeremy and his team.

Like others on our staff before them, they rose to their big moment.

4

Be Faster

JANUARY 7, 2008: *"Put on full body armor. We'll be taking heavy artillery."* Those were the first words Plouffe greeted me with after we won Iowa.

For Every Car, a Map

It was a shocker. On the morning of Friday, January 4, the nation was greeted with news of a stunning win by perhaps the freshest face in politics over one of the most familiar. Behind a record turnout of 240,000 Iowa caucus-goers, nearly twice the number posted in 2004, we pulled a whopping 37.6 percent of the delegate haul. Adding to the drama, Senator Clinton was inched out by John Edwards, who slipped into second with 29.8 percent to her 29.5.

There had been no time to celebrate in my shop on caucus night. As soon as national news outlets made the call, I emailed my teams and summoned staff over to my desk for a quick huddle. It was late in the evening, sometime after 9 P.M. One-by-one, folks emerged from the shadows of the darkened headquarters floor, trickling in from their respective work areas. Eventually, a small crowd formed a circle right in front of where I stood.

There was a lot of excitement, a bit of giddy disbelief, and a growing confidence that we were really going to win this thing. I congratulated everyone around me and told them that even though we weren't physically there, our stamp on this victory couldn't have been more evident. Along with our friends in Iowa, we had put together an amazingly tight operation. I also offered a word of caution that with the New Hampshire primary just five days away and other early state races fast approaching, we couldn't let up. Experience has taught me that defeat often comes when it is least expected.

Our candidate also had a very small window in which to savor his big moment. Shortly after his victory speech in Des Moines, Barack was on a plane headed for New Hampshire. In the wee hours of the morning, his aircraft put wheels down on the Portsmouth landing strip.

A great deal had to be done in the next one hundred hours before the polls in the Granite State opened and voting began. There were also plenty of reasons for optimism going in. Our Iowa win had suddenly transformed the Democratic primaries from what seemed to be a protracted coronation of Senator Clinton into a meaningful battle for the party's nomination.

Party in Oklahoma City

In Iowa, our staff was on a mad dash to get their belongings together. Some had to negotiate out of housing leases or find subletters, while others had loose ends to tie up before going away indefinitely. After accepting new organizing assignments, staffers compared notes and determined amongst themselves who would be going where so that ridesharing could be arranged.

Meanwhile, back in Chicago, a small team led by Jacob Roddy was assembled to support the caravans preparing to fan out across the country. His team was hard at work creating a customized packet for each staffer that would include a map, specific driving directions, and information on the prebooked hotel rooms that were spaced about eight to ten hours apart along the designated route to their appointed destination. That information was being readied for Sunday, three days after the caucuses, when convoys would depart from the center of Iowa. The plan was precise. That is, until we realized Mother Nature had other ideas.

As the departure time drew near, we received word at headquarters through an Iowa staffer that a major snowstorm would prevent direct westward movement across the Rockies toward states like Utah, Idaho, and Washington. It was decided that everyone who was headed that way should instead join the large caravan that was headed south and west, with staffers destined for states like Kansas, Missouri, Oklahoma, and New Mexico; and others continuing on to Arizona, California, and Nevada. This revised plan called for the convoy to get to Oklahoma City on the first night and then to Albuquerque for another overnight stay. On the third day, those remaining would either break due north from Phoenix to states along the Rockies or they would continue west. In all, vehicles in that caravan would ultimately find their way into about ten states. The upshot of these changes was that much of our Iowa staff would remain together for at least another night before splitting up.

Around noon on the designated day, a very long convoy prepared to move out of Iowa to start the journey down I-35. I heard it was a ragtag band of cars and trucks that set off together. Sometime late that evening, Jacob got an unexpected phone call from the hotel managers in Oklahoma City. I remember thinking that it couldn't be good news.

He reported to me that everyone had made it as planned and the rooms were full. However, the caller wanted to be sure we knew that there had been a huge party stretching well into the night, apparently extending a celebration that had begun in Iowa. I waited for the end of Jacob's story, fearing that it might involve property damage, unhappy neighbors, or perhaps even law enforcement.

To the contrary, this wasn't a complaint call at all. Rather, the hosts simply wanted to express delight over their enjoyable guests from up north. Still, to this day I remain convinced that whatever may have happened in Oklahoma City, stayed in Oklahoma City.

Speed Wins

Campaigns are a position and possession game. The objective is to control strategic beachheads first and hold them longer. This is true in everything from dominating the airwaves with paid media ads, to positioning troops on the ground, to fighting to win over key voting blocs. In all cases, you beat the competition with speed.

We won Iowa in large part because we systematically built a better organization—that, and we were faster. Then, after the eyes of the nation had followed the candidates to New Hampshire, we quietly but quickly began executing a tightly scripted and highly choreographed plan to close offices, reallocate technology, and move people to new states. It was a dizzying process unnoticeably carried out over the five days after the Iowa caucuses had finished.

Nothing about how we left Iowa was accidental. The planning for the shutdown and staff redeployment began inside my shop some five months earlier, well before Labor Day. It grew from an initiative I called get-out-the-staff (GOTS), which initially had little to do with Iowa. GOTS was a large-scale planning effort by all of my teams to prepare for a severe reduction-in-force at headquarters in the fall of 2007. We weren't planning on laying people off, but we did anticipate that perhaps a third of our Chicago staff would be sent into the field for weeks—in many cases, months—to help with voter turnout efforts in key battlegrounds.

Beginning late in the summer, when the miles of Chicago lakeshore beaches were bathed in warm sunlight, my teams were holed up in a giant conference room making plans for the days when the trees would be bare and the chill of winter would be upon us. Long meetings were dedicated to figuring out processes for transferring personnel into states, arranging for donated housing, and redistributing the heavy workload at HQ amongst the remaining staff. We began documenting all of the duties within our operations for the first time, and we made systems and policy adjustments in anticipation of the impending work force downsizing.

Because the prospective reductions at headquarters would require us to continue offering the same high standard of service to the campaign but with fewer staff and resources, I often spoke of GOTS as our own Apollo 13 project. Like the astronauts on that ill-fated space mission, I viewed this as an exercise in shutting down the powerful Command Module and fulfilling the same duties within the limitations and constraints of the less capable Lunar Module. We'd need grit and ingenuity to succeed.

Close Iowa
As we worked through the elements of GOTS, one of the working groups began considering a specific plan to shut down Iowa and the other early states operations after those races ended. The Close Iowa plan sought to accomplish three core objectives within a seventy-two-hour period. First, we wanted to have cleaned and closed each of the fifty offices and the dozens more temporary locations that would sprout up in the final weeks before the caucus. Second, all the technology and office equipment needed to be collected and reassigned so that we wouldn't have to buy more. Third, people had to be in cars and on their way out

of Iowa. Each of these elements required thoughtful deliberation by the working group and our Iowa counterparts, not an easy task at a time when we were all wholly focused on winning an election.

Seventy-two hours was a pretty ambitious goal for all of this. To be clear, our intent wasn't to abandon offices; it was to properly close and return them in their best condition to the property owners. The motivation here was simple. Our CFO, who bent every penny, wanted to be sure we got all of our deposits back quickly and in full. These were sizable sums at a time when the campaign would become cash poor. We couldn't afford to leave any money on Iowa tables. We also had another reason for wanting these offices returned in top condition. We knew that we might potentially return for the general election if our candidate won the Democratic nomination, and then maybe even again in four years. We wanted to leave the best impression behind in each of the communities that had hosted us.

Despite the good intentions and thoughtful planning by our Chicago staff, we were reliant on our colleagues in Iowa to transform our ideas into action on the ground. It was a testament to the professionalism of that crew that the Close Iowa initiative got any attention at all, given everything else going on at the time. I particularly credit Paul Tewes's deputy, Marygrace Galston. Several weeks out, she identified shutdown captains at every work site to assume the charge of leading staff and volunteers in the cleaning and closing of their offices.

Each captain was emailed a customized office closing sheet from headquarters to assist them with their upcoming chore. It included the contact information for the property owner, a monthly rent amount, the deposit amount, an end date, general cleaning instructions, an inventory listing of equipment, and specific notes related to that property and owner relationship. Office closing sheets also included the name of a Chicago staffer—one of our attorneys—who could advise and help as needed.

The collaboration between Chicago and Iowa was seamless. We not only went on to shut down Iowa in seventy-two hours, but office, phone, utility, and equipment deposits totaling in the many tens of thousands of dollars were quickly returned and cycled into our spending. When this model was scaled across all four early states, the total cash amount returned figured into the hundreds of thousands, all at a time when every dollar counted.

As part of the Close Iowa initiative, our technology team began a lengthy and detailed accounting of our computing and office equipment during the fall. In the rush of the start-up, these items were issued directly from the vendors to our early states with little documentation of how items had been assigned. Auditing our inventory was a painful undertaking, but having an accurate itemized list gave us options for systematically redistributing our assets after the Iowa contest.

Next, our IT staff outlined a detailed process for collecting and redeploying Iowa's assets since the growing staff in the numerous February 5 states would need them. We decided that we would set up regional technology drop-off centers where departing staff would be required to turn in desktop computers, office equipment, and cell phones. At each of the receiving sites, technicians would be on hand to receive and quickly "blank" the computers in the hours after the caucuses to have them ready for immediate redeployment.

In the worst-case scenario, if we lost, capturing these assets would help our balance sheet. If we won, each piece of equipment would be assigned to a new location and transported in rented moving vans or thrown into cars heading out with a caravan. The end result was that we made it all the way through the primaries without having to buy any new technology or office equipment. We just kept rolling our inventory forward as we proceeded deeper and deeper into the campaign calendar.

Ground versus Air
Easily the most gut-wrenching decision I faced in the whole of the campaign was how to treat our early state staff after their races were over. Paul Tewes pressured me for weeks to make a commitment to keep the Iowa staff on payroll and move them on into new states. While I shared his view that our organizers were our greatest weapon, I also had the report from our CFO that indicated continuing a staff-heavy organization after Iowa and the other three January races wasn't financially feasible. We were looking at costs in the millions of dollars to continue bankrolling it at existing head-count levels. The equation was further complicated by the uncertainty of our revenue streams in 2008. We

weren't sure how donors would respond if we came in second or third in Iowa—or even first, quite frankly.

We also knew that the environment we were working in would dramatically change after the early contests. While we had been able to build muscular staffs to prepare many months in advance for the four January races, the nearly two dozen contests on February 5 would feature considerably shortened runways and require us to be increasingly reliant on expensive paid media to get our message out. In Chicago, this sparked the fuse that always leads to the explosive argument in a campaign of whether management values advertising over people. The preoccupation was a distraction and a clear indication of insecurity within our work force, but it was a charge I had to continually confront at the time.

While there was general speculation swirling all around headquarters about potential layoffs and furloughs after the caucuses, I quietly worked through the specific issues of Iowa and the other three early states with Jon Carson, who was now heading our overall national field effort. I was ultimately forced to take the position that the end date for the staff in these states was the day after their respective elections, but I was optimistic that we'd be able to quickly rehire these folks if we remained competitive after February 5 and continued to see healthy revenues. I simply couldn't make a different commitment at that moment that would tie up sizable financial resources and take options off the table that the candidate and campaign manager might need heading into the primaries.

In the end, the most that Paul was able to promise our Iowa staff was that those who wanted to continue with the campaign would somehow get the chance. Together with Jon, we worked out a modest plan to offer volunteer assignments in upcoming races in other states, backed with a small travel stipend and a couch to sleep on in a supporter's home. Even then, the stipend commitment couldn't be finalized until the night of the caucus, after we knew the results and saw how the donations were flowing. Iowa staff wouldn't really know their fate until the morning after Caucus Day.

The Reinforcements

What wasn't in question during our planning was that Jon would need to get bodies into Nevada quickly for the January 19 caucus and into the February 5 states to fortify our existing troops already preparing for those races. This meant that two things had to happen. First, we needed to carefully work through all these myriad issues to ensure a seamless hand-off of the Iowa staff from Tewes to Carson. Second, while we had to be faster than the competition at shutting down and moving people out, we also had to be better at receiving them in the new states.

My shops worked closely with Carson's teams to be sure that we had welcome captains in every state and that they were properly prepared for the surge when the time came. A large part of their job was to line up temporary supporter housing well before in order to accommodate the extended stays of incoming staff. Deployment paperwork filled out by each arrival was sent in advance to the host state to help account for such detailed considerations as pet allergies and other special housing needs. In the end, the receiving teams ensured incoming staff arrived on the first day to a place to live, space to conduct their work, and an orientation to help them quickly hit the ground running.

The new cavalry wouldn't arrive without bringing a unique set of management challenges along with it, as we soon learned. In addition to these complex logistical matters, there were a number of thorny considerations that went along with receiving a huge infusion of new staff at one time. David Plouffe and I had previously been careful to space hiring waves during the campaign, partly to protect against overwhelming the local operations. But, in the run-up to February 5, people arrived en masse into these battlegrounds at the last minute. This put additional pressure on our field managers to oversee the orderly distribution of work at a time of frenetic activity and accelerated pace.

In Nevada, for example, State Director David Cohen was eager for the help. But it came with the enormous task of managing the needs of the many newly arriving now-volunteer staff from Iowa while still making final preparations for a fast approaching race. His work force probably doubled in size during those last two weeks and that only added to the everyday challenge of managing a myriad of personalities. After all, the native-Nevadan staff had already been supplemented with waves of headquarters employees, always a delicate integration process in a political campaign. That fragile work environment risked being further destabilized after the Iowans motored in.

Now each work site had a mix of existing paid staff, some with headquarters salaries and some with field salaries. Standing alongside them were the new arrivals from Iowa, far from home and no longer getting paychecks but still commanding their leadership with the fresh confidence of champions. Everyone was exhausted and working under intense pressure, making morale management a factor for our generals on the ground.

By the end of day five when Senator Obama gave his election night speech in New Hampshire, the Iowa team was firmly in place in states where battlegrounds had suddenly sprouted. They had scouted out their new living quarters, received their employee orientations, and were prepared to work the unusually long hours doing whatever was asked of them to win.

Most landed in caucus states, including Nevada for the January 19 contest there and six of the twenty-three February 5 races. Jon stacked all seven of those states with Iowa organizers to capitalize on their recent experience and familiarity with that voting model. He put gritty organizers where they could make the greatest difference.

After Super Tuesday, there would be talk that our strong performance in those contests was evidence of the Clinton campaign's failure to focus on the caucus states. I maintain instead that our success was the result of Jon's clever use and distribution of human capital coming out of Iowa.

That, and we were faster.

The Iowa Difference

Ironically, whenever I am asked how we pulled off Iowa, I always tell the tale of those five days *after* that win. The story behind the story truly illustrates the discipline of that operation and the character of our staff there. The candidates were gone, and the cameras and journalists of the national media followed them to New Hampshire. What our Iowa staff did after the world stopped watching and the paychecks stopped coming was revealing. After all, the folks there were technically done.

Many could have chosen to stay behind in Iowa and continue their celebrations. They could have walked away and left offices in "campaign condition," along with the heaps of technology and equipment for someone else to sort out. Instead, they soldiered on.

Astonishingly, more than 95 percent of our staff in that state accepted the modest offer to continue on as volunteers and dedicated themselves to their next assignments. Some might attempt to explain this devotion as some sort of drone effect, a robotic response by impressionable youngsters who were somehow drunk on Obama Kool-Aid. However, if you believe, as I do, that the personality of an organization is influenced from above, then one need only look to the top of that state's employee chart to find an obvious explanation. In my mind, you can't separate the leadership of Paul Tewes from the commitment of his staff and our performance in Iowa.

Anybody who worked for Paul became part of his adopted family. He was devoted to his staff, as they were to him in return. This contributed to an atmosphere of unity and collegiality that created bonds between the staff there that will long be unshakeable. Paul wasn't a pushover, however. He expected his people to show up fully every day, and he motivated them to work at the height of their abilities. He also held them accountable. This set the standard for the discipline and precision that was a defining characteristic of his operation. Paul got results—and he got them fast.

Paul Tewes is the fastest organizer I have ever worked with. He and his team built out that state in short order. What impressed me most about Paul was that, while he promoted an innovative environment, he respected systems and processes. I'm not saying he didn't try to push boundaries, but he didn't step outside of them. He also surrounded himself with highly organized people. As a result, he brought the rest of us along with him because his operation was orderly, predictable, and crisp—even if it was often a challenge to keep up with.

This is no small point. Some use their authority to override, skirt, or blatantly ignore systems. While they may get where they want to go more quickly, everyone else is ultimately left behind to navigate a wake from the chaos that bad managers rarely notice has formed around them. That was never my experience with Paul's organization.

I could judge the strength of his operation long before caucus night based solely on our weekly Super Tuesday conference calls. The Iowa leaders knew exactly what they needed, and they paid attention to the details and the numbers. Marygrace Galston was our key organizational contact, and she was a machine. I had premeetings to anticipate the questions she might have and potential solutions we could offer. Marygrace thought of every angle and constructively challenged every one of our suggestions. She knew her stuff, and she was organized. We had to be equally prepared.

Our unit in Chicago was sharper for each contact we had with Iowa. They pushed us to be faster so that we all advanced to the next level together. With every new outpost we took up in that state, my teams became conditioned for speed. We developed systems to quickly stand up an office, equip it, and hire staff in a matter of days. We lost no time. This became a huge advantage to us in the immediate weeks just after Iowa, when being faster really mattered.

We saw the result as we moved into the new February battlegrounds, where there would be thirty-four races in two weeks. Our operations in these states and U.S. territories had to be quickly built up and populated. Our offices and staff were fully operational many days, even weeks, before our competitors in any given city or region. This was a testament to what we'd learned in Iowa. Later, we received frequent reports coming from the field in the February states that our opponents just down the street from our locations were waiting on leases, working without Internet, or sitting in the dark without electricity. With compressed election timelines, it all contributed to the edge we gained with our speed.

Even more important than the operational advantages to our campaign, the Iowa experience provided an infusion of leadership that served us long after the caucus results rolled in. That is the untold story of Iowa. Paul did more than oversee a vote-getting operation. He was running an organizing school, and our young staffers were being mentored as leaders. They had a lot of time to learn and grow in a hands-on environment under his tutelage, having been empowered to make decisions and run critical programs. It was the unanticipated outcome of committing to Iowa early and hiring the bulk of our staff there nearly a year out. The skills they gained will benefit them for life, but they directly contributed to our broader success for the life of the campaign—well beyond Iowa.

Once the Iowa caucus was behind us, we had a cache of proven young organizers who could quickly land in other states and apply the knowledge they'd gained to their next assignments. Having won Iowa only bolstered their credibility as they became leaders among strangers in unfamiliar new states, where they were going to have to integrate with existing personnel and quickly build relationships with local supporters.

This time, they wouldn't have a year to prepare for the election; they had only days. And while our exports from Iowa could help carry out the work, we continued to rely on the principle that local residents would have to win their own neighborhoods. These arriving young leaders had valuable knowledge to share based on their recent experiences, but we could only succeed by tapping the energy and talent that already existed in communities. That would require our Iowa organizers to quickly adapt their leadership to these new circumstances.

Breaking Down Barriers

At headquarters, my staff had also grown into their leadership. Our work heading into the Iowa caucuses demonstrated an advanced level of organizational maturity that yielded impressive results for us. It also revealed an exciting new discovery for me about managing in a dynamic environment.

In the days after Iowa, I thought back to all the planning that went into the precise execution of that complex redeployment into the February 5 states. My mind drifted to being in that conference room in August where we planned GOTS, the walls plastered with large sheets of florescent paper. Scribbled across the top of each was a project label that represented a problem or an opportunity identified by members of my operations staff. Underneath that topic was a small list of names of people who had volunteered to tackle these challenges and the names of other stakeholders outside of our own departments who should be recruited to help.

The brilliance of this map was that it visually demonstrated our unique problem-solving approach. We didn't succeed by tackling complex challenges department-by-department. We formed dynamic, cross-cutting teams across the organization to meet them. For every crisis, problem, or opportunity, we had a different team.

This was an important development inside Obama for America. I had frequently lamented our hierarchical structure in the early days. During our formative period, organizing into inwardly focused, functional departments was probably the most efficient way for our new managers to bring order to the chaos of the time. But I soon became frustrated with the deliberate up-and-down nature of decision-making when we needed to be nimble and fast. Problems were outrunning solutions. Similarly, opportunities were also outracing our responsiveness. Atop my own departmental bureaucracy, I was a consistent bottleneck on the range of issues escalated for my attention when I needed to be untethered and focused across the organization. I tried to solve that dilemma by giving more decision-making authority to a tier of leaders beneath me, but that only formalized a new layer of bureaucracy.

This also created a new set of problems, since one of the distinct features of the silo-based system is that it transforms department managers into silo protectors—that is, managers who succeed in the eyes of their subordinates by fending off new work. I felt that dynamic most acutely when I convened interdepartmental meetings with our department heads and their key lieutenants to coordinate some of our campaign-wide activities at Plouffe's urging. I found organizing by consensus to be laborious and slow. It was like convening a meeting of the deliberators to decide rather than working through the doers to get things done. More worrying, the silo-oriented architecture creates an artificial boundary around staff in the middle and lower rungs of the organization. These dynamics combine to choke off innovation and cross-cutting collaboration. I was determined from the earliest days that we needed to tear the silos down.

GOTS was proof that as the walls came down, a more efficient way for getting things done emerged in this atmosphere where change came at you fast. We unleashed smart, innovative people who knew how to form a new team in any moment to solve a problem or seize an opportunity. Behind every office that was closed in Iowa, there were fluid and evolving teams—beginning with a lawyer at national headquarters working with a property owner and a local office manager, for example.

Similarly, there was a different team supporting every passenger in every car that left the state. These teams existed within departments, across departments, over state lines, and even with nonstaff. But they were fluid, fast, and adaptive. They met the organizational imperative of the time to command the fast-changing environment in which we found ourselves.

This account of the five days after Iowa may delve a bit into minutia. But these are important details because during the same 120 hours that separated our Iowa victory and the close of the New Hampshire polls, a big shift in the momentum of the race had occurred. It set up what would become a significant showdown looming further down the campaign trail. Any advantage we gained by rapidly redeploying and taking up new positions in advance of the February 5 elections wouldn't be immediately noticed by outside observers.

Ultimately, though, speed mattered.

5

Yes We Can!

FEBRUARY 7, 2008: *It was a roller coaster after Iowa. Everything after that contest was abruptly different from what we'd known that first year leading up to it—the pace, the sudden loss of control, the uncertainty of what lay ahead. It was a total shock to the system . . . and easily the most exhilarating thrill of my career.*

Chasing the Crown

Barack Obama's unlikely victory in a rural white state over his powerhouse rival set the political world on its head. It afforded his candidacy a fresh burst of credibility, even as America was suddenly scrambling to learn more about the Democratic Party's new prince. At headquarters, there was renewed urgency in everyone's step and, frankly, a little extra air beneath our feet. Just days away from the nation's first primary in New Hampshire, we had a clear sense that we were on the verge of something really big. A win could very well be enough to tip Hillary from her throne and topple the House of Clinton.

Senator Obama rolled into the Granite State with all of the energy and fanfare that Plouffe had long envisioned. The greeting awaiting us was dramatic. The reports coming from the ground describing the admiring crowds, eager volunteers, and enthusiastic press, all combined to feed our optimism in Chicago. Then, on the Saturday prior to Election Day Tuesday, a new WMUR-TV/CNN state poll showed that our two campaigns were tied at 33 percent, with Edwards trailing a distant thirteen points behind.

This was truly remarkable given that the former first lady was long thought to have an unshakable grip here. The thirty-point advantage she brought into New Hampshire in the earliest days of the competition seemed alarmingly durable even as recently as September, when a CNN poll had her lead still holding strong by a twenty-three-point margin. Additionally, the Clintons had earned a fabled place in New Hampshire political lore back in 1992. That's when breakout candidate Bill Clinton proclaimed himself the "Comeback Kid" after surging to a dramatic second place finish following his own Iowa drubbing. With Hillary's fortunes suddenly in doubt, pulling out a win here would similarly reverse the momentum in her direction and throw the race back open.

An upset victory for us, however, might just mean an early end to Hillary's hopes.

The Bully Pulpit

Excitement was building at HQ as the two sides prepared for the nationally televised debate on Saturday night. Our confidence going in was brimming, to be sure. One of my colleagues crowed that so long as our guy didn't show up drunk and endorse Republican hopeful Rudy Giuliani, the charismatic former New York City mayor, then we'd come out of it all just fine. It was the most assured we were or would be during the whole of the 2008 election cycle.

The debate had an 8:45 P.M. (EST) start in New Hampshire on Saturday night, which gave me plenty of time to get home to watch it live. The candidates took their chairs in front of the moderator, ABC News anchor Charles Gibson. Seated behind their desks from left to right were Senator John Edwards, Senator Obama, Governor Bill Richardson, and Senator Clinton. Noticeably absent were Senators Dodd and Biden, both having dropped out of the race after poor showings in Iowa.

While our candidate did indeed register a strong performance, something seemed off at the end of the night. The debate had two memorable moments, and neither of them was favorable to us. The first occurred when Senator Edwards unexpectedly stood up to Mrs. Clinton . . . on Barack's behalf. She leveled a charge from Barack's left that he had evolving positions on a range of issues, even as he'd been attacking Senator Edwards on the campaign trail for his flip-flops. This accusation directed at Barack was quickly rejected by Edwards, sitting directly to the right of our candidate. The visual of the two men sitting alongside each other and taking turns to rebut Hillary struck an odd note. This caught the attention of co-moderator Scott Spradling, who described it as "a little bit of a double-team that's probably going to have a lot of people talking tomorrow morning."

The second setback came after that same newsman queued up a question for Clinton, asking whether it was fair that she'd been characterized as having a "likability" problem. "That hurts my feelings," the New York senator replied demurely, "but . . . I'll try to go on." Our candidate clumsily attempted to soften the awkward moment, but his intervention only came off as smug and uncharitable. "You're likable enough, Hillary!" Senator Obama countered. I cringed. This one I felt certain would come back to bite us.

The following excerpt from an editorial by Maureen Dowd appearing in the *New York Times* a few days later characterized much of the pro-Clinton sentiment at the time:

> How humiliating to have a moderator of the New Hampshire debate ask her to explain why she was not as popular as the handsome young prince from Chicago. How demeaning to have Obama rather ungraciously chime in: "You're likable enough." And how exasperating to be pushed into an angry rebuttal when John Edwards played wingman, attacking her on Obama's behalf.

The outcome was unfortunate, but the debate by itself should not have interrupted the unquestionable momentum propelling our campaign through the Granite State. On the other hand, fertile soil had been tilled from which undesirable problems could sprout. And on Monday, the day before voting began, they did.

Jeers for Tears

At headquarters, staff gathered around computer monitors and television sets to watch. I imagined that something similar was happening in workplaces and homes throughout America. I turned up the volume on the television at my desk to watch the reports. We all wanted to see it for ourselves: the potential spectacle of Hillary Clinton tearing up at a women's breakfast earlier that morning was hard to imagine. Given her long and storied public career, the idea that the Iron Lady of American politics was finally showing this kind of emotion quickly became a topic of great national interest.

I looked for tears. I leaned into my television, but I didn't see any. Given the way things had gone for her in Iowa and the steam we'd generated in the days since, I thought it more likely that she was cracking up than tearing up. But there were definitely others who thought that she was acting up—that it was a staged moment.

Scrutiny immediately broke out. The airwaves were filled with chatter and speculation throughout the day—mostly by male voices. CNN's Glenn Beck and radioman Rush Limbaugh were among them, voicing opinions similar to Fox News' Bill Kristol that "no Clinton cries without calculating first." Another male reporter was said to have openly questioned if this would be her response to North Korean leader, Kim Jong-il. This fixation by men in the media over whether Clinton had shed real or crocodile tears subtly contributed to a growing perception that Hillary was being unjustly bullied.

For his part, Senator Obama was careful to avoid making headlines of his own with this fresh controversy. John Edwards was less restrained. In fact, he was pretty deliberate with his opinion that what America needed from its commander-in-chief was strength and resolve. "Presidential campaigns are a tough business," he said, "but being president of the United States is also a very tough business." That made news.

Later the same day, inside a Clinton rally, two male protesters held up signs that read "Iron My Shirt" and then began to loudly chant the peculiar slogan. The senator responded cleverly, asking for the lights to be raised so that she could help everyone see what she called the "remnants of sexism." Against this backdrop of the disruptive hecklers being escorted out of the building, Senator Clinton announced to laughter and cheers, "As I think has just been abundantly demonstrated, I am also running to break through the highest and hardest glass ceiling." The disturbance was the perfect complement to the morning's event, and it kept people checking in online to search for footage recapping Hillary Clinton's curious day.

Meanwhile, the newest CNN/WMUR findings on Monday showed we'd surged to a double-digit lead over the weekend, by a score of 39 to 29 percent. The Iowa bounce we'd hoped for was undeniable. And while a ten-point victory wasn't likely, the numbers validated our optimism. Our crowds were large, and our events routinely required overflow accommodations by our staff on the ground. This differed sharply from reports circulating that Senator Clinton's rallies were uneven, unorganized, and uninspired. Even Bill Clinton's numbers were said to be lagging well behind what our candidate was drawing.

On New Hampshire Primary Day, there appeared to be two campaigns headed in very different directions. If Hillary had let her emotions get away, I thought, it might be indicative of how badly things were going inside of her organization. Her operation seemed to be unraveling. Staff morale was reportedly low, and résumés were said to be flying out of her campaign.

Rumors of a shake-up in the Clinton camp had swirled for quite some time. Even as New Hampshire voters were stepping into voting booths and casting their ballots, the media's focus became firmly trained on a breaking story that Bill Clinton's longtime strategy giants turned CNN political commentators, Paul Begala and James Carville, had both signed on with Hillary's campaign. It was also widely speculated that the former president's footprint inside her organization would become noticeably larger. I reasoned that these developments, which never appeared to materialize, had to contribute to the overwhelming pressures weighing on Hillary Clinton.

When the polls opened to voters on Tuesday morning, there was talk in the media that we might win by as many as fifteen percentage points. Just as Clinton's team reportedly scrambled to reset public expectations that a loss in single digits would actually be a victory for her, I took deliberate steps to temper enthusiasm around me. Though all indicators said we were headed for a big day, I told my staff in our morning standing meeting to expect less than three points separating the winner and the loser. I reminded them of the predictions that Al Gore would beat Bill Bradley by nine or ten points in 2000. Gore won by just a few. I warned that one could never confidently predict the behavior of New Hampshire voters once they pulled the curtains behind them.

It turned out that my words were all too true. At the end of the day, only three points did indeed separate the winner and the loser. The bad news was ours, however, as Senator Obama came up on the short end of that count.

Play for Another Day

The race was called for Clinton later that night, and it felt like a punch in the gut. National headquarters was stunned, silent . . . and confused. When I later spoke to our New Hampshire state director, Matt Rodriguez, he was really crushed. His staff must have been as well. All external polling, he said, pointed to victory heading into Election Day. Our internal data said the same. Crowd size, volunteer support—every one of those indicators gave our New Hampshire organizers great hope. Matt was convinced that he had put together the best campaign operation in New Hampshire history. He was, of course, disheartened that the horse race wouldn't bear that out. In my mind, closing the twenty-point gap in the fall and finishing as close as we had on Hillary's turf was clear evidence that our New Hampshire staff had accomplished something truly remarkable. But the disappointment was understandable.

Soon after the call was made for Clinton, I summoned my teams over to my desk for a brief huddle. Our management was quickly taking steps to rally the troops and keep spirits lifted. Katie Johnson, David Plouffe's aide, had let me know that there would be a mandatory all-staff conference call at midnight and added that I should urge everyone to watch Barack's speech, which would be televised shortly. Just as I was wrapping up my own talk, there was movement on the floor toward each of the television monitors as word quickly circulated that Senator Obama was about to speak. I expected that inside all of our offices around the country, staff and volunteers were similarly gathering around televisions to listen to what our boss was going to say.

For me, it still stands out as the single greatest speech of the campaign. Though Senator Obama must have been deeply disappointed by the results, his concession rivaled any victory speech I'd ever heard. He kept a high tone and lifted everyone with his words. His opening included sincere congratulations to Hillary Clinton on a hard-fought victory. The senator pointed to the long lines at the polls and the record turnout as evidence of the great desire for change, and he specifically credited our staff and volunteers for the hard work that went into helping create this stirring.

Even in defeat, Senator Obama delivered an inspiring and still hopeful speech that ended with a two-minute riff reminiscent of Dr. Martin Luther King, Jr. He set up that powerful conclusion with these words:

> That's why tonight belongs to you. It belongs to the organizers and the volunteers and the staff who believed in this journey and rallied so many others to join. We know the battle ahead will be long, but always remember that no matter what obstacles stand in our way, nothing can stand in the way of the power of millions of voices calling for change. We have been told we cannot do this by a chorus of cynics who will only grow louder and more dissonant in the weeks and months to come.

"Yes we can!" he went on. Soon the audience was chanting it with him. When Senator Obama finished his speech, people in our headquarters actually applauded as if they were right there with him in the swell of the New Hampshire crowd.

In both of his post-election speeches thus far, our candidate went well beyond the usual obligatory offer of thanks to staff that seemed so automatic on election nights. In Iowa, he paid warm tribute to local organizers who selflessly serve their communities and work to improve the lives of others. His enthusiasm was evident in his proclamation that "in the face of impossible odds, people who love this country can change it." In New Hampshire, Senator Obama's address, though nationally broadcast, touched every staffer and volunteer as if he were speaking to us directly. On a night when we had suffered a jarring defeat, he saw victory in that moment and a reason to boast about the great work of his organization. He always seized opportunities to be the CEO.

Barack's speech stood in sharp contrast to the one recited by Senator Clinton shortly thereafter. Hers was fine as these things go, striking the populist tone that seemed suddenly vogue on the campaign trail. She also had a better, livelier crowd on stage behind her than the one she had in Iowa, which had been a collage of recognizable faces from the Bill Clinton years evoking the imagery of a bridge to the past.

Still, I thought one very important element was missing. After a day of heavy speculation about the turmoil inside her campaign, her speech did nothing to truly elevate her troops in that victory. The omission made Mrs. Clinton's win seem a simple accident resulting from the fortuitous timing of her earlier emotional display. My own strong hunch was that she had a powerful operation in New Hampshire that had turned in an amazing performance.

On our side, we knew that organization was the key to our success—this was true in the past as it would be in the future. It is a point that was validated by our boss, who devoted precious real estate in his post-election speech to say as much on national television. The confidence he communicated in that moment, mixed with his sincerity and determination, was passed on to the rest of us. Success begins with self-belief. We had it, and our candidate made sure we held on to it.

It was the driving message behind our campaign's inspirational mantra: Yes We Can!

Learning to Win

"Let's dump the building, Henry!" Jon Carson's voice cut through the humming chatter of the floor as he approached. It was his way of saying that he wanted to push more bodies out of HQ and into the field. Carson repeated his idea with even greater determination as he marched up next to me. "Henry, we're going to have to dump this place," my friend said with his right hand resting just off his chin as he surveyed our surroundings. Honestly, I thought we already had, but I didn't want to be disagreeable. He was pretty forceful. If Jon needed more people in the field and knew where we had them to give, then I was all for it. With that objective in mind, the two of us devoted several hours on Wednesday to shaking down department heads for additional staff that could be sent out.

Our narrow loss in New Hampshire was devastating, and from it, a new sense of urgency was born. Until that moment, rightly or wrongly, we'd all shared an unusual confidence about our destiny. Maybe it was the false sense of security that came with believing that right would prevail over might—we did think we were on the side of the angels—or perhaps it was the infectious certainty we had in the capability of both our candidate and our operation. Regardless, we'd suffered a major blow. The prevailing viewpoint circulating outside of the campaign was that this was the beginning of our end. It was a watershed moment for us. How our management and staff responded in the aftermath of the New Hampshire defeat would reveal the true character of our organization.

During the next four-week stretch, we truly learned to be winners. Twenty-five races would take place beginning with the Nevada caucuses, which were only eleven days away. That state would be close. I'd long had Nevada in the Clinton column largely because she'd had better success at winning organized Labor's support, a factor that was certain to influence the turnout wars there. A week later, South Carolina would be up. Here, our already sunny prospects were made much brighter by the heavy impact of the Oprah event in December. This left the twenty-three contests slated for February 5, a big day when nearly half the nation would vote.

Know the Way to Victory

After the long, slow buildup to Iowa, it felt as though we'd been shot from a cannon. The pace suddenly changed in a way that made every day count, every decision matter, and every mistake noticeable. David Plouffe was in the zone, however, effortlessly making on-the-spot decisions about money, candidate movement, and media strategy. I'd been working with David for nearly a year and was already impressed with his management skills as we built this organization. But it was his execution during the lightening rounds of those early races in the run-up to February 5 that I found to be particularly remarkable.

David had a steady hand at the helm and always had clarity about the way forward. I think this contributed to his unflappable response to the devastating New Hampshire loss. Understanding that better days awaited us in South Carolina just over two weeks away, he didn't overreact to the news of the moment. Plouffe kept an optimistic outlook and remained resolute in his public messaging that it had long been our plan to win Iowa, keep the scores close in New Hampshire and Nevada, and then "take the wind coming from the win in South Carolina and blow into February 5." In such moments, by demonstrating that all was going mostly as planned, David moderated the highs and lows that threatened to overwhelm us from within. This factored into the *no drama* environment that kept things stabilized in good times and in bad.

Plouffe never lost sight of the win. Even in defeat he artfully positioned our candidate as a victor. For example, while we lost the New Hampshire popular vote by 39 percent to 36 percent, Plouffe pointed out that the delegate count was tied at nine. If you added in Iowa, he could show that we were actually ahead after the first two contests. To use a baseball metaphor, a game David loves, she scored as many runs in the inning, but we were still winning the game.

Our campaign manager's attitude was infectious and noticeably influenced the rest of us. This was particularly evident in the days immediately following New Hampshire. As an example, after voters finished caucusing in Nevada a week and a half later, news outlets were reporting that the Clinton forces had soundly defeated us in the popular vote by six percentage points there. Thanks to some quick thinking and savvy analysis by our delegate strategist, Jeff Berman, David was presented with data that actually showed us edging out the Clinton campaign in the delegate count due to our performance in the precincts outside of Las Vegas. Jeff's discovery was exciting to me because it was early evidence that the precision and speed of our rapid redeployment during those five days after Iowa had paid off. Where Clinton had only enough organization to work the high population centers of the state, we were able to go wider with our coverage and, therefore, won more of the rural areas.

David went quickly out to the press with Jeff's findings. This effectively confused the story line for readers in the next morning's headlines. A friend of mine who lives in Sweden wrote me an email the following day asking, "If the European papers said Hillary won the vote but the *New York Times* said Obama had more delegates, how do you know who won?"

Tell the Story You Want Written

David always played for another day, even when he was winning. He also preferred good days spread out over several news cycles whenever possible. To this end, Plouffe was fiercely focused on the integrity of the campaign's running narrative. For example, I was struck by his disciplined and patient handling of our high-profile endorsements. Rather than simply drop names as quickly as he got them, our campaign manager was very thoughtful and deliberate about the unveiling of each. Rollouts were timed purposely. Then, when the moment was ripe and the announcement was finally ready, David resisted the lure of allowing the endorsement to become the story. Instead, he used it to amplify and support our fundamental themes. This was a unique feature of his storytelling that kept the campaign's message consistent and the larger running narrative from being interrupted with random announcements of VIP support.

Take our treatment of Kansas governor Kathleen Sebelius. I know there was pressure to stop the female flight away from us as we came out of New Hampshire. After all, "Hillary's crying moment" was said to be the number one search term by Nevada women heading into the caucusing there. Touting a woman of Governor Sebelius's stature could certainly have helped us stem that tide; particularly if quickly packaged with some other high-profile political femmes, like Missouri senator Claire McCaskill and Arizona governor Janet Napolitano, as some wanted to see happen. But rather than exploit her support and use it reactively as a response to worrying developments on the campaign trail, we used the occasion of her endorsement to tell a very different story more than two weeks later.

On January 29, the day after Governor Sebelius delivered the Democratic response to President Bush's State of the Union address, we announced her support for Senator Obama from El Dorado, Kansas. Boasting a population of only twelve thousand people, this community may have seemed an unlikely place to publicize such a prize. Certainly, we'd have drawn larger crowds elsewhere. But there was a story to be told from this spot that would help fill in some of the gaps in Barack's personal narrative for voters.

El Dorado was the childhood home of Barack Obama's grandfather, and his mother also spent part of her youth there. The senator described it as the place where his grandparents fell in love, fought through the turbulent years of the Great Depression together, and welcomed their daughter into the world. He confided to voters that they'd had a dream to "raise my mother in a land of boundless opportunity; that their generation's struggle and sacrifice could give her the freedom to be what she wanted to be; to live how she wanted to live." It was a revealing moment.

Having Governor Sebelius stand alongside Barack as he celebrated his Kansas roots and the heartland values that helped shape him was significant both for her regional stature and for the power of her endorsement as a prominent national Democrat. More importantly, her presence amplified a facet of his personal history that many Americans were discovering for the first time. It offered new clues about the influences in his life that had contributed to his general character as an adult.

The El Dorado example underscored David Plouffe's flair for drawing on local angles as a way to engage voters. During the four-week run-up to February 5, a deluge of requests came from our two dozen state directors who wanted to reserve the candidate's time in their states for large area rallies. Our organizers had quickly learned that small stadium events were the best voter contact money could buy. David pushed back on these appeals, however, because he didn't want to simply crowd-build. In response, he gave very specific guidance to our chief scheduler, Alyssa Mastromonaco. Rather than plan rallies, he instructed, we should create events that reinforced the story of our candidate as we presented him to voters in the respective states.

This accounts for the many examples during those weeks of the campaign's artful use of endorsements and local events to magnify the larger story line. In the days before the New Hampshire primary, for instance, we announced the support of former senator Bill Bradley. Bradley's return to the state where he only narrowly lost to Vice President Al Gore eight years earlier stirred memories of his aggressive dark-horse challenge. The parallels between his hard charge in 2000 and Senator Obama's current battle to defeat an overpowering, establishment-backed opponent helped recast our candidate as the clear underdog following his decisive Iowa win.

Two days after the New Hampshire balloting concluded, we attempted to rub off some of the shine from Clinton's impressive win there by trumpeting the endorsement of 2004 Democratic nominee John Kerry. This news had to be a blow to her boosters, but it was also viewed as a stick in the eye to Kerry's former running mate, John Edwards. Plouffe could have announced Senator Kerry's support a week earlier, before the Iowa caucuses, but he held it back for a more strategic moment. I thought the timing was brilliant. Were we to win New Hampshire, the Kerry endorsement would have put a bow on that gift. As it turned out, in the aftermath of our disappointing defeat, the announcement helped to once again fill out our deflated sails.

The wind was indeed at our backs after we handed the Clintons a crushing defeat in South Carolina on Saturday, January 26. We pulled 55 percent of the vote to their 27 percent and Edwards's 18 percent. It was also the end of the line for Senator Edwards, who withdrew from the race four days later.

With the win in South Carolina, we advanced past the four solo contests of January to compete in the large slate of twenty-three elections scheduled for one single day, February 5. We'd survived. The question now was whether Clinton would put us away on Super Tuesday, as pundits had long predicted. While we could see positive signs for the ensuing races in the days immediately following, how we might ultimately fare on that crucial day wasn't quite as clear.

Be a Winner

The enthusiastic crowd of young people that had piled into American University's Bender Arena in Washington, D.C., erupted into applause as the headliners entered one by one. Senator Obama proudly stood onstage alongside the three prominent Kennedys whose endorsements he was about to receive. Clearly basking in the excitement of the moment, he smiled brightly as he waved to the exuberant crowd. Then he stepped back to let the cousins, first Patrick and then Caroline, take turns at the microphone before finally giving way to the beloved Lion of the Senate.

Rumors of an endorsement from Massachusetts senator Ted Kennedy had begun to circulate in the media almost as soon as the election results were posted in South Carolina two days earlier. Plouffe had relished the prospect of this moment all throughout the previous week, and it was unfolding beautifully, just hours before the final State of the Union address by outgoing president George W. Bush.

Caroline, the daughter of former president John F. Kennedy, was normally allergic to such affairs, so her appearance was particularly warmly welcomed by the audience. The *New York Times* op-ed she'd penned entitled "A President Like My Father" had been political dynamite when it dropped over the weekend, and the speech she delivered echoed the remarks contained in that explosive piece. It was an upbeat address that she concluded by saying:

> I have never had a president who inspired me the way people tell me that my father inspired them. But for the first time, I believe I have found the man who could be that president—not just for me, but for a new generation of Americans.

Caroline's comments paved the way for her Uncle Ted, who extolled our candidate's appeal to a new generation reminiscent of President Kennedy in the 1960s. It felt eerily like the Kennedy torch was being passed to Barack.

I watched at my desk, awed by the work of our advance staff once again. I wrote a short email to Alyssa Mastromonaco, the head of that department, to say as much. They had done a consistently fabulous job all throughout the campaign, but this was a particularly polished effort. Advance Director Emmett Beliveau and his team on the ground choreographed this event to look like no other before it. This wasn't your everyday rally. It was a made-for-television production packaged for viewers watching in their living rooms at home. The imagery of the energized crowd that wrapped around the fiery Ted Kennedy—flanked by niece Caroline, son Patrick, and candidate Obama—literally offered the appearance of a nominating convention. The pageantry created a truly electric moment that filled the television screen.

I thought it was a bold move to organize such a grand event just hours before President Bush's final State of the Union address, but the contrast certainly worked in our favor. The evening's ceremony was flat, uninspired, and lacking the spark of our earlier event. Senator Obama looked large and the audience around him energized.

"Ready on Day One"

Ted Kennedy's words lingered long after the rally, and our campaign boomeranged off his endorsement with extreme velocity. During the next week, we saw huge crowds everywhere our candidate went. The rallies were staggering. We consistently registered numbers ranging from eighteen thousand to twenty thousand in cities like Denver, Minneapolis, St. Louis, and Wilmington. Even Boise drew an audience approaching fifteen thousand for an event. It all climaxed at a Southern California stop, two days before Super Tuesday voting.

Joining Senator Obama at UCLA's Pauley Pavilion was his wife Michelle, Oprah Winfrey, and Caroline Kennedy. As it was, that was a high-powered lineup. But it was the surprise entrance of Kennedy cousin and popular California First Lady Maria Shriver that electrified the arena. She stepped onstage to raucous applause, and with her endorsement, news outlets and the blogosphere lit up. This was another media coup for our campaign, and it breathed fresh life into the footage of the Kennedy endorsement event from the previous week, which continued cycling through the media.

The event featuring these four prominent women for Obama capped what had to be a difficult nine days for the Clinton campaign. Here was further proof that David Plouffe always looked to the next trophy, and he didn't need an election to pick one up. During this stretch it actually felt like we were winning every day. These successes powered our organization and drove us to work harder.

At the same time, the Clinton campaign seemed lost—even a little desperate. Their side became increasingly reliant on silly gambits they had begun employing in the fall, like mockingly parading an essay Senator Obama wrote when he was in grade school titled "I Want to Become President" and planting questions at their own town hall meetings. Those antics were starting to be replaced with harsher, edgier tactics that did nothing to lift their candidate. Accusations began to fly that a clear strategy carrying dangerously racial undercurrents had gained traction inside the Clinton camp. The charge stuck more earnestly after Senator Clinton announced just before Martin Luther King, Jr., Day that it took President Johnson to get civil rights legislation enacted.

A series of reckless musings by Clinton surrogates contributed to this growing perception. Bill Clinton was regularly in the hot seat during January for his fiery rhetoric coming from the campaign trail. The attorney general of New York stirred up controversy with a "shucking and jiving" reference to our candidate, a phrase that some complained in the media had historically been used to demean African Americans. The founder of Black Entertainment Television also ignited a separate firestorm with inferences that seemed intended to remind voters of Senator Obama's admitted drug use in his youth. Without a filter and minus a message framework that had any recognizable boundaries, every news cycle opened up a new need for the Clinton campaign to clarify, deny, or walk back remarks made by the candidate or her spokespeople.

There were some pretty big consequences here for the Clinton campaign, as evidenced in Ted Kennedy's shifting from his publicly neutral stance to a position alongside Senator Obama. His endorsement must have stung inside the Clinton camp, but the perceived motivation behind it was even more damaging. It validated an unflattering portrait of their campaign which had been slowly coming into focus. You never want your candidate to look small, but somehow the Clinton strategists seemed to be accomplishing just that with respect to theirs.

Additionally, while Senator Obama energized large crowds with his inspirational oratory, Hillary failed to generate comparable energy. In ways, she seemed isolated and alone. For example, during Barack's high-octane three-state swing with Oprah Winfrey back in December— Oprahpalooza as it was called—Senator Clinton's mother and daughter joined her for a somewhat more understated appearance together in Iowa. The diametrically opposite portrayals inspired the inevitable comparisons that characterized Senator Obama's electric stadium rock 'n' roll on the one hand against Hillary Clinton's unplugged acoustic folk on the other. It was a striking juxtaposition for her organization, once universally thought to be the undisputed political powerhouse in the race.

Election Night

On the night of February 5, results for the twenty-two voting states and one U.S. territory flashed on the television monitors throughout headquarters uninterrupted. We had speculated in recent senior staff meetings how the reporting would unfold as coverage rolled from east to west, based on when the polls were scheduled to close in the respective states and what the likely results in each might be. For the most part, it all went as we expected. Georgia was called for us first. Then, Senator Clinton got all her good news early. In came New York and New Jersey, then Tennessee and nearby Arkansas and Oklahoma. She picked up a big prize in Massachusetts—a tough result given that we'd gotten endorsements from the state's major daily newspaper (*Boston Globe*), its governor, and both U.S. senators, John Kerry and Ted Kennedy. Much later that night, Arizona and California also fell to the Clinton forces, the latter being disappointing but not necessarily surprising.

In the end, however, the scoreboard looked great for us. Eight states and the territory of American Samoa landed in Clinton's column, while we pulled thirteen into ours. We won all six mainland caucuses: Alaska, Colorado, Idaho, Kansas, Minnesota, and North Dakota. And our primary wins included Alabama, Connecticut, Delaware, Georgia, Utah, and the senator's home state of Illinois. We also eked out Missouri. New Mexico, on the other hand, was deemed too close to call and remained contested for nine days before finally being awarded to Clinton. Even then, with almost seventeen hundred delegates up for grabs, we ultimately won three more contests and about a dozen more delegates.

Ode to "Hope and Change"

The building cleared later that evening so staff could go to a local hangout and watch Senator Obama's speech. I stayed behind, alone on the headquarters floor. It was eerily quiet as HQ was rarely empty. I waited for the Clinton people to predictably press their distorted case in the media that they'd won the important states that would make them more competitive against Republicans in the fall. But as I colored in our election map to date, it painted a better picture for us. Clinton pulled the ones that Democrats were already likely to win: Massachusetts, New York, New Jersey, and California, for example. She had also won the states our party was certain to lose, like the I-40 states of Tennessee, Arkansas, and Oklahoma.

On the other hand, our wins dotted some important general election battlegrounds in the middle of the country. We won Colorado, Iowa, Minnesota, and Missouri. We also showed that we could aggressively compete against the Republicans in New Hampshire and Nevada. We'd proven ourselves better in the states that would truly matter in the general election. More importantly, the overall race was unfolding exactly the way David said it would. We took Iowa, kept it close in New Hampshire and Nevada, and then rolled through South Carolina. We carried that momentum into February 5 with great news on the other side. We won more states, more votes, and more pledged delegates. Despite the long-held conventional wisdom that Clinton would have the nomination locked down by the close of polls on Super Tuesday, clearly we had positioned ourselves to play for another day.

I took advantage of the quiet to finally click open the link to a video that had been sitting in my inbox for several days. I'd received it from New Media Director Joe Rospars with a note that said, "You have to look at this." The video was a new release by will.i.am of the Black Eyed Peas.

Joe and I—together with Chief Staff Counsel Kendall Burman and our national youth vote director, Hans Reimer—had at one time explored the idea of working with celebrity artists on music initiatives for the campaign. This was prompted sometime after the Clinton campaign's disastrous contest, which ended with the selection of a Celine Dion recording as their theme song. Kendall and I ultimately determined that because of licensing, costs, and other legal concerns, our campaign wouldn't coordinate on such projects. Produced and released without our involvement, we were free to feature will.i.am's piece on our website and promote it virally online.

With a rare moment to myself, I watched and listened as the sound of will.i.am's music filled my corner of the headquarters floor. The tinny sound that bleated from my small computer speakers and the video that was squished into my laptop screen couldn't do full justice to his riveting production. Drawing upon Senator Obama's inspired New Hampshire speech, one by one celebrities flashed into my view—Scarlett Johansson, John Legend, and Kareem Abdul-Jabbar among them—offering their own vocals laid over our candidate's masterful oratory and will.i.am's uplifting melody. Whether it was just a release of the adrenaline from the past month or the impact of his work, I noticed my eyes were beginning to well up as I watched.

The video was a moving tribute to a powerful speech, certainly. More than that, I felt a personal connection to this piece. It memorialized a transformational time in our own short organizational history when from defeat, we inside Obama for America learned to become winners. It began on a cold night in New Hampshire, when Senator Obama boldly challenged us to hold on to the belief: Yes We Can!

6

Bend, Don't Break

FEBRUARY 22, 2008: NY Times running a story about discontent among Clinton donors. One prominent backer said, "We didn't raise all of this money to keep paying consultants who have pursued basically the wrong strategy for a year now . . . So much about her campaign needs to change—but it may be too late." They have a problem!

Fired Up, Ready to Go!

We knew that good news awaited us on the other side of Super Tuesday if we could just hold our own on the day itself. We did. And on Wednesday, February 6, with five Election Days and twenty-seven races behind us, we found ourselves in a dead heat against the most formidable organization in contemporary American politics. Ahead on the campaign calendar were nine races between February 9 and February 12, with two more on the nineteenth. There would also be four states in play on March 4, including the delegate troves of Texas and Ohio.

As expected, we had strong showings in those days immediately after February 5. We won big on the ninth, taking Louisiana, Nebraska, Washington, and the Virgin Islands. We also tore up Maine the next day. I had been pretty worried about that particular state going in. I thought it was the most precarious of our post–Super Tuesday contests in the February lineup. But we proved dominant on the ground once again in those Sunday caucuses and logged another impressive win.

We stormed into the Potomac primaries of Maryland, Washington, D.C., and Virginia on the following Tuesday. We took Maryland 60 percent to 36 percent and we won the District of Columbia by more than fifty points (75 percent to 24 percent). In Virginia, we finished ahead by a whopping 29 percent. It was a big day for us. The African American vote in all three contests hovered around 90 percent, while polling coming out of Virginia and Maryland showed that we'd effectively cut into her support among women, the heart of her base. Virginia's exit data also had us performing better with white men, a consistently difficult demographic for us.

After the voting on the twelfth, media outlets began reporting for the first time that our candidate had passed Senator Clinton in the overall delegate count. Behind that good news and after an additional pickup in the Democrats Abroad primary, our winning streak was extended to eleven on February 19 when we again posted blowout numbers in two more contests. We overwhelmingly triumphed in the senator's childhood home state of Hawaii by more than fifty points, and we easily won Wisconsin.

Wisconsin was another prize for us since it had long been considered ripe for a Clinton pick-off. But the indicators were increasingly trending our way as that state's election approached. This presented both campaigns with separate dilemmas. Senator Clinton's team had to evaluate the costs of staying to fortify this key strategic position against the benefits of pulling up stakes and retreating to Ohio, where they could construct a fire wall in front of the March 4 election. Once her team made the determination to leave, we had to decide whether to hold our candidate in Wisconsin to close the deal with voters there or free him to follow Clinton into the Buckeye State.

Jon Carson made a strong case to stay a little longer than we'd originally planned. He argued that running up the score in Wisconsin would have a favorable effect in Ohio, plus we stood to nab a few more delegates. Plouffe went with Jon's recommendation, and it paid off. Our seventeen-point victory helped us pick up those extra delegates, and we did see a much needed bounce in Ohio.

The confidence we were feeling behind our wins on February 19 was further validated later that night in a moment that stood apart from the routine televised polling coverage we'd grown accustomed to. I remember it well. I watched fuming as Hillary Clinton delivered her fourth speech in two weeks following Election Day losses. She never graciously acknowledged our wins, and I resented the free air time she got after every defeat to again recite her stump speech on national TV.

Then, early into her address from Ohio, the site of a major upcoming showdown, the cameras unexpectedly cut away. Viewers were suddenly taken to Texas, where Barack had just arrived to rally the enthusiastic crowd awaiting him there. The abrupt shift of the spotlight from her stage to his offered a distinct signal to the television audience as to our candidate's new standing in his race against Hillary. It also triggered a brief celebration in my household.

Shake-Up!

The scorecard looked bad for Clinton, but the machinations inside her campaign were attracting further unwanted headlines. Super Tuesday wasn't long past when word broke that campaign manager and longtime aide, Patti Solis Doyle, was being cut loose. Deputy Campaign Manager Mike Henry's resignation soon followed.

On hearing the news about Patti, I advised my own staff to watch for the press to uncover evidence of operational failures inside the Clinton organization during the coming days. My intent wasn't to celebrate the unraveling of the Clinton campaign; rather, I just wanted to point out the advantages my teams had created for our candidate by executing an unusually tight and precise operation. After all, there is rarely sex appeal in a story about a well-run campaign. The unnoticed heroes in our operation quietly powered our campaign forward, yet received little recognition outside. In this news about the Clinton organization, there would be a rare opportunity to highlight for our staff the demonstrative difference they had been making every day.

Things were certainly amiss over in the Clinton camp. As expected, Solis Doyle's exit was paved with some highly unflattering remembrances coming from her former colleagues that were aired in the media. In addition, reports began to circulate that the candidate had been forced to make a personal loan to her campaign. Even more intriguing were the anecdotal accounts coming to us from the field that the hat was being passed at Clinton office openings—and that their staff and vendors had stopped getting paid. But it wasn't until late February that the lid finally came off.

Then, out spilled the troubling news their campaign had been battling to contain.

Disclosing Disarray

February 21 will long stand out for me as one of the more unforgettable days in the entire election. Casual political observers might recall this as the date of the highly anticipated Texas Democratic debate. I remember it for the breaking news resulting from the public disclosure filings that were newly logged with the FEC by each of the campaigns. Oddly, these government-required reports can actually be a gripping read for some industry insiders because they offer important clues about the internal workings of the competing organizations. Each report is like a packaged readout of the campaign's operational diagnostics.

Previous releases hadn't revealed anything particularly remarkable, really. Throughout 2007, the numbers reflected the nose-to-nose horse race that was consistently portrayed in the daily headlines. For example, the 2007 year-end documents showed that we had actually hit $100 million in contributions, which only narrowly trailed the Clinton campaign. Spending by the two organizations was also strikingly close.

These most recent February submissions to the FEC, however, reflected the shifting momentum of the race. The Clinton report offered data that indicated excessive spending and a money spigot that was slowing to a drip. Online blogs lit up with news reported by the *New York Times* that her campaign had laid out nearly $100,000 on food for the Iowa caucuses. Additionally, $25,000 was spent on accommodations at the Bellagio Hotel in Las Vegas in advance of the Nevada caucuses. These reports contributed to an already growing optics problem fueled just weeks earlier by a *Washington Post* piece that was also getting traction in the blogosphere. At the center of the controversy was the $500,000 in parking receipts her campaign had racked up during 2007. As one news outlet reported, the Clinton ledger looked like it was heating up dangerously.

By contrast, the numbers in our report told a very different story. Though both organizations were spending about $1 million a day during January, we posted fundraising receipts totaling $36 million for the month; the Clinton campaign showed only $13 million coming in from donors. Her campaign didn't even raise half of what it was spending, while we more than covered our expenses. Their organization had also racked up obligations to vendors totaling $7.5 million, which looked quite lopsided next to our $1 million figure. Finally, in addition to the high debt load, a line called "Loans from Candidate" confirmed prior reports that Mrs. Clinton had indeed floated a $5 million advance to her campaign.

In the everyday blocking and tackling of gritty campaign football, here was fresh evidence that, in fact, it was our operation, not theirs, that had supremely dominated at the line of scrimmage. Jim Jordan, a respected Washingtonian and former Kerry aide, summed it up in a *New York Times* article that quickly circulated electronically among our staff. He framed it in a way that I took as a high compliment:

> Obviously, some campaigns are more careful and wise with their money than others. But these budgetary post-mortems tend to follow a familiar pattern; winners are by definition smart, and losers are dumb and wasteful. In truth, campaign budgeting is hard and complicated and three-dimensional and just impossible to understand without the full time-and-place context of the whole race.

The Buildup to Mini–Super Tuesday

Though I write with some exuberance about our February run, I want to be very clear that we were not suffering from any type of post-Iowa syndrome. There was no swagger here. If anything, we were reaching deep for anything we had that could keep our spirits high in the face of a brutal battle and growing exhaustion.

Our staff had a great, unspoken respect for the New York senator. I'd even go so far as to say that we were all fearful of a Clinton renaissance. This race was far from over. With new management and a sharper message, that organization was getting its campaign legs, and her machine was still very much a threat. Nonetheless, the tables had definitely turned. Once the yapping dog nipping at the ankles of the Clinton campaign in front of us, we were now running for our lives from the enraged pit bull that was chasing us.

The next races after our wins in Wisconsin and Hawaii on February 19 would take place two weeks later, on March 4—Ohio, Texas, Rhode Island, and Vermont. Known as Mini–Super Tuesday for the sizable

370 delegates at stake, it looked like a friendly date on the campaign calendar for Senator Clinton, particularly for the edge she had in the two big states. To begin with, her appeal with the working-class white and senior demographics that together comprised a large piece of the Ohio electorate offered her an advantage. Latino voters had also been warmer to her, which lengthened our odds in Texas. But there was enough good news in the polling to lift our hopes. A mid-February survey in Ohio showed that we had closed the gap there by ten percentage points. We still trailed by twenty, but momentum was clearly breaking our way. In Texas, we had been able to slice her twenty-point advantage in half and during the final week of February we were closing fast.

Playing in Texas cost a lot of money. It was a big state with an unusual system for selecting delegates to the convention, including a voting primary and an elaborate series of caucus activities that stretched out over several days. Fortunately for us, donations were streaming in and our coffers were swelling. And since we really wanted to pull either Texas or Ohio out of the Clinton column, Plouffe dropped another $3 million on the Lone Star State at the last minute just to "keep things interesting." We had performed well in all of the caucus races so far and that's where we saw daylight we could run toward.

Soldiering On

An ongoing challenge was keeping our troops motivated and fresh since the race looked like it would drag on. Careless mistakes were beginning to show up on our side for the first time. Earlier in the month, for example, we had one of our phone vendors calling voters in Washington and addressing them as residents of another state. We also had sensitive delegate estimates somehow show up in the press. Minor mistakes were becoming noticeably regular, a sign that we all needed a break. There was no rest for the weary now, however, not when victory—or defeat—was close at hand.

The management environment on the ground remained highly complex. Many of our field organizers were in their third state in two months, and the suddenly shrinking battleground map was creating some interesting dynamics. The field of play at its widest had twenty-three races on February 5 and ten more in the days immediately following. During that time, top talent was spread very thinly across more than half of the country. This resulted in a phenomenon whereby some of the less senior staffers from early states such as Iowa or New Hampshire were suddenly thrust into higher management roles. In some cases, they were actually running smaller February states. Having acquired a fair amount of authority, these young stars suddenly found themselves taking calls from leaders at the highest levels of our national headquarters, such as communications heavyweights Robert Gibbs and Dan Pfeiffer or the candidate's schedulers and principal aides, Alyssa Mastromonaco and Danielle Crutchfield.

However, once those races were over and we moved into the March states, our staff began to compress again with far less territory in play. This had the effect of dropping some of those same young leaders back into the middle of the pack. In Texas and Ohio, where the stakes were high, our most experienced and tenured organizers filled in the layers at the top: Temo Figueroa, Buffy Wicks, Jeremy Bird, and Iowa alums Paul Tewes and Mitch Stewart, for example. Meanwhile, the less experienced talent was bunched up underneath them. The adjustment wasn't insignificant, since in a very short time some went from having been big fish in little ponds to smaller fish in much larger waters.

As the primaries dragged out and our field soldiers marched on, each person acquired new knowledge and additional baggage from their most recent assignments. Sometimes you nailed that last job, sometimes you didn't. Sometimes you attracted new fans, sometimes you acquired detractors. The role you loved in the last state might not be the one you got in the next. All of these factors were packaged into emotions that were carried into future states as staff traveled further and further along the campaign trail. It called on each person's capacity to be continually adaptable.

The taxing conditions notwithstanding, our organizers had to stay fierce in the field. The Clinton organization was a threat as long as it was alive. New Hampshire proved that there was no quit in the Clintons. Heading into the March 4 elections, I was very worried that Hillary's team was just a course correction away from getting control of this race and if they ever climbed back on top, it would be for the last time.

Sixteen races were left on the calendar, and she looked dominant in some very important states. There was Texas and Ohio on March 4, Pennsylvania in late April, and Indiana early in May. Also looming were Florida and Michigan. These two delegate-loaded states created a complicated dynamic in the race after the Democratic parties in both states defied national party rules and moved their primary elections up before February 5. Having already been harshly penalized for the violation, the decree disallowing those state delegations seating at the national convention seemed unsustainable. Clinton saw this as an opportunity and was now leading the call for all states to be counted. The issue would inevitably be revisited. This worried a few of my fellow senior campaign aides. One complained to me as we filed out of a morning senior staff meeting that in this uncertainty was an opportunity for the election to be stolen from us.

That fear kept the competition intense for those ever-important superdelegates. As of mid-February, we were still trailing by about a hundred in the superdelegate count. And because a great many were still holding out, the prospect of some seismic event that might cause the "uncommitteds" to break Senator Clinton's way consistently haunted us. A really bad day on March 4 or a fatal blow against us could very well breathe life into our nightmare scenario.

Kremlinizing Clinton

We ended February in a very strong position financially, which was why a curious exchange I had with our campaign manager late in the month took me by surprise. David approached my desk as Marianne Markowitz and I were finishing up a meeting. He hovered momentarily at an imaginary boundary on the floor several feet away and seemed sheepish about crossing it to interrupt us when I waved him over. Plouffe wasn't much for chitchat, and he looked perplexed so I knew something was bothering him. He uneasily strolled toward us while gazing intently at his BlackBerry. I braced for the news. Then he slowly looked up and said flatly, "We can't spend any more."

For a split second, my thoughts raced, rapidly searching my memory for clues as to what he could possibly be talking about. All information I had indicated money was good. Even our recent spending flurry could not have triggered a "bare cupboard" moment like the one the

Clinton camp had recently experienced. Something didn't make sense, I thought. And why was he delivering me news that I would typically deliver to him?

My private panic was quickly calmed. It wasn't that we didn't have money; in fact, we were flush. We just had nowhere left to reasonably spend it before the March 4 contests. We had unloaded our sizable war chest on them and now would have to sit tight and hold off on any new activity.

This highlighted a truly remarkable advantage that had been presented to us by our grassroots investors. With every dollar that came in, we had the ability to do more as an organization. The airwaves were saturated with our message, and we had robust voter contact operations on the ground. While Clinton was cutting staff, we were growing again. Jon and I must have hired 350 people during that one-month stretch alone, including reenlisting our Iowa contingent. In addition, Plouffe regularly pushed new pots of money Jon's direction that were earmarked for specific states ahead on the election calendar. This resulted in regular meetings between the two of us to sort through the budget details.

All of this culminated in what Marianne and I called the Cold War strategy, referring to our ability to overwhelm the opposition by outspending it. The press later referred to it as the "Kremlinizing of Clinton." Having this financial advantage so late in a campaign was more of a gift than a strategy. Our supporters had uniquely positioned us to have all the resources we needed to engage in battle at full capacity.

Our supporters were so energized that in the middle of February, just as the Clinton camp was boasting in the media that they had raised $13 million during the month to date, I looked down at our books showing us sitting at $31 million. In the five days after February 5 alone we raised more than $9 million. Marianne and I had projected weeks before, to raised eyebrows, that during January and February we'd generate more than $80 million in contributions. That was more than our best three quarters combined during 2007. Our record $55 million for February lifted us easily past that number, and we picked up our one-millionth new donor along the way as well. I estimated that was twice what the Clinton camp had. With that milestone, Joe Rospars proudly pointed out to me that one in three hundred Americans had given to our campaign.

Our scorecard heading into March 4 looked pretty impressive. We appeared strong in just about every category. We'd convincingly beaten Clinton in the last eleven races. We were ahead in pledged delegates by about 150. Our popular vote lead had stretched to over nine hundred thousand. And we had won over a dozen more states and territories than her campaign. The growing gap was becoming so plain that even Hillary's closest advisors, her husband among them, had to admit openly that Ohio and Texas were must-wins for her campaign to remain viable.

Sea Change

"For everyone here in Ohio and across America who's been counted out but refused to be knocked out, and for everyone who has stumbled but stood right back up, and for everyone who works hard and never gives up, this one is for you."

Joyfully delivered to a jubilant Ohio crowd, Senator Clinton's words pretty much summed up the election night story that filled the media narrative in the following days. Her performance was described as game changing. She won Ohio, Texas, and Rhode Island. Vermont fell in our favor, though it offered the smallest prize. While we had all hoped Hillary would gracefully step out of the race with a respectable showing, she was quite clearly sounding the call to fight on. It would extend the race at least seven more weeks, until April 22, when Pennsylvanians would vote in the next high-stakes contest.

Another dominant caucus performance by our field organizers, this time in Texas, did manage to keep the score close on March 4. In the end, Clinton ultimately won only four more delegates than we did. Although her campaign narrowly won the day, it was enough to help her stay well alive in the race. And while our winning streak of eleven since Super Tuesday had ended, we went on to take the next two contests in Wyoming and Mississippi on the eighth and the eleventh. That gave us a 14–3 record since February 5. With those wins, there was no escaping the fast-cementing perception that it was our candidate, not Hillary, who was cruising toward the Democratic nomination.

Mind the Optics

As the presumed front-runner, we could anticipate much harsher treatment by the press. We could also expect an escalation in the attacks by the Clinton campaign to be directly proportional with their rapidly declining odds of winning. After all, this was a changing reality for them as well: the race was noticeably slipping away.

David, who was always sensitive to the optics of every decision and action, for the first time began to view the contest through the prism of our campaign as the favorite. Thus, his management of it noticeably changed. The overriding consideration behind David's decision-making after the March 4 elections was that we take care not to appear to be bullying. If we were no longer able to maintain our underdog status, we needed to be sure that Clinton didn't capitalize on hers with voters and the media.

But this wasn't such an easy proposition. Emotions were rising inside the campaign. The lingering threat Hillary posed that still hung in the air, mixed with the smell of blood in the water, contributed to the highly charged atmosphere around us. We had influential staff and donors who were furious over Hillary's decision to stay in the race. If she wouldn't leave, then many thought we should actively advocate for her to step out.

Also, we were quite simply more dominant than her campaign at this point. A lot of money had been flowing in since March 4, and we were also bulked up in the field. Our large staffs in Texas and Ohio, although fatigued, were absolutely prepared to charge forward. But unlike the five days after Iowa, when our post-election movements were executed discreetly and well away from the New Hampshire spotlight, this time there were many weeks separating March 4 and the next major contest on April 22. Everything we did would be noticed and anything that made us look too muscular next to her organization could create a backlash against us. Thus, David made a very deliberate decision not to advance our field troops after those elections. Instead, he asked me to extend housing for several more days and have our folks in the field stay where they were so they could get some rest.

This showcased a special maturity on the part of our management. In this case, David avoided the trap that many organizational leaders fall into by becoming overly devoted to established methods and hardened routine. Rather than mechanically press ahead, this was an example of Plouffe effectively taking the ship off autopilot so we could manually guide it through impending rough waters. While still dangerous, this made for a safer passage.

Balance of Power

There was uneasiness amongst our senior staff after the March 4 elections. This wasn't anything like the noticeable jolt that struck after the New Hampshire loss. Rather, it was more of a low-grade angst that surrounded us. The recent results or even the frustration over Senator Clinton's determination to stay in the race had little to do with it. The common complaint that I heard was rooted in a general concern that we at headquarters had lost much of our influence with state leaders. Worry was expressed that our messaging had become uneven at the state level. Others confided to me that they thought that the candidate's repeated visits to the same cities had produced increasingly smaller crowds when we should have been getting him to the outskirts into the local diners and community halls where people gathered.

This couldn't be considered carping, nor was it finger-pointing in the wake of a narrow Election Day loss. It was a genuine observation that the nature of the partnership between headquarters and the states, an important feature of our work in January, was suddenly different. The flurry of February contests disguised this fact, but as the pace had slowed our leaders woke up to a post–March 4 world in which a palpable change had occurred.

Looking back, what we had wasn't a problem of tactical or strategic differences. We had undergone some significant growing pains that led to a sizable shift in the organization's shape. This change was largely due to the meteoric rise of our national field department. With about two-thirds of the nation voting in February, all of the campaign's energy was devoted to supporting the heavy voter contact efforts on the ground that were coordinated from headquarters by Jon Carson's growing operation.

There was nothing new or unexpected in all of this. The occasional temporary expansion of influence by one department over the others had been an ongoing occurrence in our campaign's life cycle. And while previous surges weren't universally felt, all of the headquarters components organized behind this particular wave to lift that department to heights none other had previously seen.

In this case, Field's ascent also coincided with a mostly unnoticed alteration in our organization's operational architecture whereby an administrative layer had formed between headquarters and the states. Filling that gap again was Carson's shop. This explained some of the disconnect people around me were suddenly noticing. It was a development that had its roots going back to the fall, when Jon initially took the reins as the February 5 director.

Back then, his task was to build the organizations in the twenty-two states and one territory that would vote on Super Tuesday. As those states prepared to come online, I was faced with a dilemma. I knew I couldn't treat the two dozen February 5 directors like I had the early four. That would have meant giving them the same hiring and spending authorities, despite their dramatically abbreviated tenures. To offer that level of autonomy to these states—not to mention to entrust, train, and service such a large number of people at a time when we needed to be nimble and efficient—would have failed us. There would have been costly operational and spending mistakes. More importantly, I needed to keep my teams focused on the four early states. We couldn't afford the distraction of twenty-three new partners on the ground, each with the urgent needs of their start-up organizations.

I settled on a different model to service the sprouting February 5 system. I decided that rather than work directly with the numerous new state directors, my operation would instead have just one direct point of contact: Jon. In principle, we would treat his department as the fifth early state. He would have the same authorities as those four directors while Marianne and I would have similar administrative oversight. This meant that the directors in the February states would have to work their requests through Jon's shop and final approvals would come through my office. It would also require a robust operation around him to meet the needs on the ground.

A Campaign without Boundaries

The rise of Field and the structural alteration that put more authority in Jon's hands only partially explains the changes we were undergoing at the time. Something much bigger happening outside of headquarters was simultaneously reshaping our organization more profoundly. We began to experience a form of decentralization that was unusual in a political campaign environment. It was the unexpected outcome of our advances in new media.

Specifically, we were becoming more reliant on the robust Internet community our chief online organizer, Chris Hughes, had been cultivating for nearly a year. The effects of this devolution were felt most acutely in headquarters.

A cofounder of Facebook, Chris was rapidly revolutionizing the electoral landscape by creating a social networking space for politics. Working carefully with our chief digital strategist, Joe Rospars, Hughes and his small band of online organizers put powerful tools and timely content in the hands of our supporters behind a dedicated platform called MyBarackObama.com. Also known as "myBO" by our users, Obama supporters had a way to stay seamlessly connected to the campaign 24/7 for the entirety of the election season. More importantly, with a personal computer and a cell phone, any kitchen table could be transformed into a virtual phone bank using a new online application we'd developed. Names, numbers, and a calling script were only a click away, making it possible to direct our volunteers to dial prospective supporters anywhere in the country at any time through the online phone bank.

The impact of this innovation was first noticeable after the Iowa and New Hampshire contests. In past cycles, after state races had ended and neighborhood offices were closed, supporters in these states were left behind as the campaign moved on. Local volunteers had to wait for the general election to fire up again before they could reengage—after the campaign returned and offices were again opened. In these early states, for example, that might have meant a six-month hiatus. With thirty-eight races between February 5 and March 4, we had found a way to bring these grassroots stakeholders along with us to those new battlegrounds even if they couldn't physically uproot from their homes and neighborhoods. Our seasoned early state supporters now joined forces with a national online army.

If the beginning stages of Obama for America featured headquarters as an extension of the early state operations, our organization was fast becoming a sprawling system that no longer required a centralized structure to facilitate voter-to-voter contact. Our new media and technology teams were pioneering a new political frontier by eliminating the physical boundaries that had previously constrained ongoing supporter involvement. Just as iTunes and Amazon.com made it possible for consumers to shop for specialty goods without visiting an actual store, we'd created a way for volunteers to participate in politics without leaving their homes—no campaign office or precinct organizer required. As these transaction points became less important, the traditional organizational power centers began to fall.

We were transforming into a campaign without borders.

Adapting to Change

During February and March, we experienced a dynamic period of organizational upheaval that was masked by the intensity of the competition. Change is inevitable in any business. In our case, however, because a campaign venture has a truncated existence and an accelerated life cycle relative to a typical venture, staff felt the structural and authority shifts that naturally occur even more sharply. This created a great challenge for our management since anything that affected the tender balance of power within the work ecosystem, even if temporary, could contribute to the potential for an organizational crisis. It was a vulnerability that could have led to internal volatility.

I credit our senior leadership team for maintaining unity at the top as we maneuvered through this delicate phase of the election season. In my view, camaraderie was an important factor in our ability to adapt to change when other campaigns collapsed under the weight of similar pressures. There is something to be said for maintaining a cordial atmosphere. Mutual respect is critical in good times because it is often in moments of crisis or uncertainty that scores are settled. We at the top worked harmoniously together, and that set the proper tone for the rest of our staff.

Ours was a very tight core unit that had been together for many months. Every morning we gathered as a group—Dan Pfeiffer (communications), Alyssa Mastromonaco (scheduling and advance), Julianna Smoot (finance), Joe Rospars (new media), Matt Nugen (political), Heather Higginbottom (policy), Devorah Adler (research), Jon Carson (field), Larry Grisolano (paid media), and myself in the role of chief operating officer. This was the nucleus that surrounded Plouffe and Deputy Campaign Manager Steve Hildebrand. We had long ago sorted out our relationships with one another and had proven to be collaborative problem-solvers.

In the end, I believe that of all the campaigns in this race, ours was the most pliable and our staff the most adaptable. This was evident in the perseverance of our embattled field organizers who adjusted to the unique challenges on the ground as they moved quickly through states to take on tough new assignments. It was demonstrated by our midlevel staffers who informally renegotiated the terms of their own changing power dynamic together, even as their boss's influence above them continually shifted. And it was exemplified in the example of our senior managers who responded to these sensitive developments at the top with unusual grace.

Waves came and went, but none of us in leadership dared overplay our hands or attempt to reside permanently outside of our lanes. A singular key to our success, then, was that the balance between people and departments remained stable throughout the campaign.

This wasn't a team of rivals.

7

In Crisis, Stay on Offense

MAY 3, 2008: *"We'll try not to fuck it up while you are gone," Plouffe shouted from behind me as I left his office for my family vacation. I hollered back that I wouldn't know since I'd be stuffing my BlackBerry in a drawer. Eight days later, I turned on the TV and slowly sank onto the edge of our hotel bed, shocked at what I saw. Something had gone really wrong during our time at sea.*

Spun Out

It felt like March 4 took forever to arrive, but it quickly turned into a distant memory after the elections ended. Even though Hillary Clinton's victories from that day were being trumpeted in the media as some sort of game changer, she ultimately earned less than a handful more delegates from that four-state battle. Thus, the race remained mostly unchanged, except for the sharpening reality that Hillary was losing runway fast.

We went on to take Wyoming on Saturday the eighth and Mississippi the following Tuesday. In Mississippi, we won with an astonishing 61 percent of the vote. Unlike Clinton's March 4, however, these two victories went mostly unnoticed in the press. This was aggravating since our combined nine-delegate pickup wiped out any of her gains from the week before. In fact, for the month of March, we actually won a half-dozen more delegates than the Clinton campaign.

But the media seemed to be following the script exactly as Senator Clinton had written it. She had long looked beyond Wyoming and Mississippi to instead plant a flag in Pennsylvania, billing that contest nearly two months out as some sort of winner-take-all playoff. Hillary also began hinting at her openness to a Clinton-Obama dream ticket. I thought that an interesting proposition from the trailing candidate.

Casting Doubts

The month and a half that separated Mississippi from Pennsylvania on the campaign calendar looked like a desert. There were no races. This lull would mark perhaps the most uncomfortable period in the entire campaign to date. It went by painfully slowly.

Every day that Senator Clinton remained in the race fortified the troubling anxiety inside Obama for America that there was no way of slaying this giant. Clinton's determination to stay in the race infuriated many of us. Even more worrying, Senator McCain had secured the Republican nomination on March 4. This offered him a nearly two-month head start in preparing for the general election. That was a lifetime in politics.

These tensions were heightened by a scorching media blitz we had battled for weeks that caused the temperature to noticeably spike inside headquarters. Frankly, we were all a little more tuned into the election reporting during this stretch than we needed to be. This was a problem since there was little in the news to comfort us. With the white-hot spotlight of the media now firmly trained on our organization, the outside chatter started getting into our heads. Once that happened, it became easy for doubts to prevail.

In this hyped-up environment, staff became increasingly sensitive to the incoming political mortar. Anxiety ran throughout the organization, and the stress affected everyone differently. It was demoralizing to have won March, yet watch as Clinton was somehow touted as the victor. Curiously, even a surprising number of our own staff genuinely accepted the prevailing media viewpoint that we had actually lost. While a measure of fear worked to our advantage and kept us fiercely motivated, it became increasingly difficult to keep a realistic perspective.

State of the Race

I remained concerned. I had no objection to Clinton staying in, but the nature of her attacks wouldn't help our chances in November against McCain. I calmly reassured complaining staff that it was good for us to compete in every state if it really was her intention to take it to the end. Privately, however, I worried that our candidate and campaign would be too badly damaged to contend with the Republican machine after the nomination was secured. It was disconcerting to watch Clinton sow the seeds of an ugly case against us that was certain to be embraced and adopted more heartily by the Republicans in the fall.

On March 12, a day after we'd won Mississippi, Clinton was still parading in the afterglow of her March 4 "victory." In response, David sent out what was perhaps our best public communication to date on the status of the race, beneath this subject line: Spun Out. A clip from that email follows:

> When we won Iowa, the Clinton campaign said it's not the number of states you win, it's "a contest for delegates." When we won a significant lead in delegates, they said it's really about "which states you win."
>
> When we won South Carolina, they discounted the votes of African Americans. When we won predominantly white, rural states like Idaho, Utah, and Nebraska, they said those didn't count because they won't be competitive in the general election.
>
> When we won in Washington State, Wisconsin, and Missouri—general election battlegrounds where polls show Barack is a stronger candidate against John McCain—the Clinton campaign attacked those voters as "latte-sipping" elitists. And now that we've won more than twice as many states, the Clinton spin is that only certain states really count.
>
> But the facts are clear. For all their attempts to discount, distract, and distort, we have won more delegates, more states, and more votes.

This clever piece portrayed Clinton's spin tactics as representative of her establishment ways, allowing our candidate to safely hold his outsider position even as our wins were decisively piling up. David's note offers an excellent example of how we forcefully defined our candidate and then pointed out the clear contrasts against his Democratic rival. Most importantly, with "Spun Out" we put powerful talking points into the inboxes of all our stakeholders.

In the Tank

To fully appreciate the tone and timing of David's email, it is useful to understand the stiffening head winds coming from the press that we had been battling for the better part of a month, dating back to mid-February. The uneven performance of Clinton's campaign at that time, along with the stories of internal chaos that were spinning regularly through the news cycle, disguised some of the progress her team's attacks had actually begun making in the media.

I first noticed the Clinton campaign's new, edgier message beginning to take shape with the emergence of a photo they leaked showing Senator Obama adorned in traditional African clothing. I thought it was a cheap shot meant to stir up racial divisions among voters. Regardless, I regarded it as a mostly forgettable event even though it did kick up a fair amount of dust on the campaign trail.

Things became increasingly heated after they launched a series of ads that included the memorable "3 A.M." spot. Dropping just days before the March 4 primaries, the charged piece featuring innocent children sleeping soundly in the middle of the night was meant to raise doubts about our candidate's readiness to handle a national emergency. We accused the Clinton people of engaging in a transparent ploy to "scare up votes." They countered that the clip was simply carrying a message highlighting her experience edge. We gained a momentary advantage in the exchange when the little girl featured in the stock footage they used, now a high school senior, publicly proclaimed that she was an enthusiastic supporter of Barack's. That revelation came at the end of a week of combative skirmishing, however, well after the sting of the ad had already been delivered and acutely felt inside our campaign.

The Texas debate also aired nationally around that time, and it was a strange event. More than any other before it, I eagerly looked forward to that particular showdown because I was hopeful that our candidate might put this whole thing away with a strong performance. The previous debates had been rather boring, as far as I was concerned. Sometimes I forced myself to watch them on the television at my desk or at home. On rare occasions I showed up briefly for the debate watch party at an area bar with other campaign staff.

Mostly, however, I was happy that we had people willing to carefully examine each performance, write up transcripts, and study every line spoken until the earliest hours of the morning when summaries would be packaged for senior staff and the media. The communications operation that wrapped around the debate activities was elaborate, and it reinforced an axiom of one of our PR gurus, Anita Dunn, who once matter-of-factly explained to me that debates are won after the performance, not during.

Based on that standard, I'm not sure we had won the night in Texas. I thought Clinton's overall presentation was spotty, but it was her performance that the press seemed to celebrate. This was partly because she used the platform to advance a new theme that words should matter, leaning into a flimsy charge that Senator Obama had stolen from a speech by his friend and national campaign co-chair, Governor Deval Patrick of Massachusetts.

That the media gave the matter even slight attention seemed absurd to me. Regardless, Clinton forcefully argued that if the campaign was going to be about words, our candidate should use his own. With tongue in cheek, she quipped that Obama promised change but offered little more than "change you can Xerox." It was a canned line, clearly rehearsed, and one I'm sure her advisors hoped might linger in the national conversation during the following days. The real zinger in this election wouldn't come for another two nights, however, at a less-watched but ultimately more noteworthy debate in New York City.

In a New York Minute

In every debate, both sides look for an opportunity to deliver the line that is so good it instantly changes political momentum. Mondale had such a moment in 1984 with "Where's the beef?" His rival, incumbent president Ronald Reagan, served an ace of his own in their subsequent rematch when he responded to a question about his advancing age by suggesting that he "wouldn't let the youth and inexperience of his opponent be a factor in this election."

Hillary Clinton had a similarly memorable line handed to her in New York City, just two nights after her Texas standoff against our candidate. This was a televised event that began with a simple question from the journalist-moderator to the lanky, well-poised candidate: "Is there anything we can do for you?" When the panelist responded that he was fine, the questioner refused to let it go and quickly followed up by asking, "Are you sure?" It set up the political punch line that would dominate kitchen table and water cooler conversations for weeks to come. On that night, the mainstream media was officially indicted as being "in the tank" for Obama.

Hillary wasn't in New York that night. Neither was Barack. This wasn't even an actual political debate. It was a skit from the popular late night show *Saturday Night Live* poking fun at what some felt was the easy treatment our candidate was getting in the media. Actress Kristen Wiig, impersonating a CNN anchor-moderator, popularized the line when she announced: "Like nearly everyone in the news media, the three of us are totally *in the tank* for Obama."

While the phrase was not invented by Clinton or her campaign, she quickly adopted it as her own. The characterization quickly surfaced that news outlets were some sort of appendage of our own communications shop. Senator Clinton made full use of this gift, and for the better part of two months she reminded voters of the injustice against her at every opportunity. In a suddenly transformed media environment, her campaign had new life and renewed hope.

Monster Problem

Our campaign didn't help the situation with our own sudden outbreak of foot-in-mouth disease that, unlike the Clinton campaign, had previously eluded us. The problem emerged in the days leading up to the March 4 races, when one of our prominent economic advisors characterized Barack's tough critique of NAFTA from the stump as political rhetoric. Meant to assuage Canadian officials who were apparently troubled by Senator Obama's trade position, dismissing our own candidate's economic message as a form of pandering caused quite a negative stir in the media. The episode also triggered considerable heartburn inside the campaign, both in Chicago and in the field. It was particularly acute in the days following Ohio voting when, fairly or unfairly, there was grumbling coming from the field that the fumble probably cost us eight points. Not coincidentally, we lost Ohio by that very margin, 53 percent to 45 percent.

Then, on March 7, another of our high-profile advisors was forced to resign after her impassioned interview with the British press, when she let slip a statement that Mrs. Clinton was "a monster." The comment was regrettable, first because it contradicted the senator's promise to avoid negative personal attacks, and second, because the media portrayed it as symbolic of rising tensions inside our campaign over the prospect of a protracted nomination fight. Where we had once shown great discipline, we were now committing ridiculous and harmful mistakes.

Of course, we weren't the only ones with this problem. In the first days of March, sometime just before Plouffe's "Spun Out" memo, we also found ourselves locked in an odd and unexpected squabble with Clinton finance committee member Geraldine Ferraro. The former 1984 Democratic VP nominee suddenly and inexplicably popped up from out of nowhere, howling that Senator Obama's "historic candidacy" had little to do with his qualifications. Looking at it from an organizational perspective, watching yet another of her representatives take the Clinton message off the tracks, I became even more amazed at her campaign's inability to manage its surrogate operation with any semblance of discipline. Here was still more evidence of the general management dysfunction that seemed to continually step on its own best efforts. It was remarkable to me that these problems were never really corrected.

Tensions escalated and we, of course, called for Ferraro's resignation. Clinton dismissed those appeals, citing her ally's unpaid status. You can't fire a volunteer, the logic went. Finally, on March 12, 2008, the day after the Mississippi primary and the same day as "Spun Out," Geraldine Ferraro stepped down from Clinton's finance committee. It wasn't the last we'd hear from her, however.

Reverend Wright Erupts

It struck us like a lightning bolt reaching down from the heavens. We had managed to get through the recent media drama with relative composure, but headquarters suddenly felt like a large, vulnerable target that had come under siege when the Reverend Wright crisis slammed into us. It was like a bad TV sci-fi thriller with us in the mother ship hanging alone in the sky, quickly activating protective shields as a reaction to an unidentified attacker.

The crisis surfaced after an ABC News review of about two dozen sermons by Senator Obama's church pastor, Reverend Jeremiah Wright. Excerpts from some of these fiery homilies began to appear in the news and online almost as soon as the Ferraro resignation occurred. It was as if we transitioned seamlessly from one controversy to the next. But the inflammatory nature of Wright's comments against our government and his racial views portrayed in the videos opened our campaign up to a new level of media scrutiny. Soon, there was no stopping the ensuing press frenzy to understand more about Barack's church and his relationship to the man spouting these opinions.

Our campaign responded to this crisis like none other before. There was panic as people scrambled into their positions and frantically worked to assess and manage the impending damage. We had been hit by controversy before, but not since New Hampshire had any single event sparked such a frenetic response.

Video footage of Pastor Jeremiah Wright's sermons seemed to run endlessly on TV for several days. The content being repeatedly aired gave me a sinking feeling in my gut, and it contributed to a growing sense inside our organization that the election was suddenly slipping away from us. This was just the ammunition that the Clinton camp needed to persuade superdelegates to break her way.

I wouldn't say that we in headquarters hadn't heard of Reverend Wright, but few of us knew much about him. Mostly, Barack's longtime pastor conjured up awkward reminders of the worrisome uncle that you didn't want at family gatherings. Many of us understood there was some kind of problem there; we just didn't know the true nature of it.

I avoided kicking that rock myself for fear of the rattlesnake I might find underneath, so I never broached the subject privately or publicly with anyone and shied away from speculative conversations. These were matters I assumed had been discovered and planned for by the campaign manager in the very earliest days. It was all too potentially damaging to have gone unaddressed, particularly in an organization as buttoned up as ours. I continually reassured myself that Plouffe, strategist David Axelrod, and Chief Counsel Bob Bauer had to have the whole story and a prepared course of action.

Now I'm not saying they didn't, but the campaign quickly took on water when the whole thing finally broke open. We seemed generally unready. It frankly felt like we were playing catch-up. Our researchers holed themselves up for days, emerging blurry-eyed after having viewed endless hours of sermons and culled through detailed transcripts.

I was also unhappy with our sluggish media response, which I felt was exacerbating the situation. Senator Obama initially denounced Reverend Wright's offensive comments. Then later, he scolded the media for cherry-picking from the reverend's public record over the years. But his unwillingness to more resolutely distance himself from his pastor puzzled me. As long as he refused, I feared that the Clinton campaign would club us endlessly with this one.

Even as we assured reporters that the senator had never heard the sermons being aired, I began to question my own faith in our campaign chief. For the first time, I privately doubted Plouffe. I didn't feel confident that he had fully prepared for this moment. I prayed that there wouldn't be some damning video footage that would suddenly emerge featuring Senator Obama intently listening to one of those rants from a prominent front pew.

While the whole affair mostly sickened me, I quickly determined that I shouldn't and couldn't focus on it. The event was outside of my control and something our communications and research departments would have to sort out. At the end of the day, you have to play your own position and trust your teammates to similarly get their jobs done. Hovering around the ball is of no use in a crisis. My charge was to keep my attention trained on where I was needed most.

It was striking how quickly things began to implode as the controversy developed. Some of our donors hit the panic button as soon as the crisis erupted. Though unseen, when the money people get upset, their uneasiness is noticeably felt. They're like campaign ghosts.

Joe Rospars felt the pinch online as well. He rushed over to personally communicate to me his concern that grassroots donations had dangerously slowed. I questioned Joe aggressively to understand the true severity of the situation, which I think he took as a sign of skepticism on my part. "I'm just here raising the flag," he responded. His voice was calm but his eyes couldn't so easily conceal his alarm. It's pretty scary when the money stops flowing. The Wright crisis had actually triggered a veritable stock market crash inside the Obama campaign.

Our fundraising managers were united in their appeal that we had to dramatically—and I mean *dramatically*—lower our monthly revenue goal. This troubled Marianne, our CFO, who couldn't instantaneously slow the spending, which was based on projected income. Soon, we were all spinning each other up. The spenders demanded we raise more while the raisers insisted we spend less.

I wasn't untouched by all of this. A fair heaping of criticism was directed my way, as more than one person snarled indignantly that David and I had spent far too freely. I didn't take it personally since I knew we had been very responsible with our resources. Still, I was disappointed that some of our old bad interpersonal habits from the early days reappeared so quickly in a downturn.

David and I were both convinced that this was a brief slump and not an extended recession. Plouffe insisted that I pull the fundraising team together and formulate a plan because seriously downgrading our projected revenue wasn't tenable. Steve Hildebrand and I called a summit with Julianna and Joe. Rospars came into the meeting with more confidence that our email campaigns in the coming days could get some traction and make up some of the ground we had lost. He also suggested adding an extra series of fundraising emails later in the month when we might be able to tap a more favorable news jet stream.

Thus, we reached a consensus that required only minor changes to our near-term fundraising targets. Julianna and Joe still wanted to shave money off the next month's goal as a precaution. I wasn't worried about the next month. I felt certain that things would settle back into place by then, particularly with Pennsylvania approaching and Indiana soon after that. Though I might have agreed to make that cut, I never told Marianne because I didn't want her to make any major course adjustments in our spending.

It all culminated in a good moment for the four of us. Even though emotions had run high, we were able to work together to reach an agreement on an acceptable new fundraising plan and goals, and there was unity on a way forward through the momentary cash crisis. That helped calm things inside HQ.

The political problem was a very different matter, however. Hillary used the Wright controversy to raise questions about whether Americans really knew who Barack Obama was and what he actually stood for. The argument proved alarmingly effective. It wasn't until the senator himself tackled the issue head-on that the damage was contained.

The Speech

Senator Obama's "a more perfect union" address at the National Constitution Center in Philadelphia on March 18 was immediately deemed historic. Standing before an audience on a stage draped with our nation's flags, Senator Obama courageously confronted the thorny issue of race in America by layering in his own experiences and perspective in a way that everyday Americans could relate to. It was a powerful testimonial that cast him in a warm presidential glow.

The irony is that I wasn't personally satisfied with it as a response to our Wright dilemma. I thought it was important for its content, and I certainly understood why it was so warmly received. I simply felt at the time that it didn't go far enough to put an end to our campaign woes. I was aligned more with the viewpoint that Senator Obama needed to make a decisive break from his pastor.

My failure was that I wanted a quick solution to a political problem rather than Senator Obama's thoughtful analysis of a social one. I was too swept up in the high emotion of the campaign battle to fully appreciate his address at that moment. Of course, it was an amazing speech, co-penned with his now illustrious speechwriter, Jon Favreau. And it did help us push the controversy off the headlines, prompting media coverage the next day that touted our candidate's ability to gracefully rise to big moments.

With the Wright saga seemingly behind us, our campaign quickly moved onto offense. It was a deliberate pivot. Penciled onto the communications schedule the day after his monumental address was a speech to be delivered in Fayetteville, North Carolina, commemorating the five-year anniversary of the Iraq invasion. Here, Senator Obama offered a respectful tribute to our troops, while at the same time needling both McCain and Clinton for their initial support of the war.

A few days later, largely motivated by Senator Obama's speech in Philadelphia, we picked up the endorsement of New Mexico's governor, Bill Richardson. A former fellow contestant for the Democratic nomination, Richardson was the nation's only Hispanic governor, so gaining his support was a coup, particularly since he had once served in President Bill Clinton's cabinet as the energy secretary and as the ambassador to the United Nations before that.

The sting felt on their side was evident in comments coming from outspoken Clinton ally James Carville on a Sunday morning show I'd tuned in to watch. Carville drew unflattering comparisons between Richardson and Jesus Christ's betrayer, Judas Iscariot, chirping that he would have used a Benedict Arnold analogy had it not been Easter Sunday. That drew a chuckle from my wife who overheard in the next room, prompting her to heckle back at the TV, "I don't know . . . Judas is pretty tough!"

Words Still Matter

While the Clinton campaign remained in a state of perpetual unevenness, the senator herself was a tough competitor on the campaign trail and a very strong candidate. Her own performance was consistently commanding. That's why a bizarre blunder she made in the middle of March, right around the same time as the Ferraro outburst, was so curious.

Mrs. Clinton became the target of some unwanted attention because of a tale she had spun about once having dodged sniper fire with her daughter Chelsea while on a mission to Bosnia as the First Lady. The story was one she referred to occasionally on the stump and in a speech at George Washington University. Sinbad, the comedian, challenged the veracity of her account. In a March 11 interview with WashingtonPost.com's Mary Ann Akers, the entertainer reported that the scariest thing he could recall during the trip was wondering where he would eat. As a member of the delegation that also included pop singer Sheryl Crow, Sinbad took issue with the senator's claim that the Clinton White House had singled her out for assignments considered "too dangerous, too small, or too poor."

Sinbad roared, "What kind of president would say, 'Hey, man, I can't go 'cause I might get shot so I'm going to send my wife . . . oh, and take a guitar player and a comedian with you.'"

Clinton later retracted her recollection. And though she suffered through a few laughs at her own expense, as the month ended, our candidate demonstrated that he, too, could solicit unwanted chuckles. Having gone back to the more intimate, personalized events that worked so well for us in Iowa, our campaign was again confident that as Pennsylvanians came to know Barack, they would similarly grow to like him. That is, until they saw him bowl. In a scheduled stop at a local bowling alley, Senator Obama abandoned the planned walkabout to actually . . . well, bowl.

The senator is a very gifted athlete, but I'm guessing he hadn't engaged in this particular activity for some time. The only thing worse than his reported "37" score were the pictures of him launching that ball down the lane with a tie clumsily hanging off his neck, an image the press speculated would be a gutter ball with the working-class whites we had mostly failed to attract thus far.

This set Steve Hildebrand alight. Our deputy campaign manager stomped around headquarters for days, wondering aloud in senior staff meetings if we could convince our candidate to dress down some, at least on the weekends. All the while, Hillary was getting quite a giggle off the whole thing, joking in front of cameras that perhaps the nomination could be settled with a good bowl-off.

One of Barack's biggest missteps of the entire campaign occurred in mid-April, at a private San Francisco fundraiser. Responding to a question about his declining odds in the next race, our candidate replied that political cynicism had caused folks in rural Pennsylvania to "get bitter" and "cling to guns or religion or antipathy to people who aren't like them." Someone in attendance caught his poorly phrased comments on tape and the audio clip blazed across the Internet, quickly making its way into the news stream.

Clinton pounced. "Pennsylvanians don't need a president who looks down on them," she told an audience. "They need a president who stands up for them." With about a dozen days left before voting in the Keystone State, our campaign appeared to be spiraling into a free fall.

On a Boat with No Paddle

Finally, a break! On April 26, 2008, my family departed on a much-needed, week-long Caribbean-cruise vacation. My son had been born six months earlier, just weeks before the Iowa caucus, and he had spent his first 180 days in this world as a campaign orphan. I was excited for the quality time we would get without the distractions of my work. However, the election results in Pennsylvania just days earlier threatened our plans. Clinton won big indeed. She garnered 53 percent of the vote to our 45 percent. She was also poised to do well in Indiana two weeks later. Although our holiday plans had long been booked, my wife and I struggled at the last minute over whether we should cancel.

After talking with Plouffe, I decided we would go. Things were well in hand heading into the next races on May 6. We were actually closing in on Hillary's lead in Indiana, and North Carolina seemed fine. Clinton's convincing win in Pennsylvania yielded her eighty-five pledged delegates, but that was only a dozen more than the seventy-three we added to our overall tally. That wasn't enough to significantly shift the momentum of the race. Money was once again good and things were beginning to calm down in the media. This would really be our only chance to get away as a family.

Unfortunately, our week away was a disastrous one for the campaign. Reverend Wright was back in the headlines after he had sat for an interview with journalist Bill Moyers on the Saturday we set sail. He followed up with two more speeches a few days later. I've never gone back to review those events that I missed. I just know that whatever happened must have been explosive. In a matter of days, the morale of our staff was flipped upside down. When I returned to work on May 5, the day before voting in Indiana and North Carolina, an eerily heavy feeling of resignation permeated our headquarters. It was remarkable. The place smelled like defeat.

Also around this time, just as the Wright saga had been renewed, another controversy emerged. While I was away, Hillary had enthusiastically thrown her support behind Senator McCain's proposal for a gas-tax holiday to relieve rising costs at the pumps. Our candidate responded by immediately dismissing the idea as mere pandering on the part of his two rivals, arguing that gas companies would quickly raise their rates again in response. Some inside our camp worried it was a position that wouldn't be popular with voters, but it was a fight that Senator Obama clearly welcomed.

It was no small risk to take such a bold stand given the May 6 elections were only days away. I was a little unsure about it myself. On my return to work, I took my concerns up with Pete Rouse, the Senate chief of staff and a trusted advisor to the candidate. Pete reminded me that Barack always looked for opportunities to highlight sharp policy contrasts against his rivals. Senator Obama was adamant from the earliest days that he couldn't win this election on the "cult of personality."

Frankly, finding those distinctions had never been easy in our Democratic primary field. The senator's stance against the Iraq war and his unwillingness to accept lobbyist money offered perhaps the only real daylight between him and the others. In this moment, taking a stand against the gas-tax holiday idea uniquely distinguished Barack from both Hillary Clinton and Republican John McCain.

Barack's brave stand provoked a new clash that again pushed the Wright controversy off the headlines, while also facilitating our candidate's pivot back to his preferred outsider position in the race. Riding this fresh burst of momentum, he surged in the last days to finish only two points behind Hillary in Indiana. In a state that was demographically friendly to her, this was a better outcome than we could have ever hoped for. Adding to our good news, we won North Carolina comfortably—stretching our margin of victory there to nearly fifteen points.

We were back on track.

Keeping Pressure Valves Open

The best laid plans are made and executed, but it is the unexpected—the x factor—that can quickly bring an organization down. The x factor usually grows from very human moments, emotions, or even mistakes, but it can also be prompted by persistent outside examination. In our business, the constant scrutiny of the media keeps the pressure high.

Our New Hampshire loss forced us into a lengthy, bruising primary that tested the collective mettle of our staff and forced us to learn how to win together. Furthermore, the media battering we faced, spurred by our Democratic rival's unrelenting attacks, hardened us. While we fervently wanted Senator Clinton to get out, it was in the flames of the steady stream of fireballs her campaign launched our way that we were baptized. The ragtag team that had come together just over a year before was now an aggressive army.

We had arrived.

Along the way, there were some important take-away lessons from this critical period in our organizational development. Perhaps the most fundamental was this: it is important to keep emotion from taking over in a crisis. Our candidate was known for saying that things were never as good as they seemed, nor were they as bad as people could often make them out to be. Reacting to the news of the day could have been fatal to our effort.

In fact, Barack himself can't be credited enough for his steadiness during this period. Granted, he made some tactical mistakes on the campaign trail, but given how much weighed on him, his leadership was extraordinary. He was forced to confront complex, highly personal issues, and he did so with strength and conviction. It was never lost on me that while I wanted him to cut ties with his pastor sooner—his family wouldn't formally break with Reverend Wright and Trinity Church until May 31—these two men who had shared happier times together had to be going to sleep at night deeply hurt by the unfolding events of the day. For Senator Obama, this was the man who baptized him and his children and had married him to his wife.

I could imagine Reverend Wright sometime in the not-so-distant past hanging out in Barack's backyard in Chicago's South Side, laughing over a story while the young politician grilled hot dogs. In retrospect, I don't see how the senator could have managed the public estrangement better. His delicate handling of these sensitive matters offered voters new information about the character and integrity of the man standing before them.

Another lesson from this time was to stay on offense. Despite the best efforts of his attackers, Senator Obama never allowed himself to be defined by the jarring video clips of his former pastor that were endlessly replayed in the media. Instead, he stepped bravely into the hostile news stream to confront the third-rail issue of race relations in America. It was a daring move that instantly transformed the headlines.

Later, facing the heat of another untimely Wright eruption in the media, Senator Obama again bucked conventional wisdom to stake out a risky position against the popular gas-tax holiday. His was a courageous stand on the eve of an important election. In moments of tension, leadership is required. Senator Obama never squandered opportunities to assert his.

Our management team once again deserved credit for our handling of the organization during those difficult weeks. In our rapidly changing environment, things were consistently coming at us quickly and from all directions. In fact, the challenge in this pressurized atmosphere wasn't so much deciding how to react to a given crisis—rather, it was to determine when we actually had a crisis that rose to the level of such a heightened response.

For his part, David Plouffe never reacted to worrying headlines or looming problems. He wasn't one to dramatically highlight them in staff meetings. He would appoint a team to discreetly tackle a troubling issue, but he never put everyone on it. This kept the heat down and the pressure valves open.

David's strength as a communicator was an equally important asset to the campaign. His unique ability to effectively engage our large universe of supporters offered an extraordinary dimension to his management capacity. It is common for leaders in political campaigns to treat their backers as a sort of external constituency. They construct general emails and fundraising appeals that are hollow and tactical, written as if the subscriber was little more than a full-time donor or door-knocker. Plouffe was always respectful of our supporters, treating them instead as important internal stakeholders.

In fact, while our email list at the time would soon eclipse seven million, David never lost his ability to keep an intimate tone in a medium that is often impersonal. His clever use of video as a message vehicle also helped this immeasurably. Thus, with the media landscape swiftly shifting and the news stream rapidly moving, our ability to deftly communicate with every level of the national organization allowed us all to move forward together against the torrent coming our way.

There is no question that we were emboldened by the experience of these weeks. The organization had a renewed confidence in its ability to overcome adversity. The process was messy and challenging, but in many ways it was a defining time for us. Unlike many campaigns that are reactive to the headlines, we held a steady and dedicated course.

Even under extreme organizational distress, the Obama campaign still had the capacity to drive the news.

8

Run It like a Business

MAY 9, 2008: *Goliath has fallen. Like the unbelieving villagers afraid to come out of their homes as the great giant lay motionless in the town square, party insiders are similarly frozen and slow to coalesce around us. With no real path left and certainly no money, HRC has announced she will stay in 'till the end. With six races left we labor on. Still, it really does somehow feel over.*

Winning Ugly

The last day of the primary voting season was set for June 3, featuring a doubleheader with contests in South Dakota and Montana. May 18 was a high point for us during that last stretch. An astonishing eighty thousand supporters turned out for an impressive rally in Portland, Oregon. The aerial photos that came back made it look like Barack had literally been dropped into a sea of people that surrounded him on all sides. Two days later, to nobody's surprise, we handily won the election in that state. It was an important victory because the Hillary forces really wanted to pull that one out of our column and into theirs.

Otherwise, the news wasn't all that great for us. We lost badly in the Appalachian states of West Virginia on May 13 and Kentucky a week later. We also came up well short in Puerto Rico on June 1. This helped fuel the case being made by Clinton supporters that there was a strain of buyer's remorse running prominently through the Democratic electorate in the closing days. They partly based their claim on the fact that their candidate had won more races over the final three-month period and that she had bagged 289 pledged delegates since April 22 to our 246. Hillary backers also pointed to her whopping victories during this stretch, including wins in Pennsylvania by ten percentage points, West Virginia by forty-one, Kentucky by thirty-five, and Puerto Rico by thirty-six.

But the Clinton campaign was almost out of runway following a ruling by party officials at the end of May that the Michigan and Florida delegations would be seated at half of their voting allotments, as a penalty for their attempts to buck party primary scheduling rules. With the pool of uncommitted delegates having been dramatically narrowed, their side was left with a vanishing path to victory. Still, since neither camp would leave the June 3 contests having gotten the total number of delegates needed to win the nomination, there was hope for the Clinton people in those remaining hold-out superdelegates.

Senator Clinton therefore aimed her closing argument in the final days directly at that audience. Hillary continued to insist that based on the states her campaign had won, it was she—and she alone—who could realistically take back the White House from the Republicans in November. Clinton was unwavering in her assertion that she was ahead in the popular vote, while conceding only a "slight lead" to our candidate in the pledged delegate count. This didn't square at all with our math, which showed us decisively winning in both of those categories. Plouffe was therefore specific in his direction to Dan Pfeiffer that his communications team should lean hard into the delegate number, which was indisputable, rather than engage in a debate over her scoring techniques.

New Growing Pains

On June 3, while our field organizers and volunteers were pulling supporters to the polls in South Dakota and Montana, I was having a tough afternoon of my own back in Chicago. Despite the fact that we were concluding one of the great political campaign fights in American history—one that I am sure will long be celebrated—there was little fanfare at headquarters. Senator Clinton was already far from my mind; I was now firmly focused on scaling the organization to ready it for the general election on November 4.

I was in the midst of a maze of meetings with individual department heads in an effort to shave $3 million from the newly proposed general election staffing budgets to get us through the final five months. This led to some less-than-sparkling conversations with my grumpy peers that went late into the day. On my way to one of those meetings, I bumped into an old friend, Jeff Blodgett, in the middle of a busy hallway. Jeff was the former campaign manager and senior advisor to the late Senator

Paul Wellstone of Minnesota. He was currently in town to sign the paperwork that would make him the state director there. "I can't sit this one out, Henry!" he announced enthusiastically.

When I was able to find any space at all in my busy meeting schedule, I was on the phone with my wife, who was reporting regularly to me on how the move was going at home. I had been working such long hours, from early morning until deep into the night, that I wasn't seeing my family at all. I decided that in our last months in Chicago we should get an apartment in Streeterville, a neighborhood just north of our downtown headquarters. Being walking distance from the office would cut down my commute time in the mornings and evenings, and Sine and the baby could come by headquarters for lunch more frequently.

Moving was a sudden preoccupation of mine. Later that evening, as election results streamed in from Montana and South Dakota, I inspected potential new office space several floors up. Plouffe and Hildebrand had very different visions for national headquarters in the coming weeks. Steve thought we would bulk up for the general election, while David shook his head at that idea. He didn't want substantial growth in our Chicago operation. Based on what I was seeing in the departmental budget proposals, I guessed that we were headed closer to Steve's projections. Therefore, prospecting for more square footage was necessary.

This was a distressing chore for me on what should have been a joyful night. It signaled the inevitable reality that we were about to break our campaign headquarters operation into two distinct parts on separate floors. I dreaded this possibility partly because I had heard that past presidential campaigns had taken similar steps in advance of the general election and that the decision was considered regrettable, even if unavoidable.

Typically, the practice was to isolate the business and administrative functions from the rest of the operation. In our case, there was a strong preference for moving fundraising, financial ops, and technology—as well as pieces of new media and a few other discreet functions—upstairs. That layout was certain to upset some of our managers and their staffs, and it would effectively fracture many of the departments I oversaw. Honestly, I didn't see how I could run my own operations if they were split between two floors. Marianne and I spoke often about the management challenge this posed for us. Having some of our folks pushed out to the hinterlands would take us out of the rhythm of the broader organization, resulting in serious inconsistencies.

Personally, I thought that cutting up our headquarters was a bad idea that would seriously disrupt the work flow within the overall organization. The grumbling from days past that we lacked communication and suffered hopelessly from departmental silos was long behind us. Ours was now a highly integrated and deeply interconnected enterprise. Breaking us up into isolated units could spell disaster in this kind of environment. Furthermore, moving a whole set of staff to another floor would create a class of campaign stepchildren. Morale problems would be sure to follow. The new alternative work area would inevitably become an island, effectively cut off from the excitement and activities that would be exclusive to the eleventh floor in those final months. It conjured up notions of a campaign kiddy table—nobody would want to be there and all eyes would be fixed on the grown-ups.

This was a problem I would wrestle with over the next few weeks, and it represented more than a simple logistical matter of where to sit people. It was emblematic of the myriad complex issues associated with an organization that was about to undergo massive growth in a very short time.

As I fretted over this newest problem, the day ended with voting results that had us splitting the remaining pledged delegates with the Clinton campaign. We took nine of sixteen in Montana, while they won nine of fifteen in South Dakota. The last of the uncommitted superdelegates quickly took sides and we were finally pushed over the finish line. Fifty-four contests had been completed and scored since our fateful win in Iowa on January 3, five months earlier. Michigan and Florida were also settled. Now, on the final day of battle, from a field that began with eight Democratic hopefuls, our candidate was the last one standing.

We had checkmate.

The Straight Talkin' Maverick

In the weeks just before and after we clinched the nomination, there was an abruptly noticeable lull in the campaign. It felt like we were suddenly rudderless and had gone adrift. We had been so focused on building the organization that would beat Clinton that there hadn't been much time to think past the nomination to our new adversary, Senator John McCain of Arizona.

Of all the Republican campaigns this year, McCain's was the only one that looked familiar to me. I had paid close attention to the 2000 election as a graduate student at Harvard and had spent time with some of his aides in professional settings. Based on the small doses of news I received this time around, his team seemed to be rerunning the 2000 playbook that featured a "maverick" riding from village to village on a bus called the Straight Talk Express to promote his populist message.

I had no shortage of respect for our new opponent. He was surrounded by pros, folks who had been around the block before. There was also evidence that McCain could be a shrewd organizational leader. In the summer of 2007, he made news after bravely letting some of his top advisors go and retooling his floundering organization by scaling back significantly. It impressed me that he wasn't timid. We had seen how Senator Clinton let organizational problems linger and the effect that had on her overall effort against us. McCain made those hard calls when he had to and it paid off for him later.

We also could not overlook the fact that on June 3, the day we officially began our new race against McCain, his organization had a three-month head start on us. That seemed an insurmountable lead. They'd had time to prepare a strategy and recalibrate their organization to effectively compete in the fall. Also, McCain and the Republicans had been given a clean shot at presenting his message and brand to general election voters while we remained preoccupied with our own bloody battle to the finish.

On the other hand, a protracted Democratic primary did offer us some unique advantages that would help us in the fall. For one thing, we were battle-hardened. As Senator Obama put it, our campaign had overcome long odds to beat one of the most formidable candidates ever to run for the nation's highest office.

Second, competing in every state gave us experience in some of the key general election battlegrounds. We knew the electoral terrain. Our ground troops were practiced and our message was sharpened with every new audience and voting demographic we faced. Having sewn up the Republican nomination in early March, McCain missed out on that opportunity.

Finally, and perhaps most importantly, a prolonged struggle helped Senator Obama in his effort to win the hearts and minds of party voters. There is a difference between defending one's views in a hotly contested race and showcasing them as part of the drawn-out coronation that McCain ultimately experienced in the final days of his nomination process. Both men needed a long game for different reasons; the Republican senator because conservatives had been slow in warming to him and our candidate because he was still relatively unknown among Democrats. Being urgently pressed into churches, diners, and community centers until the last vote was cast on June 3 was very helpful in building Barack's credibility.

Scaling

We were going to get really big, really fast. Our campaign had grown from nothing to become a robust organization over the course of our first sixteen months. We would now have to become truly massive in a short time since the general election was only twenty-two weeks away. The transformation we were attempting was mind boggling. Our CFO, Marianne Markowitz, half-joked that we were going to mushroom into something akin to a Fortune 500 company. I likened the feat to scaling from a corner mom 'n' pop shop into Walmart in just weeks.

In the earliest days of our organization, we were spending at the rate of about $7 million per month. During the primaries, we increased those levels to around $35 million monthly. Looking ahead, my back-of-the-envelope math had us nearly doubling that rate through the general election. While we had spent about a quarter of a million dollars during the first sixteen months for the primary, we could easily spend twice that amount in the last five if you also figured in what we might raise through the traditional Democratic Party apparatus.

I couldn't shake my discomfort over the fact that my own recent budget submission to David Plouffe reflected a quadrupling of the number of staff in my departments. I would have direct oversight of more employees than we'd had in the whole state of New Hampshire back in January. In fact, it would approach the number Paul Tewes had in the run-up to the staff-intensive Iowa caucuses. Having once skeptically complained that Paul's hiring plan must have been based on a formula of one organizer per square foot, I now brought my own budget proposal forward with a fair bit of humility.

Still, this wasn't some wish list I handed Plouffe. I knew what a hawk he was about money, so I had already done some heavy wrangling with my own managers beforehand just to get something reasonable to put before him. I was very much aware that I needed to be able to justify every last body and dollar, since I would be the person scrutinizing the budget lines of my colleagues. David actually agreed to everything I asked for, which I took as a sign of his confidence. It was also illustrative of the size and scope of the campaign to come since my departments alone would be adding about one hundred people in just a few short weeks.

Going Dark

In late May, Steve had the windows of the fishbowl papered over, and it stayed that way through June. The fishbowl was a glass-walled conference room that sat immediately behind the reception desk when you walked into headquarters. It was one of the very few dedicated spaces in the building that could be reserved for use by senior staff.

The room frequently attracted the glances of the curious as they passed by. Who was in there and what they were discussing always made for interesting speculation in HQ. Steve decided to use that space as a general election planning war room for our high-level strategists, so he pulled it off the reservation schedule and took it over indefinitely. Covering the windows with long strips of brown paper only heightened the intrigue surrounding the discussions in that room.

During this time, the campaign seemed to go dark. It felt like there was a sudden leadership void. For me, the change was made even more palpable by the fact that I lost almost all contact with Plouffe. He had made it clear from the start that as the campaign went deeper into the calendar, he would become increasingly distant from the day-to-day side of it. Over the previous nine months, David had devoted an increasing amount of his time to the outward-facing demands of the media, communications, and the strategic placement of money. With this shift of his focus, my authority inside the campaign grew wider. But in recent weeks, it reached the point where David seemed reclusive. We still met for our scheduled weekly meeting but our routine interactions in between were far fewer. This coincided with a new round of unfortunate rumors that he would soon leave the campaign.

Steve Hildebrand attempted to fill some of this gap by increasing his presence at headquarters. He traveled less and stepped more visibly into the role of deputy campaign manager, even running the morning senior staff meetings with department heads which David had stopped attending. But while David's style was to delegate work, Steve was more comfortable owning it. In the organization as it had been, this made Steve an invaluable go-to guy for Plouffe. In the organization as it was becoming, Steve, like the rest of us, had to learn to more confidently charge others with the work.

The organization was getting too big too fast for Hilde to manage himself, and he quickly became a bottleneck on many of the projects that went through him. He was in the thick of the strategic planning underway in the papered fishbowl, an activity that occupied almost all of his time late into the night. He was also working on a major restructuring of the field and political departments, something that the rest of our senior staff needed to have completed so that we could retool our own departments to align with his. As part of this reorganization, Steve wanted to upend the headquarters seating layout to accommodate the new operational structure.

Those activities were enough to take up 95 percent of his long day, but Steve also wanted a central role in the budget planning that consumed much of Marianne's and my time, and he was heavily involved in the fast-approaching Democratic convention in Denver. On top of all of this, Hilde was also working on the recruitment of high-level staff to help manage the final stretch of the campaign. I started to worry about Steve. He had been a hugely important figure in the campaign to date, but this was more than any one person could handle. I grew concerned that it was taking a toll on his personal health.

I was balancing a lot myself. In addition to restructuring my departments, hiring key staff, and managing the campaign-wide budget process with Marianne, I was spending a great deal of time at the Democratic Party headquarters in Washington to assess what steps needed to be taken to integrate our operations. This was all complicated by the fact that the strategic planning meetings in the fishbowl were moving slowly. My work was wholly reliant on the results of those discussions, which made the delay a factor in my own preparation. Without clear direction from Steve coming out of that process, it was hard to move forward swiftly on the many fronts I was managing.

Opting to Win

The gridlock was finally broken in mid-June, when we announced that our candidate would opt out of the federal public financing system for the ten-week general election period. Senator Obama would be the first nominee in more than forty years to pursue such a dramatic course. Opting out of the public financing system would mean passing on the $84 million grant made available to publicly financed campaigns. On the other hand, it freed our campaign to spend as much as we could raise through private donations. While it was a decision that was met with disappointment from the political Left and sparked outrage on the Right, from my perspective at the time it was the best choice.

Had we accepted the taxpayer-funded grant, we would have been prohibited from raising money through Obama for America. That would have meant scrapping our entire fundraising juggernaut, which had outperformed the McCain campaign by more than a 2:1 margin to date. Furthermore, that option would have left us exposed to a robust GOP infrastructure, including the unrestricted special interest groups that were prepared to pump heavy doses of financial oxygen into the McCain effort. Minus an agreement from their camp to limit party spending and refuse support from these outside influences, choosing the public financing option would have been a form of unilateral disarmament—an idea our candidate quite publicly rejected.

Besides, opting out of the system might enable us to raise close to $400 million within OFA for the general election, a possibility that would have been unavailable to us were we to ditch our fundraising operation to accept the $84 million grant. Plouffe anticipated that we could bring in close to $350 million. While that made our fundraising team nervous, I thought an amount closer to $390 million was quite realistic—partly because I guessed that Plouffe was hedging on the number he put down on paper.

But in the end, accepting the subsidy would have taken our greatest asset off the table in the final stretch: our supporters. OFA had cultivated relationships with our contributors for the better part of a year and a half. We were quickly closing in on two million donors, which blew past anything John McCain could show. That factor alone pointed to our clear edge on the enthusiasm meter. Those who had given to our campaign before were likely to give to us again, but it wasn't clear that they would actually give as willingly to the Democratic Party, even if it were acting as a surrogate for the campaign. This would certainly be true for independents and the Republican supporters we'd garnered. It just didn't make sense to risk alienating our stakeholders by choosing the option that would separate them from the campaign they'd had a direct hand in building.

Beyond the financial considerations, I also had logistical concerns. Subjecting OFA to the spending cap would have meant farming out many of our functions to the Democratic National Committee (DNC). This had been the accepted organizational template for running previous presidential campaigns, but in our case there were reasons why breaking with past practice made more sense.

First, allowing the operational center of gravity to shift to the DNC in Washington would have sucked much of the energy away from Chicago. Organizational cohesion matters in campaigns, and keeping our operation intact could be our most effective weapon against McCain, just as it had been against Clinton. Second, by transferring some of our functions to Washington, we would have risked creating two distinct power centers. If I was opposed to dividing our headquarters into two floors in the same building, I was much more strident about splitting our core operations between Chicago and Washington. In fact, public financing rules would have seriously restricted our coordinating with the DNC.

Finally, and perhaps most importantly, running our general election campaign differently would allow us to maintain a direct connection with our volunteers. It is certain that, had we opted into the system and accepted the imposed spending limits, one of the expensive functions that would have had to shift to the DNC would have been our field operations. Similar to the dilemma of divorcing our donors from the campaign, we knew our volunteers were motivated to show up for our candidate, but it was not clear that they would for the national party. This offered the most compelling argument for running our field operation through our existing organization, rather than sending that responsibility to the DNC.

Executive Courage

Not surprisingly, we were roundly criticized for the decision to opt out of the system. I understood the displeasure coming from those who viewed public financing of elections as an important way to keep big money out of politics. Senator Obama himself was a proponent of that ideal. On the other hand, I was proud that Barack made decisions on how to run his campaign based on the realities of the system we were competing in and not the system we would have liked it to be. It was evidence, once again, of his pragmatic approach as the CEO of his organization when some tried to paint him as a hopeless idealist.

McCain and the Republicans did their best to fan the controversy and seek an advantage, openly complaining about our candidate's full reversal on the issue. Our boss stood firm against the outside pressure. In a show of executive courage, the senator demonstrated first and foremost a dedication to making decisions that would keep our organization fully competitive in the fall. Despite the outcry from both sides, any verdict other than the one that gave us the best chance of winning would have been a form of campaign malpractice.

Triangle Offense

Opting out of the system made my job exponentially bigger. This was new terrain for a contemporary presidential campaign, making the weight of the decisions my teams struggled with even heavier. It was almost impossible to fathom how our organization could grow so massively without fracturing and falling apart. With thousands of brand new staff coming into the campaign, I worried that we would see some of the unfortunate patterns of rogue behavior that occasionally surfaced in our very earliest days.

I wracked my brain to understand my leverage in maintaining order as we went forward. We didn't have the natural incentives available to a typical business. We couldn't hold out the carrot of raises, bonuses, stock options, promotions, or even some semblance of job security. I worried that would make our campaign vulnerable to irresponsible spending and contracting activity outside of our approval system. I finally decided that I had to keep the organization focused on the principles that made us successful and not personally micromanage the scaling of our operational tactics. I knew I had to let go and let others lead for us to get big.

Two of the people I relied upon the most during this uncertain time were CFO Marianne Markowitz and Jenn Clark, who was now deputy COO. They were the heart and soul of our operation. What we'd accomplished together to date was pretty remarkable, especially given that neither of them had political campaign experience when I first met them. Now, only a year and a half later, Marianne and Jenn were helping scale the presidential campaign that they'd had a hand in building from scratch into a national organization. The challenges the three of us now faced were very different from those we worked through during the start-up phase. To take the campaign to the next level, we had to figure out how to respond to the newest pressures that threatened the very systems we'd built and relied upon for our success to date.

One issue weighing on my mind was a suggestion being floated to devolve the HR and finance operations to the states so that hiring and spending could be managed locally. I thought this was a bad idea, but it sprang from a valid concern that continuing the central management of these services in a massively scaled environment would create an alarming bottleneck at the top. The worry here was that meeting the needs of a few states at a time, as we had done during the primaries, couldn't compare to the new reality of fulfilling the demands of fifty states all at once. We had to prove that our systems and processes at headquarters could be adapted and scaled to swiftly and capably serve our stakeholders on the ground.

Hire Desk

We began by evaluating our capacity to on-board the crush of new employees that would ride in on a wave of national hiring. In campaigns, massive growth often occurs at times when the systems in place are not sufficient to accommodate quantum leaps in organizational size. At the crest of each of the three phases of our development—the start-up, the execution period encompassing the primary contests, and now as we scaled for the general election—there was significant stress on our personnel unit and the resources available to it.

As we moved into this latest hiring surge with new managers coming into our system, we needed to ensure that our processes and procedures were understood by all so as to minimize errors. An epidemic of hiring mistakes would have been a clear signal that our campaign was loose and undisciplined. At the same time, I wanted to be sure that we could meet the need for speed on the ground. If we couldn't effectively demonstrate our operational capabilities, I worried that a movement toward decentralization would prevail. That would have opened up our organization to uneven compensation scales across state lines and overt bidding wars between our own state leaders for existing staff.

The concern, as we were about to on-board thousands of people in a matter of weeks, was that our crude processes and limited staff resources would not meet the anticipated demand. We were still very much paper-driven and reliant on faxes and "runners." Thus, we built our existing system into a more robust Hire Desk.

Structured much like our Ops Desk, the Hire Desk system featured a single point of contact for state directors and HQ departmental managers. The process was initiated with a "request for hire" memo submitted by the state or HQ department head, which was then reviewed against the staffing plan that had been previously approved by both David and me. I signed off on the request to begin the hiring process and then again at the end before an offer of employment could be made.

Several steps were spread across various departments and teams between the request and the approval. They included vetting candidates, provisioning personal computing equipment, initiating payroll and benefits, and providing for building access permissions when necessary. In addition, there was required paperwork and new staff orientations to be completed. Jenn had long wanted a better tracking system than the Excel spreadsheets her small team was stuck with, but investing in a pricey platform was cost-prohibitive in the early days. While they had mastered the rudimentary systems available, the on-boarding challenge ahead now loomed as a major concern as states were quickly preparing a massive buildup. Simply hiring the three additional staff we were adding to her unit wouldn't go far enough to meet the demand.

To address this challenge, Jenn settled on an idea proposed by Jeff Link in our IT department. Jeff, who had been with us since the early days of the campaign, suggested a system not unlike one that might be used to track the shipment of a package online as it is processed from depot to depot until delivery. He determined that a product offered by Intuit, called QuickBase, would meet our needs.

With QuickBase, department heads could initiate hiring requests electronically rather than on paper and the entire inquiry and on-boarding processes could be easily tracked as the candidate progressed through the different sign-offs. If there was a holdup somewhere, the application could be easily traced. After I electronically approved the hire and authorized a start date, our IT department received a notice outlining the computing and telecommunications requirements for the new hire so that immediate provisioning could begin. The best part about Jenn and Jeff's solution was that it was inexpensive, it was fast, and it maintained the necessary controls from HQ while effectively servicing the states.

Accounting for Change

Marianne also needed a solution to successfully scale her expenditure approval and processing mechanisms. As CFO she made many remarkable contributions to our operation, but her system for managing the campaign's spending brought an unusual discipline to our organization. Expenditures first required a purchase order (PO) request, which was checked against the budget by one of our analysts and then forwarded to Marianne and me for preapproval. Later, vendor invoices received were checked against our records to be sure there was a PO on file as evidence that the expense had been authorized. If an invoice came through without a PO, we would call the vendor to trace who had initiated it and address the problem accordingly. These controls enabled us to quickly hone in on rogue spending, keeping it virtually nonexistent during the life of the campaign. Every single person in the campaign, from the candidate to the campaign manager to the field organizer, had to adhere to the system—no exceptions.

Now to meet the challenge of expanding our financial operations, she made two very critical moves. First, she hired a comptroller, Allyson Laackman, to bolster our accounting operations. Allyson's sharp focus and professional expertise took our accounting systems to a new level. Allyson proved to be an excellent partner for Treshawn Shields, our longtime chief compliance officer who, with director Alexa Chappell, would soon produce the largest campaign FEC filings in history.

Second, Marianne hired a team of budget analysts led by Deputy CFO Adi Kumar, our in-house Boy Wonder, to prepare the general election budget. Adi hired more than a half-dozen MBA grads from the finest schools in the country. Every one of them could have made six figures in the private sector, but they instead agreed to work for us at or near our base salary. Most campaigns hire simple spreadsheet jockeys for this kind of work, but we got these top guns because they came in late, after graduation, and they viewed the experience as valuable short-term paid apprenticeships.

Marianne lobbied hard for the creation of these roles. She won them not just based on the argument that we needed help with the massive budget we were constructing, but because they could ultimately be embedded in key departments to see, process, and track all spending in real time. Marianne was right; this team became an invaluable resource in our scaled environment. They offered us important advanced projections based on their ability to look at departmental budgets, anticipate when spending would hit, and calculate how changes in fundraising could affect our cash-on-hand position at any given moment. A campaign scaling to the size and breadth of ours was prone to wide swings on the balance sheet without precise monitoring, but Marianne's system, which I refer to as "Accounting for Change," and Adi's management of it provided us the means to understand potential financial variations up until the very last day.

As I explained it at the time, at the end of the election this team needed to land the plane perfectly and taxi precisely to the cone set before them—meaning they had to anticipate our spending right down to the last dollar on the final day. We couldn't leave a pile of unused money on the table, nor could we saddle the candidate with post-election debt. This required full awareness of how our money was managed. Without reliable revenue streams due to the unpredictability of fundraising and because of the large sums that would go out the door, this was a high bar they had to meet. In the end, Marianne's financial teams did an astonishing job in accurately hitting the spending marker we set. It was a truly remarkable feat.

One issue that remained unresolved, however, was moving Marianne's system off paper. It was similar to the problem Jenn faced. Even with our new team of budget analysts, there was no way to efficiently manage the amount of paper being processed on behalf of the fifty states and the headquarters departments. The sheer volume of spending requests and payments was going to very suddenly explode.

Marianne's financial operations department became the next target for the QuickBase solution. It enabled authorized users in state offices and HQ departments to electronically initiate spending requests or track the progress of existing ones. After the necessary review by our budget analysts, Marianne and I could log on at any time to review and approve requests or advance invoices along to our accounting department for payment. In Jeff's QuickBase world, we had a way to electronically support and continue our expenditure preapproval system that had long been the cornerstone of our fiscal discipline. Best of all, the campaign-long routine of hibernating at my table in my windowed corner at the beginning and end of each day for the time-consuming task of lumbering through the tall stack of paper requests needing my signature was gone.

It didn't take long for QuickBase to have its tentacles all over the organization. We used it to track everything from managing relationships to organizing our policy catalog to tracking hiring and spending. Growing our operation to the dimensions we were headed toward would have been impossible without this solution. The whole thing would have broken apart. But QuickBase made it possible for us to scale the principles that were fundamental to our operational success to date as we evolved the organization into the next iteration of its development.

Red-Tape Busters

The Ops Desk continued to be our primarily link to the states. Dan Jones oversaw the system that he once single-handedly managed, now with a team of awesome new recruits. He hired six managers to be based in our national headquarters. Their job was to ensure that all lease reviews, technology needs, and hiring and spending requests coming from the states were moving seamlessly through the system. If there was a bottleneck, this team was assigned to troubleshoot the problem. In addition, Dan was directly involved in hiring a capable operations manager in every state so that we continued to maintain our speed and competence edge in the field.

Along with Dan's Ops Desk, the Hire Desk Jenn managed and Marianne's Accounting for Change system combined to form our operational triangle offense. These were our hallmark processes, and they provided a foundation for the nimble and disciplined execution of our organization. Over the ensuing weeks, we aggressively worked to be sure that all incoming staff in Obama for America understood these systems to avoid rogue spending and hiring. We were particularly focused on state directors and operations managers at trainings and orientations because we knew they could best communicate these practices into the organizations they managed.

I was very specific with instructions to my staff that we take care not to be viewed as the red tape of the campaign. We were the red-tape busters. For every field office, there was a landlord with whom our campaign had to negotiate a lease. To get equipment and computing needs met, vendor contracts needed to be reviewed. Each office opening triggered a series of interactions with utility and communications companies that had complicated administrative processes to navigate. For every state in which we hired, there were government tax IDs to be arranged. Every spending receipt had to comply with complex election finance laws and accompanying reporting requirements. On the other side of every external transaction we made as a campaign was a bureaucracy our staff had to confront. The job of the people who worked for me was to break through those barriers so our organizers could concentrate on doing the jobs they were hired to do. We cut through the red tape in front of them.

Innovating for Change

Two of the hires that I am most proud of during the entire campaign came in the form of the technology one-two punch of Michael Slaby and Rajeev Chopra. After months of leaving CTO Kevin Malover's slot open and acting in the role following his departure myself, I was finally able to close the gap by splitting his job into two.

Deputy New Media Director Michael Slaby became our new chief technology officer. After an exhaustive search that included former CTOs and CIOs from Fortune 500 companies and top Silicon Valley and Seattle firms, Chief Technology Advisor Julius Genachowski and I tapped the wunderkind in our midst. We plucked Slaby out from under Joe Rospars, a move that offered both Joe and Jon Carson a talented and highly regarded partner in the development of our online strategy.

Not only did Michael and the teams he worked with develop some of the most innovative electronic tools ever packaged for a campaign, Slaby managed the complex data-integration effort that pioneered new avenues for efficiently and precisely connecting with voters. He provided leadership to a technology operation that also resourcefully harnessed existing technologies, such as GPS (global positioning system) and IVR (interactive voice response), to enhance our voter contact and field get-out-the-vote efforts. Finally, Michael was the architect of an exhaustive build-out of our technology infrastructure that accommodated historic numbers of online visitors and donors.

His new counterpart, Rajeev Chopra, had long been a fabled volunteer who just showed up in many of the states during the primaries. Rajeev was motivated by his passion for our candidate but quickly became known for his resourcefulness as a troubleshooter and his easy demeanor. It was like having a real-life high-tech MacGyver at our immediate disposal. After we hired him as our national director of information technology, Rajeev injected a mix of outside-the-box thinking, a respect for our existing systems, and the perspective of a user in the field into our systems.

His teams quickly nationalized and scaled our technology support, including hiring capable IT directors in every state—not a small task in a short window. They also streamlined our computing and office equipment procurement behind the national system of vendors he contracted and an online office profile package. Field staff needed only to populate an electronic form with the required data, which included the office size and number of staff. At the end of the survey, the program spit out a plan that would specifically address computing, phone, and office equipment needs. The proposal could then be tweaked by the organizer, sent through our office for review, and then on to the appropriate vendors for immediate fulfillment. The impressive system helped our state field offices get up and running faster than the competition at a time when speed was our edge in everything.

As we turned the corner and headed into the final stretch, our teams comprised the heart of what was quickly becoming recognized as the tightest operation in campaign history. The question ahead for us, only sixteen months past our launch and just weeks away from our climax, was whether we could scale sufficiently to compete against the imposing Republican enterprise we would be up against. I was confident that we had assembled a dynamic team that could continue to drive innovation.

Still, the clock was running.

9

Lead from Within

AUGUST 4, 2008: *There were grumblings in a recent meeting about Barack riding in a better bus. It was a modest upgrade, but there are those who think he should keep traveling "scrappy." My response was that we had to treat our candidate a little more like the next president of the United States. He needs to start seeing himself bigger, and we all should as well. It's one of the important ways we can help ready him for the highest office in the land.*

Open for Business

Around the first week of July, the paper came off the windowed fish-bowl, indicating that we had finally settled on a plan. If the campaign felt stalled at the beginning of June, things were now quickly falling into place. After weeks of wracking my brain over what to do about our space concerns, I decided we needed to stay together and crowd the eleventh floor. The space would get tight and more than a little bit uncomfortable for all of us, but I felt passionately that our organizational edge was based on streamlined communications and unity at headquarters. I caught a fair bit of grief at times for that decision, but whenever any of my colleagues complained, I simply offered to show them the spacious option available to their team on the nineteenth floor. That silenced any further complaining. Nobody wanted to leave eleven. They just wanted others to go.

Marianne and I finished the core budget and were only waiting on the individual state spending plans to be returned from the field department for final review and sign-off. It had been an exhaustive, bottom-up process that featured multiple working-group and interdepartmental reviews, layered over the traditional department head submissions. Plouffe wanted many sets of eyes on each proposal. Budgeting by committee was a little bit of hell for me, but inviting wider involvement clarified roles, eliminated duplication, and injected transparency into the process. Despite the challenge, at the end there was a feeling of real ownership by all of our key stakeholders.

Hilde had also completed the reorganization and consolidation of our field and political departments. He called the new unit "270," so named for the number of delegates we needed to win the White House. He divided the country up into six regions and formed workstations in headquarters to service each, called "pods." The pods were configured with a staffer assigned from every one of the HQ departments to work alongside each other. Much like the Ops Desk design, the idea was that there should be an easy link from the state point of contact to the regional pod designee for any specific work function. Everyone sitting in the pod was, therefore, positioned to seamlessly access the services and support within their departments in HQ on the requestor's behalf.

We now asked staff to uproot from long-held seats in a wholesale shuffle to accommodate the new organizational model. This led to a huge moving day when large garbage barrels and file boxes suddenly dotted the campaign shop floor. Most memorable was the shocking volume of trash that was discovered collecting in unseen holes over the course of sixteen months. This further validated Steve's contention that the place needed to be spiffed up a bit and get a professional makeover. He wanted HQ to take a step toward looking like the office of the nation's next leader. Staff also needed to view themselves less as rugged campaign operatives and more as employees of the future president of the United States. Cleaning house was a symbolic act that helped facilitate that paradigm shift. People even began to dress differently after that day, replacing their flip-flops and ball caps with business attire.

Here Come the Pros

Late in June, Steve and I began to prepare the announcement that new, high-profile arrivals would be joining us in the coming weeks. Some would be political campaign rock stars. These were people who had worked in past presidential and senatorial campaigns, Kerry '04 communications wizard Stephanie Cutter among them. Others were less familiar but highly regarded, folks like Patrick Gaspard and Brian Bond, both with credibility in the Labor and LGBT communities respectively. From the earliest days of the campaign, I tried to prepare my teams for this moment. Part of running it like a business meant that after you won the nomination, the professionals with long Washington résumés and deep campaign experience would soon follow. Some would even come from rival campaigns, and yes, that also meant Hillary Clinton's.

I knew this would be a source of great anxiety for some. We were all flying high after our big victory, so the idea of new people just coming in and taking over was pretty unnerving. There would be pangs of resentment, but this was change we had to embrace. Ever since the seamlessly executed five days after Iowa, I was convinced that our greatest moments came not through our innovations or ideas but when we brought unlikely teams together. When those two sides touched, sparks happened. Effectively integrating this new contingent with our existing army was the best opportunity for us to become bigger as a campaign, and not just get big. I reasoned with worried staffers that because our candidate was so close to winning the White House, the campaign needed people with unique expertise and experience at this level to help see us through to the end. While we had achieved a lot, I explained that we were entering a whole new galaxy and would need star power to help us navigate it.

Honestly, I never thought I would see this day. I was not surprised that our campaign would receive an influx of Washington insiders at this point in the race; rather, I never really believed that I would stay long enough to actually witness it. My wife and I originally enlisted with the idea that I would stay on for one year. We thought the nomination would be secured by March. Then, I could pass the reins along to capable hands and devote myself to my family. Our tidy planning was foiled, however, when it took until June for the nomination to be settled.

Leaving the campaign with only five months left seemed absurd after having seen it through its first sixteen. We determined to go ahead and take it to the end. While I was becoming fatigued, I give more credit to my wife for having the stamina to gut this out. She truly became a campaign widow, raising our son alone during his first months while I devoted all of my energy to the day-to-day management of our organization. Fortunately, Dante was warmly adopted by the campaign that had orphaned him from his father. He visited headquarters often, sporting his own staff ID badge that featured his mug shot and a unique designation displayed in bold letters under his name: OBAMA BABY.

Making Room at the Top

The integration went fairly smoothly, but it was hard on everyone involved. The new folks coming in had to penetrate an ironclad group, glued together even more firmly by our recent, unimaginable victory. On the other hand, many of the campaign's long-timers worried about getting lost in the pending shuffle. Some were nervous that they were going to be replaced. Others were tortured with the idea that they might be "layered" with a new boss. Still more were faced with the possibility that their responsibilities would be trimmed and their wings clipped.

On the whole, however, I think our staff was eager to welcome former top talent from the other campaigns. Jen O'Malley Dillon, who had been the Iowa field director for John Edwards, had joined us months before and assimilated quickly into our leadership. She was the trailblazer. But how the Clintonistas would be greeted remained to be seen.

Patti Solis Doyle was the first high-profile entrant from that camp and perhaps the most celebrated in the media of all the new faces coming in. She accepted a position with us to be the chief of staff for the newly formed VP nominee operation, and the controversy surrounding her entrance to our team received heavy play in the media. Our phones lit up with calls from Obama supporters angry at the news that we had hired one of Hillary's closest advisors. Hillary's backers were equally outraged at our welcoming the fallen turncoat. They read into the move that Senator Clinton was therefore off the VP short list.

Another newly formed unit at HQ would be an office to support Michelle Obama, whose role on the campaign trail would certainly grow. That would be Stephanie Cutter's job to manage. Also joining our senior leadership team was Patrick Gaspard and Dan Carol. Patrick took over as political director so that Matt Nugen could run our sizable national convention operation in Denver. Dan, once the director of research at the DNC, was brought on to augment the work being done on some of our most strategic issues.

Within HQ, the most excitement surrounded the anticipated arrival of Jim Messina. Jim had been the chief of staff to Montana senator Max Baucus, and he was snatched from that office to serve in the same role for us. I didn't know Jim, but Senior Advisor Pete Rouse really sang his praises, as did Plouffe's assistant, Katie Johnson. They predicted that because of our organizational styles, he and I would become fast friends.

I was relieved about Jim coming on board because it was the last piece in the top organizational structure that I thought required attention given Plouffe's shifting focus. Still, there was a lot of mystery to me about who he was and what exactly he would do. I didn't know what my relationship to the new chief of staff would be so I finally asked David Plouffe during one of our meetings. Plouffe didn't flinch. "Like us: partners," he shot back matter-of-factly.

I felt better after talking to David and even more so after actually meeting Jim. Pete and Katie were right about Messina: we did become fast friends. In him, we had a new quarterback acting as the proxy campaign manager we came to need with David being pulled to higher levels of management. The results were immediately noticeable. Jim took the controls and was clearly comfortable with them, but was also very respectful of folks like me who had built the plane that he was about to pilot to the finish. He didn't make big adjustments. Instead, he worked within the existing systems and quickly assimilated into the organization.

Jim won me over with an exchange I overheard soon after he arrived. Confronted by one of our newer staff members who had attempted to bend the spending rules, the new chief sternly cautioned, "You know that isn't how we do things around here." It was flatly delivered as if he'd been in the organization from the first day, rather than the hundred or so hours he'd actually logged at that point. For me, it signaled that Jim was committed to reinforcing our practices and continuing the discipline that had long been the hallmark of our organization.

Fresh Faces

There is no denying that the campaign I had known was no longer the campaign I was in. Things had changed everywhere I looked. The reordering of the deck at the top was suddenly evident at our morning senior staff meetings, where some of the familiar faces from many months had been replaced with people who were strangers to me. The number of us gathered around the conference table was larger too, making it feel like the longtime regulars were outnumbered. Sitting directly across from me at the head of the table running our meetings was Jim Messina, whom I had only known a week. Plouffe was also noticeably absent. He occasionally popped his head in to listen to the banter, but otherwise, he left the work at hand to his new chief.

After our meetings ended, I'd meander back to my desk, weaving through a maze of unknown bodies that seemed to be sprouting everywhere on the shop floor. Headquarters was growing astonishingly fast and quickly becoming stuffed to the gills. Our all-staff meetings now took on a whole new form. During the start-up phase, we had only enough people to loosely huddle in a thin half-moon around Plouffe's office door. During the fall and into the primary season, we required the small sectioned corner where our fundraising staff sat as a gathering spot. Now, we needed the whole north side of the building floor. The staff was so large that we actually had to arrange for an audio system to make it possible for the people in the back to hear, although the poor sound quality produced from that tattered speaker at the front wasn't very helpful.

As the campaign began to mushroom into mammoth dimensions, I started to feel the pinch personally. In fact, I was experiencing the most direct pressure from my fellow senior managers. The new ones still on their way in were pelting my inbox with questions even before they arrived. Existing department heads were hiring more senior level staff to assist them and wanted to be sure they received special attention. There were also pedigreed advisors circling the candidate with their own needs and demands. And all of these people were coming directly to me with their questions and not through our normal channels.

Suddenly, I was a client of my own departments as I scrambled to get answers for these VIP-level staff. While it was a complete distraction from my own work, it was also an absolute oversight on my part that I didn't see this problem coming. But I wasted no time on it. I pleaded with our HQ manager, Pete Dagher, to find me a capable volunteer I could hire who was both gritty and considerate at the same time. Just minutes later, he pierced the swirl of activity around me to introduce Monika Juska. I was so relieved.

I immediately recited Monika's new responsibilities to her off the top of my head. I explained that her job would be to make sure that all the department heads were happy and provided for. Some needed orientations to our processes and others needed help navigating our burgeoning bureaucracy. Her charge was to make their lives easier so that mine was too. I didn't have an assistant and perhaps I needed one, but I thought it was more important that she be part of the Ops Desk team. Just as Dan had operations managers servicing states, Monika would be the operations manager for the HQ department heads. Monika was relentless in tackling problems, and I noticed the demands on me were immediately lighter after she started. But the real evidence of the wisdom of that hire came when Research Director Devorah Adler stormed into my office to proclaim: "That Monika you just hired . . . she's a tiger!"

Managing Change

All of the departments I oversaw also experienced dramatic growth during this period. At first I made a good-faith effort to stay engaged in the interview process for new staff, but I soon realized that I needed to entrust my managers with that responsibility. If they were going to own the work, then they needed to be accountable for their hires as well. My only request was that I at least see the résumés of the finalists before an offer was made and that I be introduced to new employees during their first day on the job.

That last rule was put in place after eager new campaign staffers approached me on two separate occasions, both of which ended awkwardly. In each instance, after welcoming these strangers as enthusiastically as they greeted me, I inquired as to where they had been hired. I was embarrassed to learn that in both cases, they actually worked under me.

I also had to make adjustments for my own departmental staff meetings, given our sudden growth. Where we could once fit everyone around a table in a conference room and later assemble in a large huddle near my desk for a meeting we called "the standing standing," I now had to contact building management to rent a room on another floor that could accommodate our sizable numbers. For one of these first large meetings, I invited Jon Carson to join our assembly to explain the campaign's general election field strategy. He stood alongside me and watched in amazement as the stream of people entered the long, narrow room with rows of folding chairs that stretched far to the back. As people settled into their places, Jon suspended his gaze just long enough to turn to me and say, "Holy cow, Henry, are these all your staff?"

Despite the radical transformation occurring inside the campaign, my own day-to-day work remained mostly unchanged. The shifts around me at the top required some getting used to, but for the most part, the general architecture of our upper management was largely intact. One thing was noticeably different, however: I now collaborated on a regular basis with Jen O'Malley Dillon. Her title was battleground director, but her duties included overseeing the administrative aspects of our field operation. It was a big job with enormous responsibility. In her, I had renewed peace of mind that the mammoth budget for that department would be tightly managed and that processes would be regimented. She had immediately impressed me upon her arrival as a strong and disciplined leader.

Otherwise, the faces in my world were mostly familiar. I continued to work closely with my longtime associate, Jon Carson, now the national field director, who was firmly focused on our voter contact efforts. Another partnership that remained intact was my work with Joe Rospars and our chief fundraiser, Julianna Smoot. In recent weeks, Joe had moved his growing new media operation to our side of the building, so his staff was now sandwiched between Julianna's and my departments. Continuing a spirited yearlong discussion, the three of us were often seen huddled together in the middle of the bustling floor updating our fundraising progress and attempting to agree on monthly and long-term revenue goals, including the online grassroots piece Joe managed.

I often wrestled with both Joe and Julianna in an effort to get more optimistic projections from them. The three of us didn't always agree, and failing to reach a consensus heading into the general election, I settled on accepting two different forecasts. Of the two emailed spreadsheets Julianna regularly sent me, I only opened the one she labeled "Crackpot." It offered the rosier view that she knew I wanted. At first, she and Joe were reluctant to work off Crackpot, but they eventually came around to my point of view. It was certainly the one Marianne and I preferred for our financial planning because it consistently proved to be more accurate. Joe and Julianna were both very smart, aggressive fundraisers. For that reason, I always bet on the two of them overperforming—and they always did.

Stepping Aside to Let Others Lead

Just as we were being transformed at the top of the organization, my own departments were growing beneath me. This forced some uncomfortable adjustments on my part. Prior to Jim Messina's arrival, I had enjoyed broad authority across the entire campaign and managed much of the interdepartmental work. Steve Hildebrand, the deputy campaign manager, was out in the states for long stretches during the early races of January and February and then on into the spring, just as David's attention was pulled away from the routine day-to-day management. I had filled much of the gap that emerged at the center of the campaign, but now that we had a dedicated chief of staff under David, and with Steve mostly back in headquarters again, I was effectively pushed back more firmly over the departments I had historically been charged with managing.

The problem was that there was no longer a clear role for me back at my home base. Where I once called all the shots and directly managed many of the projects, my deputies had now firmly stepped into their own leadership. The place was mostly running itself and didn't need my meddling. All that was required of me was to step aside and let them lead. This was an important factor in a decision I was weighing as to whether I should physically move out of their way as well. This decision wasn't a small one, as it meant moving from my coveted work space in a large, semiprivate corner on the floor into an office with Marianne that was the size of a spacious walk-in closet.

My little work area was a cherished spot for me. I had a large desk right next to a floor-to-ceiling bank of windows with an amazing skyline view. Just off my desk was a small round table where I could sign daily paperwork or conduct one-on-one meetings. Behind me was the "asbestos" couch, so named because when the ugly, rust-colored sofa suddenly appeared, it looked like it had been in storage for a decade. It turned out that Dan Jones, now one of two deputy COOs and my neighbor on the floor, had arranged for it. After it was cleaned up though, it was useful for the occasional visitors to our busy corner. But my favorite thing about my work space was that I was within feet of six or seven of my key lieutenants, so that communication and collaboration easily sparked from this area. Work got done here.

The decision to abandon my little corner was ultimately forced on me as the space wars heated up during the seating upheaval spurred by Hilde weeks earlier. As part of that process, I was asked to give up my actual office, which was located close to my work corner. It was a large, beautiful conference-sized space, also with sweeping windowed views. Because I was partial to staying on the shop floor, I mostly just used it as my personal private conference room for the continuous stream of meetings I required all day long. It was useful because I didn't have to compete like our other managers for the three available meeting rooms on the floor.

Taking into account our campaign's anticipated growth and given that every other office was being packed with people, I agreed to give it up to David Axelrod. Despite David's prominent role in the campaign as our top strategist and chief surrogate spokesperson, he had not taken up a permanent place at our headquarters to date. I thought it was perfectly logical for him to move in for the general election and was quite happy to turn over my conference room. I think Marianne felt bad for me and kindly offered to give me her small office, but I liked being on the floor and I thrived off of the energy. I didn't want to leave my corner spot.

I was surprised to watch my former office get filled with, not Axelrod, but about seven new paid media department staff. Three additional desks were also parked directly outside of it to accommodate more people. Things came to a head when Ax next requested a second office. I understood that he couldn't work in the room that he had just stuffed full. But the only office left to offer him in all of HQ at this point was the last of the interior conference rooms. It was a dingy space that looked across a bank of desks and into Marianne's little office with the lovely views. Axelrod accepted and quietly moved in soon after.

Marianne suddenly got nervous. Ax often paced outside of his new station, talking deliberately to some unknown person on his cell phone while staring straight Marianne's way. Every time he passed her office, he peered in at her with his unnerving stare. I assumed that he was just lost in his brain, thinking about whatever it is communications gurus think about all the time. Marianne, on the other hand, was convinced that he wanted her office for himself, so she persuaded me to move in with her to keep from getting evicted.

Her idea was an attractive one at that point since staying on the floor was becoming a problem for me. Headquarters was getting more and more crowded. I couldn't hear myself think. At the same time, I had seating and departmental space issues of my own to reconcile with all of the new hires coming aboard in my shops. And I knew that if I relocated from my corner, I could probably stuff six to eight staffers there. I went ahead and moved a desk in with Marianne, arranging it right against the floor-to-ceiling front window so I could look out on the headquarters floor. It was from this spot that I captained the last few months.

The View from Above

The convergence of these three developments—the arrival of the pros, the coming of age of the leaders inside my own departments, and my relocation off the floor—all occurred at the same time and left me feeling strangely discombobulated. It triggered my own mid-campaign-life-crisis, as I struggled initially with how to effectively fulfill my role and position my leadership as chief operating officer in this very changed environment.

Sharing an office with Marianne did serve two useful purposes. First, I was in the money bunker when fully understanding our financial position would be crucial during the final stretch. Second, I was physically out of the way of my managers so that they could assert their own leadership without having to work through me. Still, while Marianne was an easygoing officemate, I just didn't like it in there. It felt like I was in a cave and suddenly cut off from everything. Where I once knew what was going on better than anyone else, I now had to be quickly briefed on any given issue before I could resolve a problem that had been escalated for my attention. I was now the person who knew where to get answers when I was once the person who had them.

In retrospect, I was mistaken in thinking that I was viewing the operation through an office window. In reality, I was now simply observing it from a higher level of management. Removing myself from the weeds of the work offered me a new perspective from a very different vantage point. While I didn't immediately understand this shift, from my new perch I gained insight into my own organization that I might have missed if had I remained engaged in the usual rapid-fire demands of the floor. Away from the distractions of where I had been, I was able to quickly identify a series of budding problems that, left unattended, would have quietly developed into a low-grade crisis.

For one thing, in retooling for the home stretch, I noticed that some of the high performers from the first two stages of our development weren't inherently suited to this third one. Individual skill sets didn't naturally transfer as the organization evolved. I had seen this before, when some of the creative builder-types who flourished in the start-up phase didn't necessarily graduate into the disciplined responders that were best suited to the period that included the fifty-seven primary contests—what I call the "synapse" phase. Now, not all of those were transitioning gracefully into the higher management roles that awaited them in this final growth stage.

Also unsettling was the discovery that some of the key lieutenants I had long relied on were getting tired and, frankly, bored. I could see it in the eyes of Harry Kruglik, for example, our talented correspondence manager who, after a year and a half, yearned to write speeches rather than answer letters. Some of our more experienced budget analysts struggled with a burning desire to set aside their Excel spreadsheets to focus on their first love of crafting policy. In other cases, I had people executing the very inward-facing functions of campaign management who longed for the outside contact more typical in a communications or constituency outreach shop.

As the organization grew, longtime staffers who wanted to make very big job moves regularly approached me. The dilemma, as I saw it, was akin to being the coach of a baseball team that had just made it to the World Series and having the starting third baseman ask if he could pitch. In fact, it felt like several of my most pivotal players were hungry to try new positions. It was my responsibility to ensure that we had the best people in the right spots heading into the final days and that my whole staff remained motivated.

At first I tried to resolve some of these problems by doing what managers often do: make technical adjustments to the existing organizational chart. Ultimately though, I just couldn't avoid the tough conversations. When an individual staff member wasn't equipped for a management role in our rapidly growing environment, I had an obligation to help them move aside to make room for others to step up. This wasn't the time for on-the-job training.

Also, while I am an advocate for professional growth and personal satisfaction, we were closing in on a very big election. With the future of the country at stake, this was not really the time for the career change that some people craved. I made a few moves and promotions where I could, but most of my energy was spent making the case that this was a time to set individual aspirations aside and to do everything possible to get our candidate into the White House.

On the other hand, I knew I couldn't simply dismiss this sudden stirring. I had very capable staff, ripe for being picked off by any of the other department managers who were also building their ranks and needed proven talent. My team was fidgety, and there was an abundance of jobs with the new expansion that was taking place all throughout headquarters. For the first time in our organizational existence, we had an employee's market. That left me vulnerable to losing my most valuable resources—the staff I had prepared over many, many months for just this moment.

This all hit home when one of the people I was counting on for the campaign's homestretch resigned to work in another department. It was somebody I liked both personally and professionally. But, ultimately, it wasn't the leaving that bothered me as much as the reasoning that was offered for it. This person spoke about our work as if it was somehow small. I was stunned. I knew about the lure of other departments—the exciting times on the road as part of the advance team, the shine of new media, the star power around fundraising, and the cool of communications. But, frankly, I thought there could be no better job experience than campaign management, especially running our own history-making effort.

Still, I understood how this could happen and felt deeply responsible for not recognizing this problem sooner. In our business, almost all work is very tedious and time can certainly dull the luster. Even the candidate has to perform tasks that aren't particularly appealing. However, it was the precise execution of the small that made us big. This was especially true in my shops. What particularly alarmed me was the discovery that a fair number of my staff had become as small as the details of their work at a time when we needed everyone to step into their full leadership.

Chief BIGness Officer

This revelation created an opportunity for me to devote myself to perhaps the most important challenge that I confronted during my time in the campaign. I had to reacquaint my staff with their own bigness. I would lose more talent to other departments if I didn't. This was a wake-up call for me, and I decided that I needed to check in with every one of my employees. It was time to recalibrate.

I knew I couldn't have this conversation in a large staff meeting, offering a sermon from the front of the room; nor could I accomplish this in individual one-on-one meetings. It would take me forever to get to everyone. This needed to happen in smaller functional work teams, keeping the numbers involved between four and eight people at a time. Even so, we had grown so big so fast that in advance of each of these meetings I had to ask for a lineup of the staff attending because I had not yet learned the names of some of our newer hires.

The first step in reacquainting each person with their bigness was to have everyone see themselves as more than just what their co-workers saw based on their everyday exchanges with them. Our colleagues don't always know us for our big-picture responsibilities. People instead relate to us by our job titles and our history of meeting their needs. We are typically defined by our actions, our interactions, our transactions, and even our inactions. If my staff became as small as they were viewed rather than as big as their charge, they would forfeit their leadership. For me, the consequences would be disastrous if that happened.

When making this point, I personalized examples to each of the teams I met with during the more than fifteen meetings I held over the next three weeks. In the case of our travel shop, for example, I pointed out that if a co-worker picked up the phone and spoke to one of them about booking an airline ticket, the caller likely viewed them as little more than some sort of in-house reservationist. If our people on that team in turn saw themselves simply as travel bookers, then they would ignore the hugely important responsibilities they had. I reminded the members of that travel unit that they were managers of a multimillion-dollar line in the campaign budget, the third largest area of spending. Each of them was a steward of precious resources made possible by our donors, many having stretched their own household budgets to make that contribution.

We didn't need travel bookers—mere managers who succeeded by simply ensuring the fulfillment of requests. We needed leaders who could step into the tension of suggesting to the David Axelrod's and the David Plouffe's of the campaign that if they changed planes in Denver, rather than take a nonstop flight to California, they would save the organization $400; and if they did it again on the way back, they'd save a similar amount. I recognized that it was difficult for the young staffers in this department to haggle with their co-workers and bosses about different times or routes that might save us money, but it was something we had to do. One of the reasons we brought our travel operation in-house was because we knew that our people could meet the needs of their peers in ways that some faceless person at a contracted call center in the middle of the country couldn't.

In the end, such interventions by our travel staff almost always resulted in some kind of savings, and that amount was recorded and presented to me in a report at the end of each week. Essentially, I was handed a readout of that team's leadership effectiveness measured in actual dollars. What people on the other side of that phone didn't know, I reminded my audience, was that they had single-handedly logged enough savings during the life of the campaign to enable us to run full operations in a small state we might not have otherwise been able to afford.

My parting guidance to them was that while their co-workers might see them simply as staff that helps book reservations, I see them as assistant CFOs. I deputized them as such in that meeting. Assistant CFOs were responsible for more than fulfillment. They were also responsible for money. I didn't care what title was on their business cards; they were assistant CFOs. That was big and it meant something.

The same went for the team managing the volunteer call center that received public comments. I often spoke of this operation with great pride because of the amazing work our staff and the many dedicated volunteers accomplished together. In most campaigns, receiving calls from the public through an 800 number is a function that is outsourced to an expensive private company. I remember the day that Plouffe proposed that we bring that activity in-house, after an outside vendor had managed it during the first couple of months of the campaign. His vision was for a volunteer-staffed operation taking calls from 7:00 A.M. to 10:00 P.M. daily. At the time, I worried that it would be too hard to consistently fill chairs, but our small, hardworking staff pulled it off.

While other campaign employees may have viewed our call center managers as volunteer wranglers, I saw their contribution in much bigger terms. Our leaders there professionalized that operation, turning it into a true communications shop. The volunteers answering our phones were at the front line of the public outreach work we did as a campaign, and they were the first to hear what the voters were thinking. Each night, the comments they received were condensed for distribution to our top campaign and communications leaders, giving us a snapshot of what the public was reacting to at any given moment.

Our volunteers may not have been quite as polished as trained outsourced professionals, but we had people who genuinely cared about Barack answering the phones. More importantly, we ran yet another small state with the money we saved by bringing the call center operation in-house and relying on our remarkable volunteers to run it. This was just one of many shops I could point to where we had staff performing routine work who, through tenacity and innovation, gave the campaign a serious edge that went unnoticed by their co-workers. The bigness of our call center team wasn't lost on me, and I couldn't let it be lost on them.

Not only did all my staffers have to be bigger than their daily roles, but they had also to see themselves as leaders. This was the second point I made in these team meetings. On one occasion, a staffer challenged me by arguing that it wasn't possible for everyone to be leaders. My response was that I only hired leaders. There was no excuse for a position to have been filled with a nonleader. Staffing slots were finite, and an opportunity was missed if we had hired someone who wasn't prepared to assert their own leadership in that role. Still, it was true that not every person could lead in the conventional sense. We all played a position. Not everyone could lead from the front like our candidate, campaign manager, or even the department heads did. That would be chaos.

Our success was based on having right systems, precise execution of them, and the presence of mind to quickly escalate problems or mistakes to the correct manager. It began with the standing axiom that every single person was to have a role, know their role, and be accountable for leading in that role. The failure of one would have a domino effect on the organization. If any single individual could not execute, others would feel compelled to fill the gap, but that only meant that another hole would appear somewhere else in the chain. Similarly, we couldn't have people meandering in and out of their lanes. This was a time when predictability was critical.

The "Hope and Change" Maker

As I wrapped up these check-in meetings, I had total belief in our team. We would all be challenged, but there was now a collective understanding of what we needed to succeed in the final days. This was a call to lead from within, requiring that each of us respond to the unique challenges of our individual positions with an innovative mind, a service heart, an entrepreneurial spirit, and a collaborative outlook.

An innovative mind could proactively solve unsolvable problems. A service heart had the capacity to earnestly understand the needs of the community. The entrepreneurial spirit could boldly step into the tension inherent to our leadership roles and see the toughest of challenges through to the end. Lastly, collaboration was the cornerstone for achievement in our fluid and interdependent work ecosystem. These were the qualities that had long characterized our team, and it was the best explanation I had for our success to date. It was this brand of synapse leadership that we needed to continue if we were going to win this great final battle in the fall.

Even as I worked to help my staff calibrate their leadership, I didn't arrive gracefully to my new position of leading from above. But I came to appreciate what I discovered once I got there. My role had noticeably changed through each of the three stages of our organizational development. In every instance, it required that I position my own leadership differently. To use a football analogy, during the first phase—the start-up period—I was the quarterback calling the plays in the huddle and executing on the field. During the period encompassing the fifty-seven primary and caucus races, I was on the sidelines coaching but still very near the action where I could help others perform to their highest abilities. Now, in this final stage, sitting in that small windowed office was like being in the skybox and looking down at the activity. I could see everything unfolding from afar and offer my best guidance from above, but I was no longer on the field of play. I had become wholly reliant on the performance of others for our success. That meant I had to fully invest in their leadership.

Our fate depended on it.

10

Contrast Thyself

AUGUST 26, 2008: *"Somebody needs to talk to Adi," I grumbled, concluding a lengthy rant. "I know he has huge budget responsibilities, but he leaves well after midnight and it looks like he doesn't even stop to sleep." Marianne sat before me, eyes downcast and listening intently. "I know, I know," she said, "Someone really needs to talk to Adi about his workaholism." Marianne abruptly leapt to her feet. "I'll do it, Henry!" Turning away she coyly added, "As soon as the campaign's over." Marianne liked her little joke. I could hear her characteristic giggle trail off as she charged out of the room.*

The New Reality

As we moved into summer, Senator Obama came under fire for what some on the Left characterized as his "move to the middle." Republicans preferred the term *flip-flopping*. Regardless, there was noise from both sides of the political spectrum that our candidate was disingenuously repositioning himself to appear more attractive to moderate, swing voters in the fall.

I could never put my finger on the alleged issue shifts that sparked these complaints. The news and blogs offered some clues. The Left was apparently smarting over a vote Barack cast in the Senate favoring controversial wiretapping legislation. We were also taking heat for opening our doors to the Bill and Hillary folks who began to join our ranks. These examples contributed to some of the grumblings circulating about a worrying centrist streak that Senator Obama had cleverly hidden from Democratic primary voters. To our right, Republicans were still seething over our having opted out of the campaign public financing system. They pointed to that decision as an obvious illustration of our candidate's hypocrisy and proof of a "truthiness" character flaw.

It was all very much overblown. Senator Obama had always presented himself as someone who would bridge the partisan divide, and the principles that guided his candidacy during the primaries remained unchanged. The only notable difference was that our candidate was now navigating a transformed campaign environment. He was no longer competing against a large field of Democrats for his party's nomination, and his chief rival was no longer the former first lady and junior senator from New York.

Barack was also standing before a very different audience. Where he had previously run on a state-by-state basis in Democratic primary races typically comprised of declared party members, he was now competing in a national contest for the support of all registered voters, regardless of affiliation. Prudence required that Senator Obama position his leadership to meet this new political reality. Having won the Democratic nomination, the Illinois senator now needed to demonstrate that he could lead all Americans as their president.

The New Way to Victory

Given the shifting terrain in front of us, the first thing our campaign had to do was show our supporters the way to win in the general election. The boiler-plate approach would have been to direct our finite resources to where they would be needed most. That would mean investing less in the safe Democratic states, commonly referred to as blue states, and staying away from the red Republican strongholds altogether. Instead, conventional thinking dictated, the bulk of the campaign's time and money should be targeted at the roughly sixteen key battleground states where margins were close and swing voters clustered.

Our strategy was a seismic departure from that model. We decided instead to reach beyond the accepted battleground states and wage a full fifty-state operation. In doing so, we would force McCain to play defense on his own turf, thereby making it easier to protect ours. We were committing to an ambitious all-in approach.

We only needed to win enough states to reach the 270-delegate threshold for the presidency. Our goal, then, was to win every one of the nineteen states and the District of Columbia that John Kerry did in his 2004 bid against incumbent George W. Bush. These included those blue states that ran down the Pacific West Coast and Hawaii, a large cluster of safe Democratic states in the Northeast, and the upper

Midwest states of Minnesota, Wisconsin, Illinois, and Michigan. If we succeeded there, we would only need another nineteen delegates to win the election. To that end, seven of the traditional battleground states that Bush won seemed promising for us to pick off. They were: Nevada (5 electoral votes), New Mexico (5), Colorado (9), Iowa (7), Missouri (11), Ohio (20), and Florida (27).

However, we had a chance to open our odds by expanding beyond the traditional battleground. In fact, reaching past the minimum 270 delegates would go far in validating Barack's "hope and change" agenda. This would require poaching into perceived Republican red states where we might find one or more pickups—in Indiana, Montana, North Carolina, North Dakota, and Virginia, for example. Plouffe even had a watchful eye on McCain's home state of Arizona.

The scope of our electoral strategy troubled industry insiders and political elites alike. Many viewed it as a futile approach since it was so different from what had been done in past elections. Mostly, I think they thought it smelled like arrogance coming from our campaign. Some of my political friends outside the campaign routinely lectured me that we were foolish to expand the map. In a tight contest with the typical financial constraints of a political campaign, it was argued, we needed to fully concentrate our resources on the traditional battlegrounds.

To be clear, I knew this would be a tough race and that it would likely end up very close. In May, Steve Hildebrand asked senior staff for our general election predictions to help inform the strategic planning. I presented my projected electoral map, colored in with Obama states totaling 269 delegates to McCain's 269. My forecast was for a tie, which would throw the election into the House of Representatives.

The reasoning behind my pessimism was that we had just been through a bruising battle against Clinton and I worried it had done harm to our candidate's image. I also believed that McCain's team would run a highly competitive campaign. They had very capable people at the helm. I'm not sure I believed back in early 2007 that McCain would make it through the race to win his party's nomination. But when he did, I knew the Republicans put forward what would be our toughest draw.

It's true that these factors favored the more targeted strategy that would have loaded the bulk of our resources into fewer states. Nonetheless, I wholly agreed with the wide-open approach that Ax and Plouffe ultimately settled on, mostly because I didn't really like our chances in some of the traditional battlegrounds this cycle. I wasn't sufficiently confident that Michigan, Ohio, Missouri, or Florida would necessarily go our way. At the same time, I was excited by our prospects in states like Virginia, Colorado, and North Carolina, which had been mostly out of reach to Democrats in previous elections. But the most compelling case for going wide was that, as our candidate said, this was not a time for small plans in a campaign that always thought big.

Say It Simple

Executing such a grand strategy added to the already monumental complexities before us. We were the first campaign in nearly four decades to refuse public financing for the general election. We also kept and scaled all of our work in-house rather than sending core functions to the Democratic National Committee. On top of all that, we were breaking entirely new ground by focusing our efforts beyond a narrow list of battlegrounds to run a colossal fifty-state program. These were organizational calisthenics that had never been attempted in modern American politics.

Coming off of the Fourth of July holiday, with only about seventeen weeks until the election, it would have been easy for our campaign to collapse under the weight of these pressures. The changes within were dramatic, the political environment was quickly overheating, and the scope and complexity of the organizational build-out was massive. I told David Plouffe in a private meeting that this was uncharted territory, and I worried our staff could easily become mired in it. David once again had a way to make simple sense of the mayhem by breaking things down into very easy terms.

He divided the upcoming campaign into five mini-campaigns that could be neatly dropped onto the election calendar and wrapped inside individual robust operations. The first was the upcoming overseas tour that was planned for the end of July, when our candidate would spend a week visiting with our troops and national leaders in the Middle East and Europe. Later, in August, we would roll out the new vice-presidential nominee. That would be immediately followed by our party's nominating convention. Then, in September, the debates would begin, featuring three meetings between the two candidates and a vice-presidential matchup. Finally, we would end with get-out-the-vote activities, known as GOTV.

Our message tack was also very straightforward. We would position our candidate as the choice for the kind of change the nation demanded, while casting McCain as symbolic of old Washington. The Republican, we would argue, represented a third Bush term. Americans could choose to continue the same failed policies with John McCain (McSame) or they could embrace a very different alternative in Barack Obama.

We had our plan and were now ready for battle.

Stepping onto the World Stage

July 19 was the day that *the shot* was seen around the world. Kicking off an overseas tour that included eight countries, Senator Obama reprised his performance from South Carolina the year before, this time launching a basketball across the court in a gymnasium in Kuwait. Once again, the senator nonchalantly knocked down his long three-pointer to the delight of an audience of American service men and women in uniform who cheered the feat loudly. The ball hit the back of the net and fell tamely to the floor. It was a perfect play that filled the highlight reels of news outlets for days. In that moment, the spotlight of the international media immediately focused on the senator as he made his grand entrance onto the global stage.

Senator Obama covered many miles on that trip, and he commanded the ambitious schedule with astonishing poise. In addition to sitting with leaders of foreign nations and visiting our troops in the Middle East, he addressed our largest audience to date in Berlin, Germany. Originally planned for delivery at the celebrated Brandenburg Gate, the site of President Ronald Reagan's famous "tear down this wall" speech, opposition by the German government forced us to move to a nearby open-air venue where nearly 250,000 people were packed inside the rope lines. Our candidate unleashed a powerful oratory that he concluded with these words:

People of Berlin—and people of the world—the scale of our challenge is great. The road ahead will be long. But I come before you to say that we are heirs to a struggle for freedom. We are a people of improbable hope. With an eye toward the future, with resolve in our hearts, let us remember this history, and answer our destiny, and remake the world again.

Our opponents swiftly and predictably charged that Senator Obama should be running for president of the United States and not Europe. Our candidate convincingly demonstrated that he could elegantly rise to the pageantry and weighty demands of the office.

On his return, there were exactly one hundred days between us and the November 4 election.

Foreign Threat

Sometime after the foreign trip, in mid-August, I got news that our computer network had been compromised: we had been hacked. Michael Slaby, our chief technology officer, swooped by to inform me on his way to speak to Messina about the problem. We'd had small issues before, but this seemed serious. Michael agreed to circle back later and discuss it with me further, but I was confused by his initial report. It actually sounded like he had gotten this news from Jim himself. This was information that would typically flow from us to campaign management, not the other way around.

Marianne perceived the urgency of the problem and quickly began an investigation to see if we were the victims of financial theft. Personal donor information wasn't stored on our system, so we had no concerns in that regard. But it turned out the intruder had no interest in our money or our donors. And this wasn't some two-bit hack either. I soon learned that this crime carried the fingerprints of a foreign government.

In fact, senior officials in the Bush White House first notified our campaign of the seriousness of the compromise. That explained why this was coming from Messina. McCain's campaign had been hit, too. Throughout the life of our organization we had warned staff to be on alert for phishing attacks—bad links embedded in suspicious emails that, when clicked open, would expose our network to harmful viruses. This threat was disguised in a meeting invite circulating among top staffers. But the intrusion was far worse than we had initially understood.

Over the next few days, I received updates from different people. Still, some of the information I got was rather hazy. For example, it was never clear which government was behind the attack. It may have been an eastern European operation—Russia, I thought—or Chinese. My attitude at the time was that if this was an international incident, it was probably not any of my business. People with the security clearances would wade through those issues. I just wanted the problem controlled.

It turned out that the cyberstalker was pulling emails and files from the computers of our senior staff. This ultimately led to the collecting and scrubbing of select individual equipment. It seemed odd to me that our campaign information was of such interest to a foreign government. One explanation for this cyber-espionage was that it might have been directed toward gathering information about those of us who could one day serve in the White House. If so, these hackers would be trying to build a profile on us by piecing together clues about our individual personalities, decision-making behaviors, and policy orientations. It all seemed like something right out of a James Bond movie.

I was pretty shocked by the whole episode. I never would have anticipated something like this. Slaby soon suggested that this problem was much bigger than our existing in-house expertise or capabilities and urged that we needed assistance. With the kind of outside firepower we brought to bear on this issue, I expected we would have the problem resolved within a couple of weeks. But the teams involved in defending our system seemed to begin a new battle every day against this mystery attacker. It was as if they were attempting some kind of technology exorcism over our network.

As the event continued, I learned that we would need help indefinitely. Apparently, this was a very complex virus that was too difficult to fully eradicate. Instead, we needed to focus on containing and monitoring it closely. Thus, I was told, we would just have to live with this intruder creeping around in our systems through the end of the election.

Wake-Up Call

August 22 had been a long day for me. When I left the office near midnight that Friday evening, there was still noticeable scurrying going on all around me. It was particularly busy over in Joe Rospars's area in new media, and I was pretty sure I knew why. All night, as I battled through my own concerns, my monitor had been feeding me news from a cable network indicating that the press had taken up an all-night watch at the homes of Virginia governor Tim Kaine, Indiana senator Evan Bayh, and Delaware senator Joe Biden. This was occurring in advance of reports that our VP nominee would be announced the next morning.

Having been part of a small team arranging the terms and agreements for the signs being produced for the rally announcing Senator Obama's running mate, I was among the few who knew our short list of VP nominees. I was pleased at how well the campaign had kept a tight lid on our VP choice thus far, but the fact that the media had successfully zeroed in on our short list was worrying. It indicated to me that our cover had somehow been blown. I had considered hitting up Rospars for the scoop on my way out the door, but I knew I was too burnt out. Just as I moved to turn off my TV at my desk, the news was reported that the secret service had been dispatched to the Biden residence. I was right: it was leaked.

My first thought was that this would totally screw up our Be the First to Know initiative. We had collected many thousands of new text numbers and email addresses with the promise that our supporters would know as soon as the media who our candidate's VP choice was. It turned out that the media knew first. For Joe Rospars, that meant he had an all-nighter on his hands. His launch was scheduled for later on Saturday morning, but now he had to move our text and email announcements out immediately. Due to the sheer volume of names in our database, his team wouldn't get the list requeued until around 2:00 A.M. As a result, the bulletins didn't begin to drop on cell phones and into email inboxes until about 3:00 A.M. That had mobile devices buzzing in homes all over the country during the morning's wee hours.

McCain had a response ad up on the airwaves only a few hours later. It featured a sound bite of Joe Biden from an earlier Democratic debate sheepishly responding to forceful questioning by newsman George

Stephanopoulos about his previous comments expressing doubts over Senator Obama's readiness to serve as president of the United States. "I think I stand by that statement," Biden said. It was a tough ad produced so the tension in that moment really popped out at the viewer.

The whole episode was awkward. We had always succeeded in treating our large universe of supporters like insiders. On this Saturday morning, however, those who slept through our 3:00 A.M. wake-up call later discovered that the VP nominee had already been announced and a McCain response ad was up. The disappointment was immediately noticeable. To paraphrase the words of a TV talking head at the time, it was like hearing about your sister's wedding engagement from a neighbor.

In addition to the clumsy delivery, I'm not entirely sure how supporters responded to the actual news itself. I have to confess that while I quickly became a great fan, I wasn't initially "in the tank" for Joe Biden when I first learned he was our candidate's choice. This was a well-known Washington, not-so-change-y, type of guy.

With time, however, it really sank in for me what a great pick Biden was. He compensated for some of Barack's perceived weaknesses on the campaign trail with his white working-class appeal, his deep Washington experience to offset Barack's relative newness, and a foreign affairs background that could rival John McCain's. But Joe Biden also provided a welcome internal lift to our organization. His humility was refreshing. One would expect a man with almost four decades in the United States Senate and two presidential runs behind him to be a little on the pretentious side. Joe Biden was surprisingly down to earth, and he quickly became popular among our staff.

Soon after he officially joined us, I received word to pull everyone together because Senator Biden wanted a chance to meet his new colleagues. He couldn't have been more gracious or respectful on the day he introduced himself from the front of the room. Biden joked that he was well aware that this was the team that clobbered him on the campaign trail. He enthusiastically declared that he wished he could have found an easier path in, but he was still deeply honored to be joining a staff for which he had such high regard. It was abundantly clear that Joe Biden was as excited as everyone else to be working with and for Barack Obama.

Also, it wasn't lost on me that when making his biggest hire of the campaign, our candidate proved he could back up his own talk. Senator Biden fit our ideal staff archetype that Senator Obama had described many months before. The Delaware senator was low on drama, high on respect, and an everyday guy perfectly suited to a bottom-up organization like the one welcoming him.

Convention

The foreign trip and the VP rollout behind us, our sights now turned to the upcoming Democratic National Convention. We'd had a very successful two months, but the slim lead and noticeable momentum were of little comfort. To complicate things further, it began to feel like we had a Hillary problem again as the rivalry was spinning back up in advance of the party's big gathering in Denver.

Suspicions about Hillary still lingered on our side. Rumors began to surface that both she and her husband were scheduled to have prominent roles on separate nights, making the whole affair feel more like an impending Clinton coronation than an Obama nominating convention. Growing speculation that Senator Clinton's name would be placed in nomination along with Senator Obama's didn't help ease the tension.

Those anxieties faded as soon as the curtain went up. Senator Ted Kennedy's emotional surprise entrance the first night was poignant, given that his recent surgery for a brain tumor had cast a pall over the prospects for his attendance. The house came to its feet to welcome the longtime convention favorite. "Nothing—nothing is going to keep me from this special gathering tonight," the Lion roared.

Later that same evening, Michelle Obama delivered a crowd-pleasing speech of her own, focusing on the importance of family values broadly, and introducing America more personally to hers. The two Obama daughters joined their mother onstage, as their father was beamed in via satellite from the living room of a Kansas City family's home where he had been watching. It was awkward logistically, but it made for a charming moment as viewers were swept up into a brief exchange of banter between the girls and their dad.

Hillary Clinton, Joe Biden, and former president Bill Clinton also turned in similarly inspirational performances over the next two evenings. Of course, there was a great deal of scrutiny directed Hillary's way, as convention watchers examined her every word and action for evidence of just how eagerly she would embrace her role as the party's unifier. If her commanding speech on Tuesday night left some unconvinced, all doubts were erased on Wednesday when she interrupted the official roll call vote to enthusiastically move Senator Obama's nomination by acclamation.

Overall, the convention was a spectacular event that was perfectly executed on all fronts. Still, our detractors dismissively characterized the presentation as a week packed with fluff at a time when fragile economic and national security concerns warranted a more robust, substantive policy prescription. We were also taking heat for being too soft on John McCain and the Republicans. It was clear there were those, many even on our own side, who were spoiling for a fight. But we wanted to use the opportunity of this national stage to formally introduce America to the Obamas and the Bidens. To our credit and despite the outside pressures, we effectively stayed on our convention message and executed the game plan exactly as it was designed.

On Thursday night, before a record-breaking crowd of eighty-four thousand people packed into Mile High Stadium in Denver, Senator Obama accepted the Democratic nomination to become the forty-fourth president of the United States. Nearly forty million more watched it on television. I was one of them. Fortunately for me, I had stayed behind to mind the store in Chicago, so I was able to race home from work to watch Barack's acceptance speech with my wife. After a long journey that had begun eighteen months before, I wanted us to hear the words together.

Our TV screen was filled with the hum of thousands of enthusiastic supporters who thunderously greeted the new nominee as he walked onto the mammoth arena stage. Beaming with a smile that flashed from ear to ear, Senator Obama waited patiently for the crowd to settle. Finally, his words slowly filled the stadium as he began his forty-five-minute address:

It is with humility and pride that I accept the nomination as your president of the United States.

Game on.

McCain Fights Back

It was a difficult week for John McCain's campaign. The media oxygen that followed us overseas at the end of July made the Arizona senator look left behind and home alone. His campaign seemed completely unprepared for our global foray and the subsequent attention, as if the news of our foreign trip had snuck up suddenly on their leadership team. There was a distinctly confused quality to the Arizona senator's message and movements. It all had an impulsive feel, as if he and his staff were just making it up each day as they went along.

Every night, as I watched a recap of the day's events on TV, the seventy-one-year-old seemed to show up randomly in odd and un-expected places. This offered a remarkable contrast to the images and sound bites coming back from our foreign trip that were streaming into American newscasts and running all day on cable channels. Pictures of Senator Obama wowing the overseas troops with his dazzling basket-ball escapades were set against a more serene clip of McCain motoring around in a golf cart with former president George H. W. Bush at a Maine country club. While Senator Obama was filmed meeting with world leaders, McCain was shown sneaking up on some random woman in a neighborhood grocery store and playfully slipping unwanted items into her shopping basket. The visual of Barack standing before 240,000 cheering Europeans in Berlin was noticeably different from McCain's quiet, purposeful stroll into a German restaurant in Ohio for lunch. Senator Obama was pictured speaking to reporters at the Temple of Hercules before his meeting with Jordan's King Abdullah II. Senator McCain was photographed stepping in front of a cheese display at a Pennsylvania supermarket where he answered questions from the press.

These kinds of images combined to offer two very different portraits to voters. Our candidate effortlessly navigated the world stage, while back home McCain stumbled and bumbled along. Barack came across as the future standing before electric youth-filled crowds, while mo-ments like the leisurely golf outing with former president Bush only cemented the notion that McCain was a relic from another political era. Barack appeared to be stepping onto the world stage just as John McCain was stepping off of it.

Obama was large and presidential; McCain small and shrinking.

First Blood

If John McCain's Straight Talk Express sputtered off the starting line, his message team looked to have a deliberate strategy to slow us. At the end of July, they hammered us for our last-minute cancellation of a planned visit with troops in Germany over worries that the meeting would be portrayed by our opponents as politically motivated. Instead, it was our decision to cancel that ended up being politicized by McCain and the Republicans. They also launched an online ad mocking our candidate's hubris called "The One," complete with parting waters and a starring role for Barack alongside the biblical figure Moses. The trifecta concluded with an attack on our energy plan that somehow tied Senator Obama to pop culture icons Britney Spears and Paris Hilton.

That particular television spot, called "Celeb," caught some good initial buzz. It cast Senator Obama as a policy lightweight who was hopelessly reliant on his celebrity, not unlike the two familiar costars in the clip. The whole episode was an annoyance, but Paris Hilton kept interest alive by cleverly seizing the PR opening with a video response of her own. Shot poolside sitting in an oversized lounge chair, the bikini-clad hotel heiress prescribed a thoughtful solution for America's energy future and offered this parting challenge: "I'll see you at the debates, bitches."

Some thought "Celeb" was a rather goofy spot, but I worried it would touch a nerve that made voters in swing battleground states like Missouri and Ohio say "ouch." It was evidence of a very obvious strategy by the McCain camp to discredit our candidate early and turn this election into a referendum against him. Some on his staff even confided privately to our folks with unabashed candor that their intention was to destroy Barack and drag him through the mud.

There was no real bounce for us in the polls coming off of what had been an impressively executed overseas trip. In fact, our lead was trimmed to about three points as we headed into August. But whatever headway they had made against us, their side couldn't hide the ugly truth that their candidate wasn't able to draw an appreciable audience. It became increasingly clear that while Barack Obama drew crowds, John McCain had to search for them. He began showing up unexpectedly for walkabouts and photo ops wherever people had already congregated.

One such visit was to the Sturgis Harley Davidson rally in South Dakota, where thousands of motorcycle enthusiasts gathered annually.

By all accounts McCain was warmly received, but the curious public offer of his wife as a contestant in the evening's beauty contest made news. That would be the Miss Buffalo Chip beauty contest—the same one that reportedly includes a topless runway and a rather explicit and racy talent show. After having skillfully managed our candidate through Europe and the Middle East, including sensitive war zones, I marveled at the novice advance work by McCain's campaign. This particular gaffe reflected a general lack of preparedness that, to me, was an indicator of organizational problems that appeared more and more systemic as the campaign calendar advanced.

Nonetheless, they unloaded on us over the airwaves throughout the summer, and our limp counterpunch quickly became a source of frustration among our supporters. Take the example of our response to McCain's nationally publicized remarks in Sturgis that he would "take the roar of 50,000 Harley riders any day" over a couple hundred thousand Berliners. Our paid media guru, Larry Grisolano, was very enthusiastic about a tough piece he quickly cued up in his shop pointing out how McCain's past trade policies had negatively affected the sale of American-made bikes. The problem for us, however, was that its reach was limited, airing primarily in the Milwaukee market where the motorcycles were assembled.

But the McCain campaign was urgently trying to drain its war chest to beat the FEC-imposed deadline for spending any earmarked primary funds before the start of the GOP convention on September 3. They were sitting on about $30 million, most of which they dumped on us in paid media. We weren't bound by the same financial restrictions and could hold our powder for the last two months of the general election.

The good news was that McCain's negative onslaught was a money-maker for us. During the last week of July, we could see a direct correlation between his attacks and our online revenue surges. In fact, the McCain campaign actually salvaged what had been a poor fundraising month for us. As we moved through July, Messina grew uneasy about our numbers. I tried to assure him that we always closed strong and that we shouldn't worry too much about a midmonth slump. This wasn't an unusual trend for us. But it did look dangerously like we were going to fall short of our end-of-month markers. In that last week, however, we received a surge of $15 million. That lifted us past the $50 million watermark, enabling us to eclipse our goal for July by about $4 million. A dizzying $6 million of that haul came on the last day of the month in response to their "Celeb" attack piece. It was hopeful evidence that if the McCain team remained dedicated to driving the "Low-Road Express" into the last weeks of the election, our grassroots army would make sure it cost them.

Play Offense

Despite the shorter runway beneath us, overall our campaign seemed to have had a better lift-off than McCain's. The purpose and precision that characterized our execution was mostly the result of having a strong plan to guide us. Organizational success relies on precisely managing that which you can control and effectively navigating the unexpected. It is the game of offense and defense. What separates the successful from the aspiring is that the former has a proactive strategy. Ours consisted of the five plays that Plouffe called early in the summer. They were the foreign trip, the VP selection, the convention, the debates, and GOTV. By September 1, we had executed the first three with amazing precision.

Each of our five plays was wrapped around a few major subinitiatives. As an example, auditioning our candidate on the world stage as part of a complicated production flawlessly packaged by our advance and communications teams met one of our objectives for that overseas visit. The energy of that scene in Berlin, when Senator Obama confidently addressed the huge enthusiastic audience before him, was a second. The third was framing him in the powerful images coming back home that decisively sharpened the contrasts against his rival and amplified our message.

The VP nominee selection was similarly viewed as well-executed behind a disciplined operation led by Caroline Kennedy. The process showcased Senator Obama's capacity to navigate the complex issues associated with this all-important hiring decision, even as he faced a powerful crusade that steadfastly advocated for Senator Clinton in the number two slot. Our carefully organized Be the First to Know campaign, even if ultimately derailed by events outside of our control, and the Biden announcement rally in Springfield, Illinois, were two other important elements of that rollout.

Finally, the convention was memorable for moments like Ted Kennedy's dramatic entrance, Hillary Clinton interrupting the roll call to move Barack's nomination forward, and the crowd-filled Mile High Stadium where Senator Obama delivered his historic acceptance speech.

McCain's side was less precise on offense during the summer of 2008. Despite the steady stream of early attack messages, his campaign routinely sputtered. But with the Republican convention about to commence, our real test lay ahead. Unbeknownst to us, McCain's leadership team had pulled a page from the back of their campaign playbook that mapped out a surprise option they were prepared to try. The call was a risky one, but McCain made it. I think it's fair to say that they ran something our way that nobody saw coming.

It was an immediate game changer.

11

Know Where to Be to Effectively Lead

SEPTEMBER 20, 2008: *Hockey legend Wayne Gretzky once said, "I skate to where the puck is going to be; not where it has been." I consider my boss to be one of the most skillful political athletes of his time. Like Gretzky does on ice, Barack similarly looks far down the campaign trail and positions himself where he can best assert his leadership.*

Enter Sarah Palin

I sat on the floor, gazing at my television screen while slowly tying my shoes. I was captivated by the breaking news bulletin being aired. My BlackBerry laid arm's length away with a half-written note waiting to be finished and sent. Twelve hours earlier, from the same spot in my living room, I watched Barack Obama step forward at the Democratic National Convention to accept our party's nomination for president. It was a moment I hoped would linger a long time.

Our fortieth-floor, one-bedroom apartment was quiet and very still. My wife and baby were both soundly asleep in the next room. The large floor-to-ceiling window to my right framed a spectacular view of the Windy City's southern skyline. Firmly in the center, on the other side of the Chicago River, was the high-rise that housed our campaign headquarters. The eleventh floor, occupied by Obama for America, was the only one that remained consistently lit deep into every night from one end of the building to the other. On this Friday morning, before the sun came up, that very floor was still glowing as if it never shut down the day before.

I had already been up for several hours finishing a few documents and browsing through my email from home. As 9:00 A.M. came and went, I worried about running late. I wanted to get into the office, but news coverage speculating about McCain's choice for his vice-presidential nominee kept me glued to the TV. The BlackBerry note I had started was to my friend Kent Lucken who lived in Boston, and it was intended to congratulate and welcome him back to the campaign trail. It looked to me like former Massachusetts governor Mitt Romney would soon be announced as McCain's running mate. A longtime supporter, Kent had close ties to Romney and had helped him during the Republican primaries. But I hadn't heard from my old friend since his candidate had left the race.

Earlier reports suggested that on the short list with Romney were Minnesota Governor Tim Pawlenty and former Arkansas governor Mike Huckabee. However, Huckabee dashed any hopes attached to his candidacy with a statement that he had not been vetted for the job. Pawlenty, too, was apparently not in contention. This left only Romney. His reentry would mean Kent was back in the game. Still, I decided to wait and see for sure what the outcome of the announcement would be before I hit *send* on my BlackBerry.

Reporters began hinting that McCain may surprise everyone by instead choosing a little-known, first-term governor from Alaska named Sarah Palin. Now I really couldn't pull myself away from the television. I talked myself into believing that on the morning after our convention, I could get away with staying home a bit longer to watch the announcement. After another hour of channel surfing and sifting through the cable news chatter, networks began to cut over to the Republican rally in Dayton, Ohio, where the introduction of their VP choice would be made. McCain and his team certainly deserved credit: they had kept their secret. Now the event was getting the buzz it was due.

If our convention looked majestic the night before, I was watching something very different now. My television screen took me inside what looked like a small gymnasium, though it turned out that there were actually fifteen thousand people crowded inside Dayton's Nutter Center. The atmosphere had a folksy appeal, almost like a school pep rally, but it was a scene everyday people could relate to.

A team of cheerleaders warmed up the raucous crowd to set the mood for the big moment. Then it happened. McCain and his family walked onstage to a rock-star greeting from the audience. I looked for clues in my television picture as to whom he might have chosen, but saw no immediate evidence. His initial remarks were equally unhelpful.

Then, things came into focus. The person Senator McCain began to fawn over, and the one who ultimately burst into the arena to thunderous applause, wasn't Mitt Romney. It was someone I barely recognized at all. I'm pretty sure I let out a hoot intended to alert my wife in the next room. The Arizona Republican had chosen a total unknown to be his running mate. McCain actually picked Palin.

I watched, aghast. Sarah Palin's political résumé included less than two years as governor of a state that wasn't even the size of our candidate's state senate district. Her national security experience was limited to her command of the Alaska National Guard, a responsibility that came with her brief half-term tenure as the state's chief executive. Prior to that, she had been the mayor of a town that had a population smaller than our political rallies—smaller even than the one I was currently watching on TV. At that moment, it appeared to me that McCain had really jumped the shark with this call.

Later, during a brisk walk to the office, I slowly talked myself out of my giddy state. These were smart people we were up against. They had to know something that wasn't immediately apparent here. I turned the event over in my mind, replaying the words and images. They had leaned into some interesting aspects of her background for a Republican figure. A former union member married to a "proud member of the United Steel Workers Union." A hockey mom. The daughter of an elementary school teacher. The current governor and former mayor who they claimed had a proven history of reaching across the aisle to get things done.

I had to admit that Palin herself had been impressive—very impressive, in fact. Her remarks were sharply written and solidly delivered. She owned that podium and confidently claimed her place on the stage with a comment in her speech that she was the rightful beneficiary of women who had fought for and won the right to vote eighty-eight years before. It was really quite powerful.

She then craftily shifted the focus toward two notable pioneers before her, paying warm tribute to, of all people, Democrats Hillary Clinton and Geraldine Ferraro. She took listeners back to Denver just days before, where Hillary had rightly boasted that she'd left eighteen million cracks in our nation's highest and hardest glass ceiling. Palin bellowed to raucous applause, "But it turns out the women of America aren't finished yet, and we can shatter that glass ceiling once and for all."

They were going after the Clinton coalition, I realized. Honestly, that was a soft spot for us. Even in the afterglow of the convention, I was worried that we had not fully achieved the unity we sought. Hillary was fabulous, but it didn't feel like we had completely closed the deal with her supporters. Still, it was hard for me to believe that someone with Palin's profile could actually succeed in luring the Clinton following away from us.

When I got to the office, I was very careful to present a poker face to our staff. There was something here that we had to take very seriously.

Eighteen Days of Sarah Palin

As soon as the announcement was made, Bill Burton, our gritty deputy press secretary, pushed out a statement to the media that read, "Today, John McCain put the former mayor of a town of 9,000 with zero foreign policy experience a heartbeat away from the presidency." That ended up being the only hard fastball we directed Sarah Palin's way.

Three days later, the Republicans gathered for their national convention in St. Paul, Minnesota. It was an unremarkable affair except for two great weather events: Hurricanes Gustav and Sarah. Gustav was the one I'm sure the McCain people wished had never blown ashore. It revived unfortunate memories of President Bush's mishandling of Katrina three years prior. Governor Palin blew in on the third night to accept her nomination as vice president. She lit up the room with an electrifying performance. More than thirty-seven million people tuned in to watch, surpassing anything Hillary and Joe Biden could muster the week before and falling just short of Senator Obama's viewership numbers during his acceptance speech. There was no arguing that Sarah Palin captivated America. Some loved her and some loved to hate her, but everyone was talking about the Republican Party's explosive new star.

The Palin pick was game changing on many levels. For one thing, it got McCain his swagger back. For another, it abruptly evened the score after we had carefully built up a lead over the summer behind the foreign trip, the VP rollout, and the convention. Most importantly, Senator Mc-

Cain was able to quickly pivot to his newly recast image as the outsider in the race. Running as the *experience* choice wasn't working for the political veteran in an election where people were clearly yearning for change. But because McCain had also long branded himself a maverick during his career, choosing Governor Palin reminded voters of his unconventional streak. This was helpful in countering the unfavorable image of him as the candidate representing establishment Washington.

If some thought the Arizona senator's choice was a desperately thrown long ball, the political Right caught it and was now running with it. The enthusiasm spike was noticeable. Palin was his greatest gift to the Republican base. For the first time in this election, McCain's vision for the future was clear, and win or lose, it was embodied in Sarah Palin. With one single play, he succeeded in both energizing conservatives and opening a path to the middle running as a maverick. It was a uniquely rare moment in American politics: choosing Sarah Palin undoubtedly and suddenly changed the dynamics of the race.

This wasn't all bad news for us, however. Even as Palin fired up the Republican base at their party's convention, our online donations were heating up. As soon as she walked off the stage, we had our highest unsolicited contribution spike ever. The reaction to her was so profound that Rospars's shop slipped out a note to our supporters via email from Plouffe at 1 A.M., just to help prime the pump when our supporters woke the next day. Money poured in, and my BlackBerry blew up with notes from Clinton friends who were now fully behind us. Sarah Palin actually accomplished something that even Hillary Clinton couldn't fully achieve at our convention; she almost single-handedly galvanized the support of Democratic women behind our candidate.

McCain Rising

At the conclusion of the Republican convention, McCain and Palin hit the road together. Worries about McCain's past problems collecting crowds were apparently still fresh in the memories of his staffers, some of whom now seemed downright giddy over the size of the rallies this new duo was attracting. For all of the attacks their campaign had leveled at our candidate as some sort of celebrity, Palin had something that John McCain wanted—attention. The man who had to seek out audiences a month ago now had an in-house crowd builder, causing his team to profess a commitment to keeping the two closely tethered in the run-up to the election.

Things got hot fast. Their team returned to the trail ready to rumble, and we were quickly on the defensive. Our campaign stumbled through an accusation that Senator Obama had called Governor Palin a pig. In fact, Senator Obama had suggested that the new McCain-Palin *change* mantra was nothing more than "lipstick on a pig." Their campaign successfully twisted that into a bad story for us by referencing a favorite line of Palin's: the difference between a hockey mom and a pit bull is that one has lipstick. On another front, we drew fire for an ad they had launched promoting a silly notion that our candidate wanted to teach sex education to kindergartners.

The public's fascination with the freshest face in politics had grown into a frenzy. The unknown had everyone wanting to know more, which I think became part of Governor Palin's appeal. Though the hyperactive rumor mill that cranked up must have been hurtful to the Palin family, the curious speculation definitely benefited McCain. This fueled remarkable interest in her first big national press interview, a one-on-one with ABC newsman Charlie Gibson. Scheduled to air the evening of September 11, the anniversary of the terrorist attacks on our nation's soil, it was the first time Americans could sit down with Sarah Palin since she had been drafted onto the Republican ticket.

Sarah Palin's highly anticipated performance was only good enough to keep the speculation that surrounded her at a fever pitch. If you didn't like her, there was plenty to validate the opinion that she wasn't ready for national office (for example, her fumbled response to a question regarding the "Bush Doctrine"). If you were a fan, it was also easy to invest in the argument that Palin continued to be unfairly badgered by the media (for example, being questioned about something called a "Bush Doctrine"). It would have been foolish to underestimate her though. Media strategist Larry Grisolano later told me that the audience dial testing conducted during her interview broadcast showed quite clearly that everyday people really liked her.

Hanging in the Balance

Soon after the interview was aired on Gibson's program, our campaign slipped into another period of crisis. It was likely triggered in part by worries that Palin's performance was received better than any of us wanted to admit, which sparked fears of her as a threat to our election chances. The panic surfaced at headquarters in a pattern that was by now recognizable to me: it began with the proverbial untraced grenade tossed from outside by key influential supporters, and followed by the predictable taking up of arms from within by a handful of others on our staff who seemed hypersensitive to this outside turbulence. The alarm had been sounded.

Polls suddenly showed us trailing McCain by three points, which struck up the all-too-familiar chorus from our past: the candidate couldn't throw a punch; our campaign lacked the killer instinct; we couldn't hold a lead. It felt like many of our allies had quickly turned against us. Democrats in Washington blamed our campaign for jeopardizing the party's efforts at winning a filibuster-proof Senate, which required a sixty-seat majority. According to some of my Capitol Hill acquaintances, there was open resentment that our not attacking McCain more forcefully over the summer and at our convention resulted in a missed opportunity to define him before a national audience.

It didn't stop there. Our support among rank-and-file union members was also reportedly crumbling. My friends close to organized labor privately warned that, although shop stewards left union halls armed with election literature, it wasn't getting out of the trunks of their cars and into their jobsites. Big donors were also nervous that their investment was futile and failing. Our candidate was getting booed at events. Even my wife heckled me as I walked out the door each morning, shouting that we needed to fight back harder.

Plouffe must have been sensitive to the growing discontent because on September 12, he sent around a strategy memo describing "the first day of the rest of the campaign." In it, he assured our supporters that our campaign would firmly hit back against McCain's alarming tactics and "take the fight to him" on issues of importance to the American people.

In the two weeks after the arrival of Sarah Palin, I think it's fair to say that we were reeling. This was as bad as anything I had previously seen. I gave regular pep talks to my staff to keep their heads in the game. One attempt at lifting spirits inside HQ went sour when a promised and highly anticipated visit from Senator Ted Kennedy was abruptly cancelled at the last minute. Also around this time, Senator Obama and David Plouffe checked in for a long overdue all-staff call that somehow flopped. Both men were uncharacteristically flat and seemed unprepared, as if the phone meeting was a distraction from another more important matter. There was a fair bit of chatter among staff during the rest of the day expressing universal disappointment. I suspect these views were simply a function of the general crankiness that had crept into our work force. Still, if the call was meant to pull things together, we did not accomplish that objective.

Sarah Palin hit the scene with a dozen weeks left in the election. To borrow an analogy used at the time by Republican strategist and former boxer Ed Rollins, this election was a twelve-round fight. With nine weeks to go, John McCain's running mate had delivered the first three rounds for him.

We were definitely on the ropes.

View from Within

As the drama unfolded on the campaign trail, there was a growing interest in the inner-workings of the campaign among the general public. Despite the demands on me at work and at home, I relished the chance to share my experiences. I spoke to a variety of groups in these final days, including high school and university students, business groups, and even a delegation of European executives. Perhaps my most memorable talk was to a local second-grade class that visited our headquarters.

Accommodating the request of one of my staffers seemed like a fun idea when it was proposed days earlier, but now I was anxious about being away from my work. Partly because of my time pressures and also being mindful of my young audience, I decided to keep the talk short and the concepts simple. So I carefully explained to this fidgety bunch what a campaign was, how voting worked, and what I did for the organization. Then I wrapped up my talk and opened the floor to questions, expecting that from the mouths of babes some amusing banter would follow that would carry me through the day.

The first question came: "Why didn't you pick Hillary as the vice president?" I stumbled through my answer, relieved to move on to another questioner. "How are you going to be able to pay to put everyone on health care?" asked the brassy little girl in the front row. Now I was scanning the area to see if there was any press in the room. My imagination became active as I teased out a scenario in my head where I'd single-handedly lose the election with an embarrassing answer to these hyperinquisitive seven-year-olds that got recorded and went viral.

I eventually regained my footing and pulled the discussion back on track, but not before fielding another pointed question probing my opinion on big money in politics and the "ridiculous" cost of running a presidential campaign. This was a tougher crowd than my business executives from the day before. After that session, I made a rule that if I was to meet groups that included anyone under twelve I would be sure to eat all my vegetables and get extra sleep the night before.

Leading from the Middle

National headquarters was now beginning to crank up to the election's climax. The pace was fast, the floor was loud, and tensions were high. It was really crowded. We ended up stuffing people into our space like sardines in a small tin. I endured many complaints from staffers who were fed up with the elbow-to-elbow seating arrangements. Trash was everywhere. And then there were the dirty restrooms. Some people actually used facilities on other floors or down on the shopping court level at McDonalds. But we kept the campaign together until the last days, and I still viewed that as an important factor in maintaining our hallmark organizational cohesion and discipline.

Things had changed for my teams. We used to be the launch pad—the start-up incubator. There wasn't a state operation, headquarters department, or general function that we didn't have a hand in building and launching. Success at Obama for America ran through us. Now the car was built and we were the engine running through the entire campaign. Our presence was everywhere.

It was fascinating to have watched this organization grow and evolve over time. The silos were long down and we were now highly integrated. Many of my staff didn't even sit in my area anymore. This was true for all of the department directors. In our new system, we were organized into teams as much as we were departments. The new seating chart reflected that change. Most of my "fly-away" staff was assigned to one of the pods I mentioned earlier, servicing six multi-state regions across the country. Each pod, or workstation, was headed up by a national regional field director to whom they were also then accountable. Dan Jones's operations managers, for example, all met as a team at his desk first thing in the morning, but then fanned out to their respective pods for the rest of the day. Adi's team of budget analysts also sat with the departments they supported.

This integrated system made for a sensitive dynamic as most of my staff now had to balance the demands of two bosses, including a department head from my area and a manager in their new host department or regional pod. Additionally, they had to meet the needs of the stakeholders they served in the states or another area of the campaign. In that way, just about everyone who worked for me had a mix of relationships to tend, services to provide, and a budget line to manage.

For this reason, I remained fiercely focused on helping my staff command their leadership in this hyperdynamic environment. In my view, our campaign management had a direct stake in staff leadership because any failures in this regard would show up in our financial bottom line later.

Money mattered in these last weeks. We had a fragile cash-on-hand position that was complicated by the fact that we would soon have to lay out a lot of money for paid media. It could even put us temporarily in the red. This was tricky terrain for our campaign and a big responsibility for our budget team. Their success was based on everyone in my departments executing their roles with precision. I knew I could count on Marianne and Adi to fire the flare as quickly as they detected a problem in our financials. My job was to make sure there wasn't a preexisting leadership breakdown somewhere in the system that would lead to a cash crisis later.

I doggedly worked with my managers to make sure our young staffers were fully aware of the stakes associated with every transaction. If anyone who worked for me took it upon themselves to play workplace sheriff and assert authority over budgets and policies too enthusiastically, their co-workers would lose confidence in our ability to meet their needs. They would ultimately find another way to meet them, probably by going rogue. They might also escalate the problem to their supervisor, which could result in interdepartmental tensions. In other words, respond too stridently too regularly and a staffer risked death on the shop floor. Dead leaders were useless in this environment.

On the other hand, if any of my staff was too loose with their stewardship of our resources and practices, then we were vulnerable to losing control of the sizable pieces of the budget and operation each of them managed. If anyone avoided conflict too readily, or even became a full-time advocate on behalf of the stakeholder to one of our own principals, it was an indication that they were not working actively enough on our behalf. Just as I couldn't have dead leaders on the shop floor, neither could I have any that were too alive. That was an indication to me that they were too cozy with the partner department or prone to avoiding confrontation. This, too, would make them ineffectual. I needed everyone to be just enough alive to lead another day.

Each of our staffers, then, needed to be able to confront the natural conflict inherent in serving multiple stakeholders with competing demands while also being respectful and dedicated to proactively finding solutions. Leading in the middle was a skill everyone had to master. The old paradigm of one leader at a time wouldn't serve our organizational needs. In our challenging omnidirectional environment, success was based on everyone leading in every moment.

I wasn't cultivating soft skills. It was about getting work done. These were hard skills in my opinion. Thus, after all these months and with all the twists and turns of this organization, my management ethos had remained the same. I still viewed myself as one part chief executive officer, one part chief people officer, and one part fire fighter. If I properly tended to the first two, I had fewer fires to fight.

The Meltdown

On the morning of Monday, September 15, the nation's attention was nervously focused on Wall Street. Reports had swirled all weekend that investment banking giant Lehman Brothers would be seeking bankruptcy protection. Speculation was rampant regarding the possible market fallout behind what would be the largest Chapter 11 filing in U.S. history.

Very different responses to the emergent crisis on Wall Street came from the campaign trail. McCain at first issued a statement that the "fundamentals of our economy are strong," a stance he soon attempted to walk back. Days later, after initially expressing opposition to a rescue package for the financial industry, he announced plans to suspend his campaign so he could go to Washington to help write the bailout legislation. The Arizona senator brazenly challenged our candidate to follow suit. McCain next floated the idea that he would skip the first debate unless a measure was passed in Congress. He again taunted Barack to make a similar commitment.

For his part, Senator Obama was less reactive to the events as they unfolded. He dismissed the call to suddenly drop everything and return to Washington, instead sticking to the campaign trail while staying in contact with policymakers. He was particularly adamant about his intention to be at the first debate, reasoning that this was exactly the time that voters needed to hear from their candidates. Despite the forceful pressure coming from McCain, Barack never ceded his position close to the voters.

Senator McCain's new enthusiasm for the House bill under consideration was apparently not welcomed by all of his colleagues at the Capitol. The media reported that lawmakers on both sides of the aisle characterized his involvement as an effort to turn the bailout negotiations into a McCain rescue package. When the initial vote failed, the stock market plunged 777 points. McCain quickly cleared out of Washington and headed back to the campaign trail, where he could get some distance from the fallout. Several more suspense-filled days passed before a deal was finally struck. Then, on October 1, McCain joined Senators Obama and Biden on the Senate floor where all three men cast their votes supporting a new $700 billion measure.

Trouble in Camp McCain

These two weeks marked a strange reversal of fortune for the McCain campaign. During the first eighteen days of the McCain-Palin ticket, we saw the eight-point lead we took out of our convention at the start of the month collapse as soon as Republicans assembled in St. Paul a week later. By the time "Sarah Barracuda" and the McCain message bulldogs really got their teeth into us, we were actually behind. But on the heels of McCain's unfortunate reaction to the financial crisis in mid-September, Sarah Palin badly mishandled an interview with CBS News anchor Katie Couric. Footage dribbled out over several days, including features that were aired on two consecutive evening newscasts beginning September 24. Things on the campaign trail seemed to downshift into slow motion as that political train wreck played out. It looked painful: like having a root canal without the Novocain.

At the same time, money was flowing in for us. Jim Messina and I always checked in together at the end of every day, generally sometime after 9 P.M., and often closer to 10 P.M. During one of our discussions midway into September, as we were poised to blow past the all-time one-month record of $66 million we had set the month before, I confidently announced to Jim that we would shatter $100 million in donations in September. I even went so far as to brazenly suggest that we could actually hit $150 million. I was slightly embarrassed to learn that Jim later shared my provocative musings with the campaign manager. Messina eagerly reported back a day or two later that my prediction was met with a momentary pause from Plouffe, followed by a contemplative, "Well, Henry would know."

I felt a little on the hook after that and watched the fundraising results nervously every day for the rest of September. Heading into the final week, I worried we would come up well short of my forecast. All the while, outside speculation was entirely focused on whether we would break the $100 million-in-one-month barrier for the first time in American politics. It wasn't until three weeks into October—just in advance of the FEC filing deadline for the previous month—that the world learned what we had known for many days: Obama for America ended September with a record-setting $150 million cash haul.

The Gloves Stay On

Also heading into the last week of September, we had pulled ahead in the polls again and were now gaining noticeable momentum. McCain needed to deliver spectacular performances in the three upcoming presidential debates beginning on September 26 in order to pull his team out of the spiral. He didn't. In fact, the failure of his debate prep operation was badly exposed. During the entire ninety minutes of the first meeting, McCain didn't once look at Barack. This offered reporters an unflattering story line about Senator McCain's temperament that circulated relentlessly in the news over the ensuing days. In the second debate on October 7, McCain quickly resurrected the controversy from the first matchup with another flourish of contempt directed our candidate's way, this time brusquely referring to his rival as "that one." Making matters worse, the town hall format for this particular meeting also exposed the Arizona senator for pacing around the stage while our candidate spoke. Thus, the McCain "wander" offered additional laugh lines to late night comics and filled humorous monologues and sketches much of the following week.

But it was his fascination with a man dubbed Joe the Plumber in the final debate and in the days following that had me really scratching my head. America had been introduced to Joe just days before that final October 15 debate, after he had stopped Senator Obama, who was door-knocking residents in his Ohio neighborhood. Their ensuing exchange over tax policy quickly became news and the event caught McCain's attention. As with Palin, the Republican presidential hopeful once again found a way to lift a fresh face from obscurity to sudden celebrity. John talked about Joe endlessly in that last debate.

The whole thing smacked of a grand gimmick. To begin with, Joe's real name was Sam Wurzelbacher. We also soon learned Joe wasn't actually a plumber; he wasn't licensed anyway. In fact, I thought Joe was a plant when he first crossed Barack's path—that he'd somehow been put up to the whole thing by the McCain campaign. Then, I heard a rumor that Joe once got a speeding ticket outside of Palin's Wasilla, Alaska, and instantly became intrigued by the thought of a previous connection between the two somehow. I waited eagerly for my hunch to be validated in the media but of course nothing came of it. Regardless, my own conspiratorial musings drove home for me just how much the Joe sideshow had further clouded McCain's already erratic message at this critical moment when closing arguments were being teed up for voters.

Now, with the debates behind us and momentum in our favor, the fight would shift to the field for the final stretch.

The Leadership Election

Many claimed after the fact that America's economic meltdown in mid-September positioned Obama to win. I maintain that our candidate positioned himself where he needed to be to achieve victory. There is a difference. One argument is invested in Barack as the beneficiary of external factors, while mine credits his assertiveness.

It's true that polls had long showed voters had more confidence in our candidate's capacity to manage the country's economy. But the Wall Street collapse didn't turn this into a referendum on who would better manage the economy. Rather, it was a disruptive moment in the campaign that suddenly caused voters to focus on how the two men managed their leadership. Ultimately, it was Senator Obama who emerged as the leadership candidate in an election that became about leadership.

To demonstrate this, I have a framework that I believe reflects how voters make judgments about the candidates standing before them. It is based on three criteria; I present it as a triangle. On one side of the triangle is *self-definition*. On the second side is *credibility*. And on the third is *competence*. Thus, the candidate who most convincingly meets the tests of all three sides of this triangle has the greatest chance for success. Using this framework, we can compare how the two men performed, beginning with the financial crisis.

Side 1: Define Thyself
Again, the first side of the triangle is focused on how the candidates defined themselves—particularly against one another. There is a rule in

politics: "Define thyself lest you be defined." The job of the campaign is to define your candidate, and to define theirs too. In our case, Senator Obama staked out a clear position as the candidate who represented hope and change, while typecasting McCain as the one who stood for continuity with the existing establishment.

The Arizona senator, on the other hand, never fully settled on a specific posture. It wasn't clear whether McCain wanted to be the experienced candidate who battled his way to the front of the 2008 Republican pack or the maverick from the 2000 election. He vacillated between both, placing the two sides of his own political personality at war against each other. It often appeared as if McCain's inner-maverick was striking back against the Washington-insider devil on his shoulder. That made it difficult for him to maintain a convincing and commanding position on this edge of the triangle because his decision-making was random, disjointed, and prone to whichever John McCain showed up on a given day. It's hard to lead with two minds.

Side 2: Credibility Counts

The second side of the triangle is credibility. On the campaign trail, you must always have or work toward building a base. An important factor for the candidate, then, is the alignment of creed and deed—self-definition and action—because this is how you hold your credibility within a universe of voters. People want to know where you stand. This can play out around stated policy positions or issue priorities, of course, but it can also be based quite literally on where you position yourself in the eyes of those whose votes you seek.

For example, in the days after the September 15 financial crisis, the bottom-up outlook that appealingly defined Senator Obama's candidacy since the beginning of the election was fortified by his insistence on maintaining a position close to the voters on the campaign trail. Barack's actions were consistent with his image as a man of the people.

McCain's reaction, fleeing the campaign trail to take refuge inside the Capitol where he could help write legislation, was at odds with the maverick image he wanted to project. Furthermore, his establishment instincts offered a favorable contrast for our candidate. Senator Obama's was the confident voice emanating from the crowds surrounding him in the communities he visited, while McCain's was the muffled monotone echoing from the halls of Washington. Despite McCain's best efforts to get our candidate to abandon his proximity to the voters—first by urging him to join in suspending his campaign and returning to Capitol Hill, then challenging him to also skip the first debate—Senator Obama held his ground. His reaction fit neatly into the choice we had long framed for voters as this election being about change versus more of the same.

Side 3: Mind Your CEOness

Finally, competence is the third leadership criterion on the triangle. On the campaign trail, the candidate's integrity, management style, decision-making, and record of achievement are constantly under examination. Furthermore, you are judged on your ability to lead in the organizational environment of the moment.

The reactions of the two candidates in the wake of the economic failure communicated distinctly different information to voters about the decisiveness of both men. The crisis exposed McCain's reluctance to focus on more than one thing at a time. Additionally, his reflexively bounding back and forth between the campaign trail and the nation's Capitol conveyed an impulsive streak. All the while, Senator Obama demonstrated resolute confidence as a CEO.

Barack asserted from the very earliest days of the campaign that if voters wanted to understand what kind of president he would be, they should watch how he ran his campaign. Behind his leadership, our staff backed up his words by competently handling the rapid-fire demands coming our way. Looking through the new leadership prism for this election, voters saw two very different CEOs emerge. One came across as unpredictable—even episodic—as he presided over an organization that seemed to regularly lurch. The other consistently projected steadiness and command.

Answer Risk

Other events on the campaign trail, when viewed through the leadership-triangle framework, reinforced these same perceptions of the respective candidates' executive decision-making. Take the selections by the candidates of their respective running mates in August. These weren't inconsequential decisions to voters. The VP nominee would be the most important hiring decision the two men would make in the campaign.

Sarah Palin was clearly the choice of maverick McCain. But this again interfered with McCain's image as the experienced choice on the self-definition side of the triangle. Teaming with the unseasoned Alaska governor undercut his most important argument: that his rival, Barack Obama, would bring a thin political résumé to the Oval Office. It was ultimately confusing for voters.

It could be argued that McCain's nod to Palin was aimed more at lifting his own credibility with a specific segment of voters. Remember, the second side of the triangle focuses on the candidate's standing with a desired community or constituency. If this was the case, McCain's running mate selection may have seemed brilliant. Palin clearly energized the Republican base where he hadn't. But Senator McCain also had an enthusiasm problem with moderate Republicans and independent voters. Unfortunately for him and his campaign, despite early signals that Palin might woo Hillary Clinton's supporters, the Alaska governor was unwilling to leave the extreme right edge of the political spectrum. Swing voters would have to come around to her instead. Governor Palin was very precise about where she positioned her leadership, and it wasn't near the middle. This was a serious problem for the McCain campaign. Holding Palin close to the base might have worked if the candidate himself could have pulled in the center, but McCain struggled to generate any excitement at all.

This leads to how the choice of Sarah Palin as his VP nominee reflected on McCain's CEOness, *competence* being the third side of the triangle. McCain was hurt by a running perception that his choice was made brashly and at the very last minute. This opened his campaign up to questions about the vetting process surrounding her selection, and it intensified the scrutiny of Palin's readiness to step suddenly into the nation's top job. Finally, Sarah Palin seemed to be a divisive influence inside their organization. Incessant rumors in the media about the emergence of dual power centers and a rift between the McCain and Palin camps did little to give the impression that this was an effective hiring decision.

Ultimately, picking up a second maverick opened up fresh worries over what McCain's rogue ticket might mean in the Oval Office. While Sarah Palin's dramatic entrance initially appealed to the hopes and aspirations of many Republicans, her uneven performance mixed with the nagging doubts about her qualifications made her selection representative of all that was wrong with the McCain campaign.

Joe Biden had a different effect on our ticket. Where Barack's inexperience may have been a worry for voters, Senator Biden's long Washington credentials were helpful to our candidate. Also, the process behind Biden's selection reaffirmed the perception of our operation as competent and precise in its execution. And our new colleague, even given his many years in the Senate, couldn't have been more unassuming on his way in the door. Once inside, Senator Biden contributed positively to the harmonious atmosphere that was the hallmark of our organization. We had only one camp and one power center in the Obama campaign.

In the final analysis, Joe Biden had the kind of background and experience that could help relax concerns about our candidate. The unintended consequence for McCain adding Palin to his ticket was that it instantly positioned him, not Senator Obama, as the dangerous choice in this election. For us, tempered with a dose of Joe Biden, Barack's *change* drumbeat seemed suddenly less threatening to voters.

This triangle framework is not merely a convenient way to explain the events of the day. Throughout the election, different elements of our organization contributed to the narrative associated with each of these three leadership criteria: our candidate's self-definition, his credibility, and his competence. Whether it was our message and paid media teams reinforcing the candidate's image, our constituency and communications teams connecting his values to voters, or those of us focused on the management of our operation, we all had a place on the triangle in every moment.

I often turned on my television late at night to find chief strategist David Axelrod vigorously sparring with a news host or an opposition spokesperson to define our candidate and contrast him against McCain. David Plouffe had wide responsibilities in our campaign, but I regarded him first and foremost as our chief optics officer. Barack's credibility in the eyes of voters, including how he was presented to the electorate by the press, was David's primary charge. And when it came to the integrity and performance of the business of Obama for America, I viewed that as my job. I worked hard every day to ensure that Barack had a campaign behind him that lifted his credibility with voters as a supremely capable CEO.

This positioned our campaign in the final days to be right where we wanted.

12

Close the Deal

NOVEMBER 4, 2008: *"[To] the best campaign team ever assembled in the history of politics—you made this happen, and I am forever grateful for what you've sacrificed to get it done."—Barack Obama, from his election night speech at Grant Park in Chicago*

The End of the Road

The night before the election I got home at midnight. Three hours later I was up again and shuffling around my apartment. By 4 A.M., I was back out the door. Before I left, I fumbled around in the kitchen for a pen and a piece of paper. Having found both, I scribbled some words for my wife and left the note on the counter for her to see when she woke up. I wrote:

> *Dear Sine,*
> *Thank you for taking a chance on me once again. Our new life begins after today.*
>
> *Love, Henry*
> *(The former COO at Obama for America)*

Sine had left my Boiler Room credential hanging neatly on the front door of the apartment. I appreciated her for that, as I would have surely forgotten it otherwise. The Boiler Room was where the action would be at HQ on this particular day. Only a very small number of staff had been issued the laminated badge that would grant them access to the secured and guarded private space on the nineteenth floor. Over the past few weeks, the Boiler Room had been prepared to serve as our national command center for this day.

It was Election Day morning, and my walk to work through the dark streets and over the bridge across the Chicago River was eerily quiet. I felt confident about our chances, but I also noticed the butterflies in my stomach. I could see the steam of my breath in the cold November air. I noticed that my breathing was heavy, just as it had been the very first time I walked toward that downtown high-rise after getting out of a cab on busy Michigan Avenue. This was going to be a long day, but at least I wouldn't have to take the time to go vote. I took care of that duty several days earlier, when I managed to tear myself away from the chaos of headquarters to stand in a two-hour line at an early voting site across town. I passed the time in line answering a flurry of emails and busily fielding calls on my BlackBerry.

During my walk to the office, my mind was on the events of the previous two days. Our Nevada state director, Terence Tolbert, had died from a sudden heart attack. He was only forty-four years old. I didn't know him personally, but I was well aware of the great work he was doing. He left behind a young family, which was heartbreaking to contemplate. Then on Monday night, I learned that one of our very dedicated volunteers in Florida was accidentally struck down by a car at an intersection while participating in a campaigning activity. The details were still sketchy in HQ, but I was told that he was seventy-five years old, married, and a very enthusiastic supporter. And of course, there was the sad news that, on Sunday, Senator Obama's beloved grandmother passed away. These events were a reminder, once again, that behind the slogans and rallies and the bustle of everyday campaign activities, this was all very human stuff. As the polls opened across the country this morning, there were families associated with our campaign that were grieving those they had lost.

Later, when the will of the voters was finally revealed, the staff and volunteers of the losing campaign would confront a different type of grief. I have known that particular feeling. It's surprisingly wrenching.

Even the winners experience a form of anguish after it sinks in that the purpose and community, which was such a prominent part of the campaign life they had come to know, will suddenly vanish. The intense personal emotions that accompanied the work—sometimes threatening to distract from it—were what I dealt with every day. Campaign management, in the end, is about people. In the rancorous back and forth of politics, that somehow often gets lost.

Winding Down

The eleventh floor was lifeless when I arrived at the office. I strolled around headquarters that morning before others arrived, taking advantage of my last few moments alone with the house my team had built. This would be the last day of its existence. I could see there would be a lot of trash left behind. The place had really become a mess. We would have a small wind-down unit stay behind after the election to shut down headquarters, close the books, and oversee the roll-up of all the offices and operations in the field. Win or lose, that was my final job to manage for the campaign. It wasn't the most glamorous one, but it was the post-election role that I wanted and had long expected. It was the responsibility of the COO to close out the campaign.

To help me with that monumental job, I hired Josh Gray just weeks before Election Day to be the assistant COO. I knew I was exhausted and would mentally collapse as soon as the voting was over. I needed a wind-down manager to help drive us through this complex and laborious process. I wanted the execution of the shutdown to be crisp and mistake-free—nothing that would end up in the press. Bills had to be paid, offices restored to proper condition, and all of our vans across the country returned to leasing companies.

I was proud of myself for that hiring decision. Josh had long been a valued volunteer and I was impressed with his work on the Campaign Mystery Shopper project we had done together earlier in the campaign. I needed someone I could trust to dig into the details of the wind-down who wouldn't be distracted by the activities of the election. Josh quietly interviewed operations staff in advance and built an elaborate shutdown task list with day-by-day deadlines. In fact, he was already working with some of my staff to begin execution of some of those chores on the day of the election.

If we won, Chief of Staff Jim Messina and Senior Advisor Pete Rouse would immediately move on to help command a very large and complex operation that would prepare and plan the new Obama administration, officially known as the Presidential Transition Team (PTT). There would be no respite for anyone tapped to join them in that monumental effort. I had already been working with representatives from PTT for a few weeks to fill out their rosters of open positions. Some members of my staff were actually scheduled to leave for Washington to join them early Wednesday morning, just hours after the election results came in. Anyone who wasn't going on to PTT might ultimately end up on the Presidential Inaugural Committee (PIC). PIC was the operation that would prepare the vast array of formal parties and the ceremony to swear in the new president on January 20.

Things would slow down for me, however. It was one advantage of staying for the wind-down. I was looking forward to spending more time at home with my family and enjoying the holidays. But I didn't know how long the wind-down activities would carry me or what I would do next to generate income, so I had to get a career plan quickly. Chicago wasn't our home, and if we lost the election, I faced the prospect of soon being out of work with no immediate possibilities for new employment. Even if we won, my future was uncertain. But my wife was pregnant again, and my family was counting on me. Now I worried I had the same bad economy awaiting me that we had featured in all of our recent election talk. These thoughts added to the pressures of the day.

Eighteen Days

On the morning of the election, there was every reason to feel hopeful. I wasn't certain about a favorable outcome, but I felt like we were right where we wanted to be. This was not necessarily a comforting thought, however. I had experienced similar pangs of nervous confidence on past election days, only to end up on the losing side at the end of the night. For this reason, while there was a fair bit of exuberance building around me as the day broke and headquarters filled for one last time, I remained guarded.

Many on my team and in headquarters were hired after the primary season was over. If they didn't come from a rival camp, this would be the only election they knew in this campaign. Some had not been with us for Hillary Clinton's New Hampshire surprise back in January. Even fewer had experienced the disappointment that I did working on the 2004 election, when positive early exit polling falsely inflated the hopes of Kerry supporters and later turned out to be badly flawed. In the end, President Bush edged out Kerry in a race that came down to a couple of counties in Ohio. People forget that had Kerry won that state, the Massachusetts senator would have become president. There was also the historic election of 2000 I worked on as a volunteer, in which Bush beat Gore by a few hanging chads.

These examples motivated me throughout this campaign. I never let go of bitter losses. That feeling of being punched in the gut was what drove me to do that little bit extra every day. It's why I pushed those around me so hard. I didn't want to lose and later think about what we could have done better.

Plouffe had been similarly cautious since the last debate in mid-October. Despite McCain's strong performance, there was a growing consensus that the election was ours to lose. David recognized this and quickly pulled an all-staff conference call together with Senator Obama three days after that final debate. Both men wanted one last opportunity to check in with us. With less than three weeks left before the election, we couldn't afford to let up in the final days.

Whatever may have gone wrong with the previous conference call, they definitely nailed this one. Senator Obama spoke first, urging us to close the deal we had made with the American people. He must have witnessed something that bothered him because he tersely admonished that anyone seen high-fiving, backslapping, or acting as if this race were in the bag could expect to have an unpleasant personal conversation with him. Senator Obama was clear that this contest was far from over, and all of us needed to remain attentive and focused. He wanted us to finish what we started, and that meant we had to see this through to the very last vote.

David followed up on that point with one of his best riffs ever. "Eighteen days," he said. His monotone voice rang out unevenly from the many desk speakers and telephone earpieces across the otherwise quiet and oddly motionless building. "A lot can happen in eighteen days," he continued.

Plouffe reminded staff about the eighteen days following our Iowa win, when some in the media began to prematurely position our candidate as the presumptive nominee. We went on to lose New Hampshire and then split Nevada. Going into the last of the early state races, there was open skepticism about our ability to close the deal in South

Carolina. David also reminisced about Super Tuesday, a day that many speculated we would lose. Not only did we deliver a strong performance, we won all eleven contests that followed during the next two weeks.

But good days gave way to bad ones. David revisited the rocky road leading to Texas and Ohio on March 4, the Reverend Wright pounding in the media following our Pennsylvania loss, and the last two and a half weeks of the primary season when Clinton kept winning races even after her mathematical odds of getting the nomination were virtually nonexistent.

Finally, Plouffe recalled the healthy eight-point lead we took out of our convention, only to watch it slip away after the announcement of the new Republican VP nominee in Dayton. He remembered the ensuing period leading to the market collapse as the eighteen days of Sarah Palin. Sounding the same urgency as Senator Obama, Plouffe pointed out that anyone who doubted the possibilities of what could happen in the last eighteen days of this election need only look back at the campaign calendar.

Eighteen days. That talk now seemed like ages ago.

Fire Fighter

As we came out of the final debate on October 15, the polls showed us surging ahead into the double-digits. Republicans, on the other hand, had pulled up stakes in Maine, Wisconsin, and Michigan. Money was tightening over there and the battleground map was suddenly shrinking in our favor.

The campaign trail had gotten really hot. The crowds around McCain and Palin looked increasingly agitated. Perhaps this was evidence that, despite Palin's strong performance against an equally impressive Joe Biden in the VP debate earlier in the month, their supporters saw no real way back into this race. Regardless, the sharp rhetoric coming from the Republican duo seemed intentionally aimed at fanning these emotions.

I was personally alarmed at the news headlines his campaign generated each night when I tuned in to watch the day's recap on TV. The speeches by McCain and Palin were edgy to say the least, but it was the jeers coming from some of the audience members around them that were chilling. In one clip, references to our candidate sparked loud taunts such as "Kill him!" and "Terrorist!" Things were definitely getting out of hand.

At first, McCain seemed willing to roll with it. But soon even he looked out of place at his own rallies. On at least one occasion, he was rebuked by one of his attendees demanding that he "pledge to represent our anger." The crowd rants became so intense that, in another instance, Senator McCain took it upon himself to defend our candidate against a charge by an audience member that he was a terrorist. This sparked a stirring of boos.

Just minutes later, he pulled the microphone from the hands of another upset supporter, rebuffing her remark that Senator Obama was an Arab. This offered a compelling contrast between the two candidates, as every night, television sets across America depicted very different scenes. One showed Barack before large, adoring crowds; the other had McCain in front of smaller, angrier ones.

Campaign Hothouse

I was feeling the heat directly around me as well. Heading into the last weeks of October, I was in full emergency-response mode. In mid-October, three of our field offices in as many days received mail containing dangerous-looking substances. A small team from HQ was working with those offices and with the necessary local and federal authorities, but this was an alarming development. I became worried that the fiery emotions on the campaign trail were creating a dangerous situation for staff and volunteers in our field offices. In the wake of these incidents, I put the final touches on a memo for our sizable staff—now approaching six thousand—alerting everyone to be cautious with any envelope or package that had unusual labeling, excessive postage, uneven form, or evidence of white powder or other visible substances. Any suspicious activity was to be immediately reported to the authorities and to the emergency email address that went directly to Dan Jones.

I was also focused on another ominous development in advance of our upcoming FEC filings at the end of October, this one playing out in the media. At issue was a charge long circulating in the conservative blogosphere that our system for receiving credit card contributions did not safeguard against potentially fraudulent activity and that we were therefore willingly receiving bogus donations. Our processes were completely FEC compliant and we had an extensive back-end system for addressing malicious activity. But these rumblings were the gasoline that erupted into flames after being sparked by a story in the *New York Times* on October 9.

The article, which highlighted the challenges to campaigns of receiving questionable online donations in an outdated federal compliance system, used our most recently posted FEC report as the source for much of its analysis. McCain's campaign was also mentioned for similar problems, but I was aggravated that we figured so prominently in this piece. We weren't fingered for unseemly activity. In fact, the story rightly pointed out that the related issues were a very small part of our intake, and the quoted watchdog sources mostly focused their critique on the system's deficiencies. Still, I was distressed. Our operation was becoming a media story for the first time in this campaign.

At first blush, this was an annoying story and one that would not lead to any great shift in the election dynamic. The problem for me was that our upcoming FEC filings on October 20 (for September) and October 23 (for the period of October 1 to 15) were going to invite further scrutiny of our reporting. This would be complicated by the revelation that two-thirds of our record $150 million for September came through our online channels. The reports being compiled by our compliance team would be the largest FEC filing in history, the second eclipsing 175,000 pages. The reporting schedule was also compressing in front of Election Day, which increased the burden on our finance and compliance operations. We had bulked up our efforts in recent weeks by putting more eyes, more search tools, and more capacity into the backroom operation to keep up with the flood of donations into our system. But this kept the pressure high on many of our staff in those final days.

Cakewalk

During these last days of the campaign, the loud hum of activity on our floor stopped uncharacteristically one afternoon to accommodate a very special celebration. Dante arrived at headquarters late in the afternoon sporting a blue button with a large ribbon on his tiny shirt that read simply: 1st Birthday.

Still a novice walker, Dante dropped his hand from mine as soon as he reached the HQ floor and clumsily walked solo along the cleared pathway, cooing and singing to himself the whole way as he motored along. He seemed unaware of the cheers that broke out along his route, which was lined with desks on either side of him. Smatterings of applause were interrupted with shouts of "Happy birthday, Dante!" and "Go, Dante!" as staff interrupted their busy chores to acknowledge him as he passed by.

Beginning at the front reception desk, Dante first made his way through headquarters operations where Pete Dagher and company sat; then on he went past Heather Higginbottom, Carlos Monje, Danielle Gray, Larry Strickling, and the gang in policy. Dante cut through communications—with press on one side and research on the other. The crew in scheduling and advance offered a standing ovation from the back as he motored by. Next, after he got past the First Lady and VP operations, he turned the corner in front of Katie Johnson and Kristin Sheehy who'd both always received him warmly. He darted past campaign management—where Plouffe had a small office next to a larger one shared by Messina and Rouse—then he cruised alongside the room that was the 270 nerve center hosting Hildebrand, Carson, O'Malley Dillon, and Political Director Patrick Gaspard. Dante then made his way through the long stretch of pods that comprised the 270 operation. He arrived at my work area to the loudest applause and scooted toward Monika Juska, who took his hand and led Dante to the party area she had prepared for him at the end of the pathway. He lumbered through new media to more cheers before he got to Smoot's finance department, where his mom was hastily putting the final touches on the site for his little bash.

As a dad, there couldn't have been a more thoughtful gesture coming from the more than two hundred of my co-workers who broke away from the demands of their work, only a week and a half before the election, to come over and wish my son a happy birthday. My absence from home during his first year made Dante the campaign's orphan who the staff had kindly adopted. He held the distinction of being the only child born during the campaign who also turned one before Election Day. Our staff generously threw him a big party to celebrate, complete with Winnie-the-Pooh cake and a time capsule for him to open when he turns seventeen—just days before the 2024 election.

One by one, staffers came forward to offer up campaign memorabilia that they slipped into a large trunk during the time-capsule ceremony. There were even handwritten notes from people I had never met, field organizers who wanted to share their personal experience from working in a given state for this candidate in our historic effort. The last item to be placed inside was a letter I wrote. In it, I expressed for the first time my own confidence in our chances on Election Day. Though my wife and I never had any plans or aspirations to work in the administration if we were to win, I do remember writing, "Who knows? Maybe a year from now you will be playing on the White House lawn."

Election Day

And now it was finally here! Election Day is like none other in a campaign. We had seen our way through the scheduled fifty-seven primary and caucus races during the first five months of the calendar year, but now a similar five-month span separated us from our last contests back on June 3. I realized that I missed the excitement of Election Day. Suddenly it was back, like an old familiar friend. During the primaries, everyone on my staff dressed up for the big day. It was a tradition born during the earliest races. On this day, the gang again looked sharp in their finest business attire as they trickled into work.

Nonstop Election Day news coverage blared from the large televisions and monitors that dotted the floor and walls throughout headquarters. I had also been given access to a portal on my laptop, which would reveal the sensitive exit poll data that would pour into our Boiler Room. But even as campaign workers and volunteers were busy across the country, election days were always slow for me. At this point, my job was done. There was nothing left to build and launch. Resources had been pushed out to where they needed to be. The only difference on this particular day was that we might have to spend last-minute money in the field to help our get-out-the-vote effort. Jen O'Malley Dillon and Jim Messina worked closely together in the Boiler Room to evaluate reports coming in from the field and assess our needs.

Jim had a sizable pot of money to work with going into Election Day. This was made possible by a last-minute blast of online donations. In the final days of the campaign, we cut down on our online fundraising efforts and instead pointed our website visitors to get-out-the-vote (GOTV) pages. Marianne and I still worried that the donations had trickled to a point that it threatened our end-of-campaign targets so I made a hard plea to Plouffe for a late appeal to our supporters. He was reluctant to interrupt GOTV but finally agreed to an email prepared by Rospars that had tested remarkably well. It was a well-crafted bulletin using Marianne as a messenger to explain the complexity of GOTV and asking our backers to help us fund the costly operations that were so critical in those last hours.

It will long be remembered as the "Markowitz Surge," so named by Joe because it generated a few million dollars that spared Jim and I from any more heartburn on that last day. Money became one less thing for us to worry about. I originally anticipated that the two of us would be engaged in a litany of conversations about what we could afford to spend as the hours progressed, but thanks to our supporters, he was armed with all the money he needed. I think we only checked in together once or twice that day, when Jim wanted to drop some extra cash on Pennsylvania to keep things out of McCain's reach there. That last financial push was just one way our loyal backers helped us close the deal.

The game was on the ground now as the country was buzzing with campaign activity, the scale of which had never been previously seen. The battle was in its final stages, and highly complex operations that had been planned for months were afoot. In neighborhoods everywhere, volunteers were hopping out of vans for both candidates with orders from their precinct captains to find previously identified supporters and make sure they got to the polls. A flurry of paid ads saturated the airwaves, and the Internet was alight with voters searching for last-minute clues as to whom they should vote for or to find nearby polling places.

It may all seem random to the casual observer, but when done right, this is a day that is carefully choreographed long in advance. My colleague in the advance department, Ellie Schafer, called it "running the play." You spend months planning, preparing, and practicing. On Election Day, it all comes down to execution.

Then, the best organization wins.

Grant Park

As Election Day faded into the evening, I was awed at what we had built. Only eighteen months had passed since the birth of this massive organization, back when we were hiring our first staff and getting computers out of boxes. These were the last moments of its life as it spun itself out in a maze of voter contact activity on the ground and a blaze of ads shooting over the airwaves. The next day, it would be lifeless. The streets would quiet again, and things would return to normal.

Around 8 P.M., I called my wife to have her come down to headquarters. The pop of champagne corks provided background noise as I dialed her number. I was among the last to come to terms with the idea that we would actually win. It still seemed too early to celebrate. I never fully lost that anxious feeling from the election night in 2004, when some of us working on the race huddled together around computer monitors until sometime after 10 P.M. to watch the county-by-county reports from Ohio where the Bush-Kerry battle was ultimately narrowly decided.

Now, with Pennsylvania having just been called for us, I finally began to let myself believe. Sine had been through past elections with me and said over the phone that she hadn't liked the way the early results were going. She eventually changed the channel to the Food Network to pass the time until I called. As soon as we hung up, she and baby Dante were out the door, but it seemed like forever waiting for them to arrive given they were only a short walk away.

Unbeknownst to me, Sine was stuck outside the building that she had so easily accessed during her many past visits. I forgot that the entrance she typically used had been closed off to the public today. In the chaos and confusion, Monika Juska had to go rescue her. Ultimately, my wife succeeded in talking her way past security by showing the Obama Baby staff ID that Dante always wore to work. When she finally made it inside and up to the eleventh floor, Sine noticed a strikingly different atmosphere from what she was used to at headquarters. It was festive, and staff was uncharacteristically relaxed.

We didn't have time to hang out, as the senior staff shuttle was soon departing for Grant Park where Barack would deliver his acceptance speech. I think I was in a state of shock, and things were happening fast. I wasn't fully confident that I understood the arrangements, so I pulled away from Kevin Malover, who had come down to HQ to congratulate me, and asked one of my most reliable longtime aides, Lindsay Masimore Mueller, to help escort my family to our ride. I was still in a daze as she confidently led us through the bustle and off the floor, but I was suddenly and sharply broken from my fog the moment we stepped off the elevator and into the building lobby. There, we were greeted by enthusiastic applause coming from the friendly building and security staff that had so generously accommodated us for the better part of two years.

Lindsay quickly pushed through the swirling crowd in the lobby and led us to a spot just outside the building where we caught our specially designated trolley. As our vehicle made its way onto the streets that had been emptied of all other traffic, it suddenly became quiet. We turned onto Lake Shore Drive, normally a busy thoroughfare but now oddly wide open, and our trolley rambled slowly alone on the vast stretch of highway. In a hushed voice, I assured my wife that all signs were good. Dante rested peacefully in my arms as I presented her with a briefing of the top-level numbers. Honestly, though, I think I was still trying to convince myself of our victory.

It was dark, but the outline of Lake Michigan ran along the left side of the trolley to the east. To the west, as we came over a small hill, a great glow emerged. Approaching it more closely, a continuous blazing white light illuminated the thousands of people who had already gathered in Grant Park. As soon as I saw it, my heart skipped a beat. It was shocking. The spectacular crowd filled the view in the windows to our right as we drove along. It was an impressive scene that I will never forget.

Once inside the park and off the trolley, the three of us wandered down a lighted path that led to a private, tented area. On our way, overjoyed well-wishers grabbed my right hand to shake it; people slapped my back and offered hugs of sincere congratulations. Many I knew, but there were a number I didn't recognize at all. We were like movie stars going to our film premiere.

My badge granted us full access to the massive backstage tent complex. We freely strolled from the senator's tent where Oprah Winfrey and her entourage were gathered, to that of the VP nominee, before finally settling on a friends and family tent that seemed to have the most life. There we found an open table immediately next to one occupied by Brad Pitt. He very graciously made himself available to supporters and volunteers, who bashfully approached to ask if they could pose with the Hollywood movie star for a picture. The activities at his table offered interesting entertainment, though our attention was occasionally pulled to the other side of the tent, where such recognizable political figures as Tom Daschle, Rahm Emanuel, Jessie Jackson, Jr., and Chicago mayor Richard Daley randomly appeared.

Our need for food overcame our interest in people-watching, so we gave up our prime seating to go forage. This took us into another section of the large tent where an even livelier party was underway. Behind the loud hum of the enthusiastic chatter, television monitors were trained on the up-to-the-minute election and polling coverage. We continued to receive occasional congratulations from our neighbors at the new post we took up standing alongside a tall table in the congested space.

Suddenly, a wave of applause and cheers erupted from outside, where the crowd was gathered. It whooshed through and enveloped our tent, surging like a hard-charging train. It was thunderous. Confused and quickly trying to make sense of the commotion, I glanced up at the television above us to see what caused this outburst. Dante was cuddled neatly in my left arm where I stood, so I tugged on my wife's sleeve with my free hand and directed her attention to the screen just behind her. With polls having just closed in Washington, Oregon, California, and the senator's home state of Hawaii, TV networks were calling the election for Barack Obama. I still can't describe the emotion of that moment as we embraced—me, my wife, and our baby. Competing against the loud cheering around us, I could hear Sine sobbing in my right ear as she quietly repeated over and over, "We did it!"

Acknowledgment

We couldn't stay for the entire celebration at Grant Park. Baby Dante was a trooper, but there was only so far we could push him. That was also the reason we decided not to venture out into the vast crowd, where a spot was reserved for our family near the stage. We chose to hang back and listen to the newly elected president speak from our tent. That left us alone back in the emptied space at our old table next to Brad Pitt and his small party, who had apparently also opted to avoid the crowd. We kept to ourselves, and he appeared to be enjoying his moment of peace, though he sparred enthusiastically with his friends.

Eventually, we strayed into the courtyard that connected the small tent city. In the few minutes we were out and about, I exchanged hellos with Obama confidante Valerie Jarrett. I also used my son as an excuse to meet news commentator Lawrence O'Donnell. I explained that Dante and I faithfully watched him on *Morning Joe* every day at 5:00 A.M. It was about the only "daddy 'n' me" time we ever got, I remarked. O'Donnell very kindly tolerated our intrusion and congratulated me on our successful campaign. He was quite friendly.

A few minutes later, we somehow became acquainted with Dr. Dean Ornish, whom my wife recognized from TV. Dr. Ornish was very charming, excusing himself from our conversation only long enough to embrace his friend, Oprah Winfrey, as her large party made a noticeably grand exit from the president-elect's tent. She and her entourage slowly sauntered off and vanished into the night, absorbed by the Grant Park crowd impatiently awaiting the victorious candidate.

Sine and I decided to pass up our invitation to see and congratulate the president-elect. It was getting close to midnight and hours past Dante's bedtime. He was in the earliest stages of finally melting down. As much as we wanted to stay and hear Barack's address, we knew it could be some time before he finally went onstage—though Oprah's movement toward the crowd was a clue that he was starting in that direction. We began making our way back to the trolley, following a path that was now virtually empty. Behind us a sudden cheer went up and then I detected the booming voice of my now-former boss. He acknowledged the work of our campaign, calling it the best team ever assembled in the history of politics. For me, as the chief operating officer, those were sweet words to hear.

President-elect Obama actually specifically mentioned David Plouffe in his remarks. Such direct praise and gratitude to a campaign manager had never before been expressed in a presidential acceptance speech, but it was appropriate coming from a candidate who continually demonstrated an appreciation for his organization and the people in it. Sine and I arrived at the departure point and boarded our trolley.

As we drove off, Barack's words became fainter and fainter, eventually blending unnoticeably into the night noise of Chicago.

After Words

JANUARY 20, 2009: *"... let it be said by our children's children that when we were tested we refused to let this journey end, that we did not turn back nor did we falter; and with eyes fixed on the horizon and God's grace upon us, we carried forth that great gift of freedom and delivered it safely to future generations."—Barack Obama, from his inaugural address*

Closing Shop

Early the next morning, I made my way to campaign headquarters. There wasn't much reason to be in so early, except my wife needed the baby stroller that we left in my office the night before. It was dark inside, but the television sets were still aglow, flashing images of the joyful reactions and street parties from all over the world. Otherwise, my surroundings were already unrecognizable. HQ Manager Pete Dagher and his squad had stripped the walls bare of all campaign signage, and piles of cords and equipment were evidence that Rajeev's team had begun sorting through the technology debris.

Just days before, I issued notice to all but about seventy-five staffers around the country that their last day on payroll would be the Friday after the election. The rest would have limited assignments as part of the wind-down crew. At headquarters in Chicago and offices around the country, staff was instructed to clear out their belongings in advance because they would not have access after Election Day. There was really no reason for anyone to come in after voting ended. We completed on-line checkouts and staff evaluations in the last days before the election.

For the rest of the week, the outpouring of kindness shown to my family continually surprised me. In addition to the notes that streamed in on my BlackBerry with warm words thanking me personally for electing Barack Obama president, as if I had done it all single-handedly, I also opened a package from Dr. Dean Ornish. Inside was a signed copy of his book, accompanied with a long, handwritten letter tucked inside the front cover. I was really struck by his thoughtfulness. At home, my wife received flowers and cards and care packages. Some were from friends who were enthusiastic Obama supporters and others I knew voted for John McCain. Not since Dante was born had we been the recipients of such thoughtfulness.

I was very happy that Sine was getting the recognition she deserved. In many ways, hers was a much greater sacrifice than mine, particularly because it was mostly unnoticed. Having been either pregnant or chasing after a baby (or both), she couldn't go to the big events that other spouses got to attend, and she hadn't been to any of the candidate's big rallies before Grant Park. She never even got to meet Barack. She never asked. But Sine was definitely at the front of his fan club, even if her commitment to motherhood kept her away from campaign activities. She let me pursue my dreams at no small disruption to our family.

Postpartum

Headquarters quickly became a lonely place. In less than a week, aside from the two dozen people directly around me, I felt suddenly cut off. Our small remaining staff was swallowed up once again in the huge eleventh floor space that only days ago had been unwieldy with all of the people and bustle. Now it was quiet; library quiet. Quiet like the ride to Grant Park, quiet.

I rarely strayed from our corner but was bored one afternoon and determined I should stroll the floor to see how we were progressing with the cleanup. The place was very different now. The same path Dante traveled only a few weeks earlier for his birthday victory lap now revealed only empty desks and large, growing mountains of technology and office equipment rising from the floor. In one heap was a clump of the black telephones that once graced each of our desks. In another was a giant collection of computer and phone cords. Next to that was a high stack of keyboards. The piles continued until a yellow rope of tape separated the technology collection site from a small corner where the remainder of our staff was gathered and quietly working.

My fellow senior staffers and longtime friends had vanished to take up new positions; some at PIC to plan the inauguration, some at "Transition," and others I suspected on a beach somewhere. As I knew he would, David Plouffe immediately handed over his BlackBerry as soon as the election was over and walked out. Many months passed before I saw him again. Occasionally, a note from him showed up in my inbox with a request to help settle some outstanding items, but we quickly lost touch with each other. He invited me over to a celebration or two at his home in D.C., but I could never make it. As he suggested in the days before Dante was born, I had some making up to do with my family on the back end of the election. David was now also getting cherished family time as he, his wife, and his son enjoyed the arrival of a new baby girl into their home.

The last I remember of David, he was celebrating our "beautiful map." I, too, colored one in on Election Night, after my family got home from Grant Park, and marveled at it. I was still wound up so I sat at the dining table with my computer to see for myself exactly how we did. Just as was hoped, we won all nineteen Kerry states and the District of Columbia. I highlighted them in blue, one after another. Then across the middle of the country I noticed we pulled away Nevada, Colorado, Iowa, Indiana, Ohio, Virginia, and North Carolina from the Bush 2004 column. Along the bottom of the map I added New Mexico and Florida, which we had also flipped.

States like North Carolina, Virginia, and Indiana—these were huge prizes. North Carolina hadn't backed a Democrat in more than thirty years, dating back to Jimmy Carter's run. In Indiana, Republican nominees prevailed in each of the last ten presidential elections. When the dust finally settled, we took 53 percent of the popular vote to McCain's 46 percent. Our delegate count was a whopping 365 to 173, particularly impressive when compared to Bush's 286 to Kerry's 252 four years earlier. David was right: it was a beautiful map.

Now, the most difficult thing for me was the emptiness that accompanied the severing of my connection to Barack. After two years of monitoring his movements and managing the day-to-day activities of his organization, I felt a strange separation anxiety of sorts. Gone were the morning senior staff meetings. Gone were the campaign press clips. Gone were the endless emails. My BlackBerry, which once blew up with hundreds of notes every day, was silent now. The constant annoying flicker of the red light on that device, which had directed my life for two years, flashed only occasionally. Sometimes I sent a test message to myself to see if it was even working.

One President at a Time

I didn't watch the news anymore. It only gave me the feeling that I had somehow been left behind. I made a specific decision to stay in Chicago at headquarters so that I could spend time with my family, and I was happy for that chance. It just required a big adjustment on my part. Occasionally, when I did turn up the volume on my TV to hear the latest, I found that the post-election plan for the president-elect was being executed precisely as we had mapped it many weeks before. Our Transition team followed a clearly prescribed principle that there should only be one president at a time.

The country was still reeling from the financial crisis and looking to the newly elected president for cues. But Barack Obama remained in Chicago away from the spotlight of Washington, D.C. Rather than participate in grand meetings in the nation's capital, he opted for smaller, understated private visits at his transition headquarters near his Illinois home. Despite being pressured to weigh in on the hot issues of the moment, the president-elect made it clear that he would wait his turn.

The Call to Serve

The phone call came the day after Christmas, exactly two years after the fateful one I received in 2006 that led to my joining the campaign. This time, it was an offer to work for the president. Serving in the administration had never been a personal ambition. My wife and I wanted a quieter life for our family. I aspired to being less a president's man and more a family man. But there could be no greater honor than serving in the White House for this, the forty-fourth president of the United States.

I said "yes," and once again committed my family to a whole new journey. Sine left the campaign the way she arrived: pregnant. This time she was carrying our second son, Zane Alexander, who would be born in May, right on the cusp of the hundred-day mark of the new administration. We had a White House baby to join our campaign baby. That made them the first such sibling tandem in the administration. They were the "Obama Babies." Dante and Zane eventually became fixtures around the White House, sometimes romping just off the back colonnade near the Rose Garden with First Dog Bo, or making an occasional visit at the Oval to see Mr. Barack, as they call him.

My first day at my new job was both vivid and surreal. I left the home of my friend Danny Sebright in Logan Circle, where my family was staying for a few days until we found a new place to live. I kissed my wife and son good-bye at the banister just in front of the door and began my trek to my new office. Sine and I had decided to forego our great seats for the swearing-in ceremony because, though it was a beautiful day, the freezing temperatures would be too cold for a baby and a pregnant mother. Instead, I would be among a select few to enter and commence the new White House at 12:01 P.M.

I walked to work on quiet streets that were devoid of traffic and the noise of cars. I was alone for much of my walk. The roads had been cleared of vehicles in deference to the more than two million people expected to descend on the Capitol for the inauguration ceremony. As I approached the White House complex, there was commotion. Music. Dancing. Celebrations in the streets.

Then, at a security checkpoint I showed my ID to the secret service agent and was admitted to a private path that led me to the entrance of the White House. Walking alongside the Old Executive Office Building, I was alone again. The silence grew as I moved farther and farther from the festivities. There was a howling in the distance that sounded like the wind, but was really the low hum of the appreciative crowd that was packed into the National Mall to watch the president's inauguration.

As I stood at the top of the Navy Steps outside of the Old Executive Office Building, waiting to be processed in, I looked across the small, empty street to the West Wing. Aided by overhead speakers placed along Pennsylvania Avenue, I listened intently as a booming voice flooded the air around me. Though he was speaking from the steps of the Capitol a mile away, President Obama sounded like he was directly in front of me. Two and a half months separated his Grant Park speech from this moment. His words are back again, I thought, as he offered his inaugural address to the nation.

The Pictures (Once Again) Tell the Story

When I was first escorted into my new office, the walls were bare and empty. It took about a month before I could dress them with four framed jumbo-sized photographs. Three were scenes from the inauguration taken by the president's brilliant chief photographer, Pete Souza. They were a source of great pride for me during my service. The other was of my own swearing-in as a member of the president's senior staff.

The first was a close-up that showed the president accepting the oath of office. Among the onlookers were the president's family, Vice President Joe Biden and his wife Jill, 2004 presidential hopeful John Kerry, and a very proud Ted Kennedy, who attended his last inauguration on that day. I loved the expressions on each of their faces and the others who surrounded the president. Next to that photograph, I had a second shot that dramatically captured Barack Obama at the very moment he stepped from behind the curtain to confront the vast crowd at his inauguration. Souza's staff called it the photographer's "money shot." The view from behind showed him with uncharacteristically hunched shoulders, as if Pete had actually caught the moment when the weight of his new job suddenly bore down upon him.

Finally, a third jumbo image was the one I showed off to visitors in my office with the greatest excitement. It was an aerial view of the inauguration crowd spanning the whole of the National Mall, stretching from the U.S. Capitol to the Washington Memorial. It held special meaning for me because for many years as a young organizer, I dreamed of completely packing that space with people committed to one good cause or another. After a few noble tries, I decided that filling the Mall was an unattainable dream.

The day I hung that picture on my wall, it stood as evidence of one of the greatest feats of my career. Although the election ended on November 4, a distant two and a half months before, this photograph represented what I considered the true last day of the campaign. The organization that I helped build from scratch was ultimately responsible for assembling the vast, sprawling crowd shown in that photo. It was historic: the largest-ever gathering at the National Mall. Reports had upwards of two million people attending President Obama's inauguration.

I also liked to show visitors my beautifully framed Commission, featuring the signatures of both the president of the United States and the secretary of state. It was closure for me seeing Hillary Clinton's signature on that precious document beside Barack Obama's.

But it was a simple unframed eight-by-ten-inch photograph that sat on the mantle of my majestic fireplace, hidden amongst the pictures of my wife and sons, which had the greatest personal meaning for me. Also taken by Souza, it was an eye-to-eye portrait of the president and me clasping hands just as we had both assumed our new roles. I remember that conversation captured by the president's photographer quite fondly. It was our first since I had been reunited with my boss. President Obama told me that he was glad to see me here, and he warmly inquired about my family. Then he firmed his grip and sharpened his gaze as if to get my attention.

"Keep it tight, Henry," he said. "You know how I like it run tight."

Acknowledgments

I AM REMINDED OF A note that President Obama scrawled out to my youngest son on his second birthday. It read in part: "Zane, dream big dreams."

Growing up in the 1970s in my little town of Three Rivers, California—with a population of less than two thousand—I imagined the White House was a faraway place that appeared on the television news every night. This was long before *The West Wing* series gave us any romantic ideas of what it was like to work in the political hothouse environment. It was also before 24/7 cable news. My most memorable early glimpses of Washington politics came to me through a small black-and-white screen with a dull picture and fuzzy reception on one of three network channels. That's when I discovered my first reality television show, *The Watergate Hearings*.

Despite this drama playing out in our nation's politics, I grew up believing that government service was a noble calling. And while it was hard for a rural country boy like me to imagine I could ever find my way to the White House, I thought I was destined to work there someday. I attribute the sense of possibility I possessed to the people in my life that encouraged me to dream big.

My parents were both educators and actively worked at helping me and my brother see a world bigger than ourselves, whether it was through their obvious commitment to others or scrimping every dime they had to take us to places you could only get to on an airplane. In fact, it was at the conclusion of my very first flight that I would get to actually see and walk through the White House when I was eleven years old.

Because of the influence of my elementary and high school teachers like Bobbie Harris, Steve Fleming, Glen Bennett, and Richard Robinson, and my immediate and extended family—my mom and dad, my grandparents and relatives, Father Evan Howard and the Brothers at St.

Anthony's Retreat House, the Henning family (my Swedish exchange family), my Three Rivers classmates and neighbors, or my younger brother Mark and exchange sister Hildy—I learned to believe that if I kept the faith and worked hard, my vision for myself could become reality.

Helping elect Barack Obama president was the experience of a lifetime. I relished being in the bunker with Steve Hildebrand, Anita Dunn, Jim Messina, Pete Rouse, and the rest of our leadership team at headquarters. It should be quite obvious from this book that I am a very big fan of David Plouffe's. I miss working with him and I am forever grateful that he believed in me enough to make me the chief operating officer of this historic campaign.

There were literally more than 150 people who worked directly for me during the campaign. And it was my honor to work for you. Perhaps the highest compliment I have ever been paid came from one of our crack budget analysts, Ellen Kim, who once introduced me as "a mentor of leaders." I hope the first part of that statement was true, because the last part certainly was.

This was a team effort. But there were a few people who led our part of this historic endeavor that should again be given a final ovation. Marianne Markowitz was an incredible copilot. I especially valued both her seriousness and her wonderful sense of humor. Jenn Clark was a joy to work with. Among other things, Jenn was our fixer. I always appreciated that she tackled some of our toughest problems so I didn't have to. Dan Jones and Adi Kumar punched above their weight every day—and won commandingly. Treshawn Shields, Allyson Laackman, and Chief Staff Counsel Kendall Burman—whose desk lamp was always the last to go out at night—rounded out an amazing operations management team. I don't think we had even one good fight among us. Ever. It was a great privilege to work with such a smart, dedicated, and collegial group. Finally, the two people I may have leaned on the most and could never thank enough were Alison Stanton and, later, Monika Juska.

We also had a remarkable team of tech innovators who stepped up at different times. Kevin Malover expertly got us up and running, while Michael Slaby, moving over from new media, and Rajeev Chopra became our not-so-secret weapons. I was also grateful for the guidance and support I personally received from our technology advisor, Julius Genachowski, just as Campaign Treasurer Marty Nesbitt and Campaign General Counsel Bob Bauer consistently offered me and Marianne sage and invaluable advice that made us better with every contact.

If my personal road to the White House was unexpected and in ways unlikely, my path to becoming an author was even more so. This book was actually begun nine years ago—a full year and a half before I signed on with the Obama campaign. I had started a book highlighting leadership lessons from the campaign trail based on my experience to date that was mostly a disaster. I called it, "Campaign Principles for the Principled Campaign." One agent literally commented that "this hurts my eyes." But even through the disappointment I never let go of the words of my writing mentor at the time, author and entrepreneur Eve Hogan, who confidently announced the first time we spoke: "It sounds like you have a book in you, Henry!" I guess she was ultimately right.

I suspended that project to work on the Obama effort. During the campaign I kept a leadership diary. It was sloppy and rambling, but I thought it would be fun to leave behind for my children. Inside, I tested the success principles from that early failed writing project in my new campaign laboratory. I never intended to write a book, however. Quite honestly, I'm not sure at the outset I thought we had much of a chance of making it past Hillary in the primaries.

Then just days after the election, I got the idea to write this particular book from a childhood friend of mine from Three Rivers. I hadn't seen Glenn Smith in twenty years but he carefully laid out for me in a phone conversation exactly how it could all come together. Against the backdrop of the 2008 campaign, I saw how the principles of success from my earlier writings could be highlighted in this victory. Were it not for Glenn's call, this book would not exist.

Having the University of Iowa Press as my publisher was a great gift. When Elisabeth Chretien agreed to pick up my manuscript, I knew that I could not have a more perfect home for this story. This was partly because of the warm feelings I held for Iowa and the significance of that state in our 2008 run. It was also, quite frankly, because of the superior reputation of this press. As a first-time author, I couldn't have had better support. Before I worked with Elisabeth, I had a great story. After collaborating with her and her team on the manuscript, I had a great book.

Finally, a word about my wife. Sine lived this story. Then she read it. And read it again. And read it still again. Every time she did it got infinitely better. Sine is a talented screenwriter, and she helped me portray this experience in a way that invited the reader into campaign headquarters as it evolved from a blank space in the earliest days into a dynamic and bustling community at the end, to experience history-in-the-making. Sine made sure I wrote in pictures.

My wife lost me to the campaign; then she lost me to the White House. And after that she lost me to the early days of my obsessively writing this manuscript because I believed deeply that we had a unique view and had made a special contribution into a precious moment in our nation's history that needed to be told to our children—to all of our children. It is our story, certainly. But it is a uniquely American story.

The day she said "yes," we began the journey of a lifetime. I got to serve our country, and it was a high honor. Sine sacrificed for our country, and that was an act of much greater virtue.

Thank you for reading my story.